Riding *on* Luck

— SAGA OF THE USS LANG (DD-399) —

Rex A. Knight

CENTRAL POINT, OREGON

HELLGATE PRESS
P.O. Box 3727
Central Point, Oregon 97502-0032

(541) 245-6502
(541) 245-6505 fax
info@psi-research.com e-mail

Book designer and compositor: Jan O. Olsson
Cover designer: J. C. Young

Knight, Rex A.
    Riding on luck : saga of the USS Lang (DD-399) / Rex A. Knight.
       p. cm.
    Originally published: 1998.
    Includes bibliographical references and index.
    ISBN 1-55571-551-6 (paper)
     1. Lang (DD-399) 2. World War, 1939–1945—Naval operations, American. I. Title.

D774.L318K 55 2001
940.54'5973—dc21

00-143907

Hellgate Press is an imprint of Publishing Services, Inc., an Oregon corporation doing business as PSI Research.

Printed and bound in the United States of America
First Edition 10 9 8 7 6 5 4 3 2 1

 Printed on recycled paper when available.

Contents

Foreword

Rex Knight is the proud son of Randell J. Knight, who served as a young sailor aboard the destroyer USS *Lang* (DD-399) during World War II. Rex was an attendee at the 1998 *Lang* Reunion in Myrtle Beach, S.C., and we met for the first time on that occasion. I was there to perform the duties of after-dinner speaker at their banquet, and after that task was completed, I had the opportunity to talk with Rex. He told me that he was writing a book about *Lang*, and when I evidenced interest in it, he was kind enough to give me a preliminary copy. I very much enjoyed his narrative, and therefore had no hesitation in agreeing to do this Foreword when he requested me to undertake it.

As a young Ensign, less than a year out of Annapolis, I had the good fortune to be assigned to USS *Sterett* (DD-407), and served aboard that destroyer from her commissioning on 15 August, 1939 until 7 April, 1943, when I was wounded, and had to be evacuated to the Base Hospital in Espiritu Santo, in the New Hebrides. During my years on *Sterett* I served successfully as her Assistant Engineer, Communication, Gunnery, and finally Executive Officer. I therefore was able to observe that particular McCall Class destroyer from every vantage point, and in every phase of her operations. As a bonus benefit, I also acquired a close acquaintance with the characteristics, as well as a few of the personnel, of the other three ships of Destroyer Division Fifteen; *Lang*, *Stack*, and *Wilson*. *Sterett*'s first rendezvous with those division mates was in October, 1939, in Vera Cruz, Mexico, where we took turns shadowing the German liner *Columbus*. It quickly became apparent to *Sterett* sailors, that *Lang* was the outstanding ship of the three. Naturally, no *Sterett* sailor would have concluded that any other destroyer was more outstanding than his own ship, but at that juncture an accurate and honest assessment would probably have graded *Lang* as even better than *Sterett* — but my *Sterett* loyalty compels me to say, it would have been by just a little bit! My reasons for classifying her as the number one ship of the division are first, that she was the Division Flagship; all tactical and operational signals, whether by flag-hoist, flashing light, or radio, originated in and were transmitted by *Lang*; her signalmen and radiomen from the outset, demonstrated consistent, smart, rapid, and highly skilled communications techniques; they rapidly gained a reputation for faultless, heads-up performance, and *Lang*'s reputation as an outstanding destroyer division flagship grew with that of her personnel. Finally, the ship was smartly and skillfully handled by her captain and deck officers. Those of us aboard the other ships of Destroyer Division Fifteen were proud to have her flying our division pennant.

I distinctly remember *Lang*'s first skipper, Lieutenant Commander Felix Johnson, who frequently came aboard *Sterett* to see Lieutenant Commander Atherton Macondray, our own skipper, who we greatly admired and respected. It was obvious to us that Macondray looked up to and admired Felix Johnson. *Sterett*'s officers accepted Macondray's opinion, of his contemporary, and shared in his admiration of him. On a few occasions, we had the pleasure of Johnson's company at dinner in *Sterett*'s ward-room, and we enjoyed his wit and his friendly manner. We were also very aware of the fact that Felix Johnson, while in every way respectful and correct in his manner and attitude toward the division commander, was in no way awed by his imperious persona. Having had a taste of the division commander's medicine when he temporarily shifted his pennant to *Sterett* for a few days, we sympathized with *Lang*'s officers and crew. On *Sterett* he had ridden the entire ship's company with the zeal of a martinet. Our empathy for *Lang* was reinforced by our appreciation of what they were enduring.

As is already apparent from the foregoing paragraphs, Rex Knight's book evokes a thousand memories, a tribute to his painstaking research and his obvious under-standing of what it was like to be a destroyerman aboard a McCall Class destroyer during World War II. His descriptions of operations with the attack carriers, of convoying troop convoys and logistic support units, of night surface actions, and the run into the Mediterranean with *Wasp* and HMS *Eagle* to deliver Spitfires to the belea-guered island of Malta (I was *Sterett*'s officer of the deck and had the conn when the British and American ships which comprised the task force, sortied from Gibraltar and joined up for the dash to Malta. It had been a dramatic few moments), reawak-ened memories of those same or similar experiences aboard *Sterett*. No one can read these pages without realizing that the destroyer sailors of World War II were kept very busy; that they were "Jacks of all trades," with the skills necessary to defend the heavy ships from submarine or air attack; to bombard enemy positions ashore in support of our troops; to fetch downed aviators from the sea and return them to their parent carriers to fight another day; to take on enemy surface units, often against overwhelming odds, and emerge victorious; in short, to meet every challenge and never flinch.

It is obvious that the author of *Riding on Luck*, through listening to his father's accounts as a young boy, and later as a young man through his discussions with a considerable number of *Lang* veterans, has acquired the same loyalties to and pride in *Lang*'s outstanding record, as those long held by her crew. His love for the ship and her men is apparent on almost every page, and it is refreshing and encouraging to those of us who fought that war, to see such loyalty and patriotism in this son of a veteran. Hopefully, this book will bring inspiration to other youngsters who are privileged to read it.

One of the dominant themes coursing through these pages is the constant awareness of what was happening in the war, not only in the theatre where *Lang* was operating, but in those theatres on the other side (or sides) of the world. The author has done a remarkably good job, involving a great amount of research, in keeping the reader informed regarding the Big Picture. I found this to be unique in books written about specific ships, which in my experience, usually concentrate on the locale in which the subject ship is engaged; and it is a bonus to the reader, who is bound to come away from this read with a reasonably comprehensive summary of World War II.

The reader of *Riding on Luck* will also become aware that the author pays tribute to the ship itself. He is especially enthusiastic about the McCall Class destroyers. They were all one-stackers (having only one smokestack), they were all relatively small (designed at 1,500 tons vs. the 2,100 ton Fletchers and 2,200 ton Sumners which followed), they were all very fast (all of them were capable of from 38 to 40 knots), they were all very maneuverable (having turning circles of 700 yards), and with their original suit of 16 torpedoes and 4 five-inch dual purpose guns, they were the most powerful destroyers in the United States Navy at the time of their commissioning. All of them gave a magnificent account of themselves in battle, against other enemy surface units, enemy aircraft, including the dreaded kamikazes, and against enemy submarines. After my own experience aboard *Sterett*, I share his enthusiasm for ships of that Class. But we must keep in mind that the Japanese Navy had in the interim constructed the 2,250 ton Fubuki Class destroyers, which carried 6 five-inch guns, and no matter how many torpedoes, theirs were the infamous "Long Lance" variety, with a speed almost double that of our "fish" and a range of at least twice our 10,000 yards. So we can be thankful that we had the McCall Class to fill the vacuum in the first years of their existence, but we can also be thankful that we had the larger and heavier Fletchers and Sumners in time to help offset the Japanese advantage. Of course, to those of us who were there, the real difference which offset the enemy's strength was in the industrial strength of the United States, and the truly magnificent performance of our entire citizenry — not only the military, but the civilian element, which united and gave it their all. Please God, if the need ever arises, let the American people react the same way again.

Rex Knight has been attending the annual *Lang* reunions for several years, and in fact was instrumental in organizing and establishing the reunion tradition for *Lang* veterans, who had not been in the habit of getting together every year. I believe other old salts will agree with me that this is in itself unusual, that the son of a veteran was not only motivated, but possessed the qualities of leadership required to successfully launch a reunion program for men of his father's generation. By his attendance at those reunions, he has made friends with and bonded with *Lang*'s crew. In the process he has grown to understand them, to respect and admire them, and to appreciate their selfless contributions to the victory at sea which they achieved. This book is a tribute to them — his way of thanking and praising them. He has done it with grace and devotion, and some of his descriptions are almost poetic. It has been a noble effort, and it deserves an enthusiastic and resounding "Well Done!"

Charles R. ("Cal") Calhoun
Captain, U.S. Navy (Ret.)

Acknowledgments

The opportunities that I had at re-opening the minds of many former *Lang* sailors to their past, listening intently to each story as long filed away facts were recalled from deep within their memories, was every bit as special as being the first to gaze upon some long lost treasure. To feel the emotions, to see the laughter and the tears of the storytellers made each sharing of their recollections so much more personable, and real. My only wish is that I had the talent to relate with simple words such powerful expression. Perhaps I can be forgiven for not endeavoring more forcefully to deliver in this text the full gamut of emotions as experienced by the wartime sailor. But, in truth, such an endeavor was never my intent.

This history, due in large part to the six and a half years it encompasses, required a certain balance of the whole account which allowed few opportunities to truly detail personalities or relate their personable stories. A few such stories are scattered throughout the text, yet they are purposely kept to a minimum to ensure accuracy and balance.

First and foremost, this is the history of USS *Lang* (DD-399). Though very difficult to separate, I continually had to keep reminding myself that it was the warship and not the officers and crew that was the subject. Certainly each man that served on this destroyer's decks was a critical part of the life she exhibited. But it was *Lang* that was the common bond to the men who served her. She brought them together. They were her soul, but she was the mechanism from which was displayed their united spirit. She was their adoptive mother, and they her adopted sons. They took what she was able to offer and lived and worked and fought, and were endeared to her for a lifetime. Never would they say, "We brought her home!" No, not once did I ever hear such statement from any of her former crew. It was always, "She brought us home!" And, indeed, she did, and through one of the most turbulent times in recorded modern history.

Secondly, this is a war history. One of the unique things about *Lang*'s career is how closely it was interwoven with so many of the great events of World War II, and especially so in the Pacific campaign. For this reason it has been possible to give considerable insight into the war's progress, while duly noting how certain events directly effected *Lang*'s role.

Obviously, *Lang* was just one of a multitude of warships that had a role in the conflict comprising World War II. Many ships made their mark in history during those most destructive of years. Other officers and crews were just as proud of their ships as *Lang*'s were of her, as well they all had a right to be.

Indeed, each ship was unique in its own way. Yet none independently won the war. The massive challenge of both the Atlantic and Pacific campaigns assured a massive team effort in procuring the victory. And for this reason, a good portion of the credit for *Lang*'s success must be attributed to the expertise of a great number of other ships' officers and crews, pilots and support crews of each the Navy, Marines and Army, and a superior leadership.

Still, *Lang*'s unequaled ability at obtaining good fortune is quite evident throughout her career. Just by her classification as a destroyer she had from the outset been assured an important and vital role in the contest. No other warship type was to suffer more losses, whereby the war's end a total of 71 American destroyers — and a great percentage of their crews — would not return home. That *Lang* survived the conflict from beginning to end while participating in 11 major campaigns in of itself was quite a feat, but to do so unscathed was near a miracle. Truly, other ships also had careers blessed with good fortune, but it is doubtful any surpassed that of "Lucky *Lang*."

With respect to this written history, however, I must admit I had much to learn when it came to documenting such a story. The process proved itself much more difficult and time consuming than initially expected. Therefore, as compared to other histories, this documentation might not be of equal plane. But I have given my best effort.

At this point it should also be stated that there is even the possibility that some of *Lang*'s former crew might find reason to disagree with portions of this history. It did not take many interviews to quickly learn how each man saw a particular event differently. Actions were often quick and clouded in confusion. Men portside of midship did not get the same view as those starboard or those on the bridge, while men below decks often received their understanding of the action second hand. To get the most accurate account of any action it required that the author compare numerous sources, official and unofficial, before determining how the action truly played out. Hundreds of hours of research and study went into each chapter. Every effort was made to be as accurate as possible. Still, I was not there. It is firmly believed that what is documented in this history to be correct, but I will not argue against those who witnessed the moment firsthand. Simply stated, to challenge the veteran's personal recollection is both rude and disrespectful. For, indeed, errors are possible. And should any part of this history be proven in error, please accept my sincere apology.

Certainly, as stated, every effort has been given to make this history as complete and accurate as possible. Yet, let it be known that such effort would have been near impossible without some very special help. Indeed, a great many former officers and crew of *Lang* gave special assistance, providing eyewitness accounts, diaries, documentation, and photography in the research for *Lang*'s past. To these men I give the following acknowledgments: Carlton R. Adams, Robert Allbritton, Kenneth R. Arthur, Lyle Beattie, Leonard C. Bisgrove, John T. Bland III, J. A. Browning, Eldon Coward, Frederick T. Cretors, John Crosson, Robert E. Glass, Don Kenzie, Francis E. Lihosit, Scott McIntyre, Raymond P. Novak, Harold Payson Jr., John H. Potthoff, Donald P. Racette, Thomas T. Sapp, James A. Smythe, Pemberton Southard, Vernon R. Stark, Charles W. Stirrup, Harold D. Symons, William L. Walden, Alvin G. Weber, and Leonard J. Wood. My thanks to each of these gentlemen for their timely and unselfish willingness in offering their knowledge and personal keepsakes.

Additionally, there is need to express thanks to two dear friends of my youthful past for their encouragement in my quest for history. George W. Dennis, himself a former *Lang* sailor, was one of the first to plant the seed of desire for my learning about the past; his first contribution being a gift of a Confederate $5 bill which is still in my possession this day. His love for history, especially American history, was contagious and incurable. Second to George was Arthur Gagle, a former Army engineer who served in Alaska during World War II, and another who influenced greatly my desire for history. Arthur loved books and writing, and, despite my shortcomings as a well groomed writer, I seriously doubt anyone would have been more excited of this history — "My boy's book," he would've proudly announced — than this uniquely special connoisseur of the written word. Without having had their influence this written history might never have happened.

Then there is my father, Randell J. Knight, to whom I am most appreciative. Himself being a former *Lang* sailor, he too contributed heavily to my knowledge and understanding of *Lang* and life aboard her. Yet more importantly, his support for this effort — even when the effort seemed to falter — never ceased to be present. Thanks Dad! Oh, and my mother's strong support was no less meaningful. To her too I express my sincere thanks.

My wife and children somehow put up with me as well. My researching and writing often took my time away from them. Certainly the dollars spent on research and writing materials they would have much preferred some alternate use, as they too had a long list of wants. And, when my writing efforts were sometimes frustrated, my disappointment would often boil over, occasionally even to spill out upon them. Yet they rarely complained. I have been most fortunate to have had them as part of my support group. Thanks Linda, Shane, and Shauna, your unconditional love is a rare commodity in our world of today.

Above all, with the greatest amount of respect, I thank God for allowing me this wonderful opportunity, having given the tools and the ability to make this history possible. If there is to be any success from any work, it is by Him. Therefore, much like *Lang*, I too have been very fortunate. And certainly never was I alone in my endeavors.

Chapter 1

1939

The sight was not so unusual, a ship speeding swiftly across the moderate surface of the coastal Atlantic, her bow raised while pushing aside tons of water in a determined effort to reach some distant harbor. Somewhere far beyond the horizon a powerful storm of dreadful proportions was brewing, and typically the vessel's course and speed seemed evident to her attempt to avoid the fast approaching danger. Rushing torrents of air passed through her tightly stretched stays, creating a constant high-pitched tune while confirming her great velocity of movement. Yet, despite her obvious efforts, she was in fact unknowingly racing headlong into the storm's destructive path. Indeed, destiny was already determining this vessel's course, and only providence could safely guide her through the treacherous passage.

That which threatened the ship's security was not at all a new phenomenon, but was destined to be of an intensity far greater than so far experienced by mankind. Neither were its gathering forces of natural origin, its destructive winds being of the man-made variety, bred by hatred, greed and all other essence of evil. Furthermore, the hands of time had long since passed the hour when the storm's destructive conclusion could have been safely avoided. There were to be no detours, no turning back. What had begun for this ship as a maiden voyage destined toward a hoped-for long career of service was ending with only a promise of future uncertainty.

Yet the immensity of the threat to her small stature notwithstanding, this vessel stood able and ready to meet each pending hazard. Her displacement of 1,725 tons and dimensions of 341 feet in length and 36½ feet at the extreme beam gave her a delicate appearance, but her small frame, when propelled by the two powerful steam turbines housed within, could reach speeds that could rival that of the fastest shipping afloat. Furthermore, her design incorporated power far beyond that of speed; like young David of Biblical record, she had the ability to destroy an enemy many times her own size, demanding the respect of all adversaries. Indeed, her reason for being was for the very purpose which threatened her future. This vessel was a warship, a destroyer by classification.

By 1939 destroyers were certainly of no new concept; they had origins dating back to the 1870s and Robert Whitehead's invention of the first self-propelled, underwater "torpedo." With the newly developed torpedoes naval warfare was revolutionized, allowing small, quick vessels the potential of destroying even the largest of seagoing shipping. Obviously, such potential was not to go unnoticed, especially by the British, who had a particular interest in retaining a long held naval superiority in the world. Soon the Royal Navy was successfully testing and incorporating the new design, classified as "torpedo boats," within its own ranks.

Success of the new torpedo boats, however, created a new problem for the Royal Navy, that of proliferation of their new ship's design among the other world navies. Such might not have been so disturbing had it not been that the design's greatest success was that there lacked any real effective means by which to defend against it. Therefore, to counter their own concept the British were compelled to design a new ship capable of catching and destroying the small, speedy torpedo boats, thus leading to the concept of "torpedo boat destroyers."

The first true torpedo boat destroyer, HMS *Havock*, was produced by the British in 1893. A thin hulled and cramped oversize of the original torpedo boat design, the vessel proved to be a complete success. And not only did the new destroyer have the speed, maneuverability and firepower needed to catch and destroy the pesky torpedo boats but, by carrying its own arsenal of torpedoes, also the capability to destroy larger shipping. Suddenly a whole new era in naval warfare was born.

In 1897 a new invention, the Parson's steam turbine, added even further to the uniqueness of the destroyer, greatly increasing its speed to as much as 36 knots at a sustained rate. With such speed few ships were capable of outrunning the destroyer. Still, the destroyer's mission remained limited.

Not till 1914 and the eruption of the First World War did the destroyer's role begin to expand. Germany's early success with the U-boat, followed by British inventions of hydrophones and depth-charges, quickly introduced the world to an even newer and deadlier concept of ocean warfare. And it was the destroyer, in possession of its great agility and speed, which was to inherit the task of stopping the newly bred underwater hunters and the new threat they posed.

Additionally, the success of the airplane as a weapon of war, both during the First World War and in tests afterward, was also to lead to even further development of the destroyer. Though never to the extremes he desired, during the naval tests of 1921 General William "Billy" Mitchell had successfully proven the airplane an effective weapon against shipping. No longer could these new weapons be ignored by the world navies, and soon all warshipping, including destroyers, were being provided defense systems against the new threat.

Indeed, the ships, most notably known to American sailors as "Tin Cans," had evolved to be much more than just a torpedo boat destroyer; they had become a weapon of universality and necessity to all navies. And the destroyer's appeal, its reputation and glamour as a proven fighter, would make many a sailor proud to serve upon their decks.

Certainly the crew of the destroyer which continued in its speedy course to port were proud of their ship. She was just completing a wonderful voyage, having visited such tropical Caribbean ports as San Juan, Fort-de-France, and Nassau. Each visit had allowed the crew opportunity to check out many lovely sites, not the least of which were the many beautiful girls, while having the occasion to sample the regional refreshments and the rhythmic native music of each host port. In fact, the voyage had allowed many of the men their very first occasion to visit outside their home in the United States. Truly such occasion, journeying to beautiful islands, enhanced by beautiful sunrises and sunsets, was to set the stage for what was destined to be a wonderful career of a new destroyer in the United States Navy, and thus was the shakedown cruise of USS *Lang* (DD-399).

Lang's existence had begun with the order to lay down her keel at the Kearny Shipyard, Kearny, New Jersey, on 5 April 1937. Sixteen months later, on 27 August 1938, her empty hull was christened by the wife of Admiral William D. Leahy and then officially introduced to the salty dark blue liquid that would be the roam for the rest of the destroyer's career.

Following another seven months of fittings, *Lang* was finally ready to become an official member of the U.S. Fleet. And at 11:10 A.M. on 30 March 1939 Rear Admiral C. H. Woodward, Commandant of the New York Navy Yard, gave the formal order which placed *Lang* in the commission of the U.S. Navy.

A cold mist of rain had been falling that morning and the ceremony, with all its traditional character, highlighted by the shrill sound of a boatswain's pipe and the raising of the red, white, and blue commissioning pennant, progressed quickly. For the crew the shortness of the ceremony had satisfied their wish for brevity. Still, it was a proud moment, awarding each man the title of "Plank" for being a part of the commissioning crew; though the event had yet to fully develop that pride. A great deal more time combined with the mystery of seamanship, drawing ship and crew toward one personality, would be needed before such pride would be fully realized.

Indeed, though the time needed to mold *Lang* and her crew into one unified team had begun with the commissioning, the molding itself would prove a career long process. In the beginning it would be imperative that a strong nucleus of experienced crew, those who would one day be the *old timers* of the ship's company, be created. These would be the men who would give the ship its greatest strength and wisdom. To gain them would require a special attachment to the new home where they were to eat, sleep, and work. Yet being special was never to be all that difficult for *Lang*.

Since the end of 1934 the United States, through the vast efforts of President Franklin D. Roosevelt, had been turning out new and innovative designs of warshipping. The steadily increasing building program was designed to return idle ship workers to work during the depressed economic hard times while strengthening and modernizing the U.S. Navy to treaty strength.

The ability, however, to meet the threats posed by a fragile global political structure was an ever increasing challenge for the U.S. Navy. Rumblings in Europe, amplified in powerful speeches of defiance by both Germany's Adolf Hitler and Italy's Benito Mussolini, were again pushing the nations of the world toward another full-scale war. Yet, while the world focused primarily on Europe's insecurity, the U.S. Navy directed most of its attention toward the threats coming from the western Pacific regions of the world, and with good reason.

Following the First World War there was a sincere desire by almost every nation of the world for a return to a secure peace. Many treaties were signed, not the least of which was the Kellogg-Briand Pact, outlawing war. Included among the signers was the nation of Japan, an ancient culture, long in self isolation and only recently interested in worldwide cooperation.

Having emerged from the world conflict as the world's third largest naval power, Japan was finding itself pressed by many world leaders, especially from the United States and Britain, to come to terms on an naval armaments production treaty. The positioning was very timely; in seeking to establish a role in world leadership while in turn strengthening economic ties with the west, Japan's liberal government showed itself very conciliatory. And in 1921 Japan readily agreed to sign the Washington Naval Treaty, agreeing to a naval warship restriction of a 5:5:3 ratio with the United States and Britain, Japan retaining the smallest number of the ratio.

Though promoted as a positive merit by the government officials who signed it, Japanese Naval leadership looked upon the treaty as a betrayal and were furious, arguing their constitution gave them sole authority over their own numbers. The civilian government leaders held their ground, however; and in 1930 they again agreed to sign yet another naval limitation treaty, the London Naval Treaty, renewing the earlier made restrictions.

Despite their anger, the officials of the Imperial Japanese Navy (IJN) bided their time and complied with the despised treaties. In the process, however, they developed many ways to overcome their limitations; not the least of which was their ability to introduce high quality innovative designs into their warships, and especially so with their destroyers.

Indeed, officials of the U.S. Navy were highly surprised when in 1929 the Japanese introduced their new special type Fubuki Class destroyers onto the world scene. Much larger than any other conventional design and heavily armed with three twin-mounted 5-inch guns and nine 24-inch torpedo tubes, the Fubuki outclassed any other destroyer of its time.

Combine the vastly improving quality of Japanese warships with a growing nationalistic movement and include Japan's illegal invasion of China in 1931 and it is easy to understand the U.S. Navy's decision to come out of hibernation. The need for modernization of warship designs, especially with destroyers, was quickly evident, and U.S. naval engineers were quick to respond to the challenge.

Catching up to the Japanese, however, proved to be quite difficult. The Farragut Class destroyers laid down in 1932 were merely an act of desperation, their designs of 1916 concept and already antiquated. Only a marked improvement in firepower, with new duel purpose 5-inch guns (the Japanese had already incorporated the world's first duel purpose guns on the Fubukis) assisted by the new Mark 37 director, gave the Farraguts conventionality.

By 1933 the new Porter Class destroyers was on order, and finally the U.S. Navy had a competitor for the Fubuki. The Porters had the size, speed, and firepower, mounting the first U.S. introduced twin 5-inch guns (though not duel purpose) and two quadruple torpedo mounts. Still Japanese destroyers retained their superiority.

Furthermore, the IJN had by 1933 made great advances with their torpedoes. Besides having reloadable torpedo mounts, a luxury unknown to U.S. destroyers, the IJN had a new secret weapon, the type 93 (Long Lance) torpedo. By the time U.S. planners learned of this new menace it would be far too late for many American sailors. Yet, to match the known torpedo threat, additional torpedo batteries were added to the next class of U.S. destroyers, the Mahan Class, raising the number of torpedoes carried to twelve.

Following the Mahans, the Gridley Class was to mark the last major change in U.S. destroyer designs prior to the Second World War. Since the end of the First World War the U.S. Navy had seen their destroyer designs progress from the small four stack "flushdeckers" to the larger two stack, broken (split-level) deck designs of the Farraguts, Porters, and Mahans, and finally reverting to a smaller single stack, broken deck design of the Gridley. Yet, being armed with four to five duel purpose 5-inch guns and four quadruple torpedo mounts, the Gridleys could still effectively meet the challenge of their Japanese counterpart. And though they were smaller, the space required for their armaments had been obtained by uniquely trunking the ship's two boilers into one stack, and without any loss of power.

The Somers Class was the next generation of destroyers introduced by the U.S. Navy. An intended upgrade to the Gridleys, their design did not meet expectations, proving too top heavy and requiring some reductions in armaments, specifically in the number of torpedo mounts.

The next class of "single stackers," the Benham Class, was designed to improve the top weight problem while retaining the firepower required to meet modern adversaries. Of the Benham Class, USS *Lang* was the third to be built.

Yet, despite all its building efforts, by the middle of 1939 the U.S. Navy had been surpassed by the Japanese in naval strength in the Pacific. The Japanese government had refused to agree to any additional naval limitation treaties, and in 1937, when the earlier agreements expired, they took full advantage of their new freedom by launching into a massive new building program. Though the number and quality of ships in the U.S. Fleet also improved greatly during this time, when the war began the single stack destroyers were still the mainstay of the U.S. destroyer fleet, remained that way during the first two years of the war, and were destined to perform excellently throughout the conflict till the bitter end.

As a Benham Class destroyer *Lang* carried armaments of four duel-purpose 5"/38 caliber guns (two forward and two aft), four .50 caliber antiaircraft guns and sixteen 21-inch torpedo tubes (two quadruple mounts midship port side and two quadruple mounts midship starboard side). As time progressed, however, so would the destroyer's weaponry, vastly improving her ability to meet the variety of challenges of ocean combat.

On the outside *Lang* was every bit as powerful as she was sleek and speedy. On the inside, however, the crew was to find her accommodations lacking considerably.

In the crew's quarters, both forward and aft, bunks were layered four high with foot-locker space beneath the bottom bunk. Entry into the foot-lockers made necessary the bottom bunk be raised, an arrangement that sometimes, depending on his size and temperament, proved quite a bother to its occupant.

Work areas were even more confining. Engine rooms and boiler rooms were full of obstacles on which to bang one's head, with piping, duct-work, conduit and railing mazed throughout.

The ship's mess offered the greatest space, taking the width of the ship near its center. There, steel tables occupied most of the interior while a large vat for making coffee and a fenced off scullery occupied one corner.

Other areas of the ship included the galley, chiefs' quarters, officers' quarters, and staterooms, wardroom, sickbay, machine shop, armory, magazines, and handling rooms for the main batteries. These areas were also small, utilizing only the necessary space. What areas remained vacant — there were few — became space for storage, something there was never enough of, especially during the war years. Everything had its proper place, leaving little room for additions. Even when in the future changes would be made, to accommodate weight requirements, additions in one area would usually require deletions in another.

Regardless *Lang*'s cramped conditions, each sailor soon found enough space aboard to claim as "his spot." Some would find their "special" place to be upon the tapered uptakes, where on cool nights one could relax on the cozy warm surface to study the stars as they seemed to glide from side to side with each sway of the ship. Others might choose one of the bitts, where one could sit in relative safety as cool blasts of salty spray filtered through the air and rainbow colored sunlight to pelt against one's exposed skin. Wherever chosen, whether at one of these or some other location, it was there where the men would most often think about home, read a letter from loved ones, dream about the future, and, with the arrival of war, hope and pray for a tomorrow.

Certainly in the beginning *Lang*'s future looked very promising. Her newness was overwhelming. Machinery worked with precision and crispness, unhampered by excess globs of grease or rust. Polished brass fixtures sparkled, as did the crystal clear port lights. On the inside the smell of fresh paint had yet to be overcome by the future odors of mildew, sweat, ether, smoke, and oil. She was a new ship with a new crew, both untested and neither yet truly bound to the other as a unit. To the naked eye they were a sight to behold, but the real polish had yet to be applied. *Lang* and her crew were far from being a real fighting team. Time and training ... time and training ... only these and spirit would set the foundation for such teamwork — world events would do the rest.

Momentarily, however, no one could have accurately guessed the future of this haze-grey configuration of war. Although war by the Spring of 1939 was more closely reality than thought, most Americans were in agreement that any outbreak of war in Europe would be European affair of which they would have no part. Few would have wagered that in less than three years, *Lang* would be in the thick of fighting a second world conflict. And, though Japan was already embroiled in war with China, causing great deterioration of relations with the U.S., it would have been difficult for many to picture this the enemy to whom this ship would dedicate three full years of attention.

In fact, the only early hint of the destroyer's future was in the numbers painted upon her bow; the initial observation occurring on commissioning day when two passing sailors noticed the numbers with great interest. One said to the other in a prophetical tone, "Now there's a lucky ship!" "How so?" asked the other. "Why, just look at her number," was the reply, "Any 'Black Jack' player knows those numbers are lucky." Indeed, the number "399," when added, equalled 21. For now, however, the hint of luck was to remain just that, only a hint.

As for *Lang*'s crew, they too were unsure of the future. They were a varied lot. A few had been serving the Navy for some time, having had previous association with ships and the sea. Yet the majority of this new complement were young recruits, barely of the age to be called adults. They had come from diverse backgrounds and diverse areas of the country: from upper, middle, and lower income families; from the north, south, east, and west; from cities, towns, country homes, and farms. For most, worldly experience had been confined to a few miles radius of where they referred to as home, and for this reason — at a time when many economic problems persisted throughout the land — most had viewed the Navy as their only possible opportunity at seeing the world and meeting new people. A few of the men, however, were present strictly due to family tradition. And yet an even smaller number were there purely in search of the home and family they otherwise never had. Even so, despite backgrounds and reasonings, the future was sure to bear to all a common adventure.

For at least one man, however, the future was a little more focused. Usually to be found at his special perch upon the ship's bridge, the tall, slender, and handsome figure stood proudly at his place of command. His eyes stared straight ahead, momentarily oblivious to any movement around him. Just for a moment he reflected upon some past event and challenge which had led him to where he stood this day. Then, with a sudden return to the present, he began to admire his new ship and crew. He watched as below him men busied themselves with duties at various stations, acknowledging and carrying out orders with near perfection. Moments like this he had worked hard for; only in his dreams had he been here before. Leadership was now reality, and he must now establish that leadership correctly. He must mold a ship and crew into a team, a real fighting team. The task would not be simple, but he was ready to meet the challenge. Certainly he would give it his finest effort.

Lieutenant Commander Felix L. Johnson was somewhat a mystery to his crew. Although they had been under his command for several weeks, few of the men had determined exactly what kind of commander this fellow was destined to be. Obviously, the glow on his face and the pride he displayed were not hidden, but these were not so important to the crew. The crew was much more concerned with this man's attitude, demeanor, and strictness — with great emphasis on his strictness. Only time would accurately answer their questions of him, questions possibly even he had yet to answer for himself.

By 25 July *Lang* had completed her trek back up along the eastern seaboard and was dropping anchor at her home port of Tompkinsville, Staten Island, New York. As compared to future duties at sea the voyage had not been all that long, or nearly as dangerous. Yet, aside from all the excitement generated by the ship's newness and the adventure of travel, nothing would ever compare to a safe return to home. This was a happy time for the crew and they greeted the opportunity with broad smiles.

Obviously, there was much to smile about. The shakedown had been successfully completed, and the ship and crew had worked very well together. Perhaps the highlight of accomplishments had been the speed test, during which *Lang* had cranked out 38.44 knots, not only producing a mighty wake but also producing a great sense of pride in the crew toward their new ship. And it was a pride well deserved, for the crew had solidly established their destroyer among the fastest of the fastest class of warships ever in the history of the United States Navy.

There was no doubt that the crew had returned from *Lang*'s maiden voyage with a whole new spirit. Captain Johnson had noticed it; his ship and crew were displaying the common bonds that define a unit. Certainly it was the beginning of a great and growing relationship — a fine beginning, yet only a beginning.

This was not to say, however, that every aspect of every one of the ship's functions had worked perfectly. There had been some problems, mostly mechanical in nature, found during the recent trials. These were not totally unexpected. One of the reasons, of course, for the shakedown was to locate any flaws in the ship's machinery. Once located and diagnosed, flaws could be corrected. The few problems found on *Lang* were quickly adjusted for, and only a few days passed before the ship was once again on the move.

Lang's next departure from New York Harbor took place on 12 August, a date that was to mark a most memorable moment in her career. On this day the destroyer embarked on her first official duty, as the escort for the cruiser *Tuscaloosa* (CA-37).

Commissioned in 1934, *Tuscaloosa* had been in service considerably longer than *Lang*, yet she was still new as compared to many ships of the U.S. Navy. One of the first capital ships to be produced during the administration of President Franklin D. Roosevelt, she was but one of a growing list of new ships created in the effort to put people back to work while bolstering the Navy to treaty strength. She was certainly a powerful looking vessel, nearly twice the length of *Lang* and carrying armaments of nine 8-inch and eight 5-inch guns. There was little wonder that she had become an honored symbol of the president's policy.

Indeed, on this day *Tuscaloosa* was a very special ship. Destined for the summer fishing resort of Campobello Island, in the Bay of Fundy, New Brunswick, Canada, the cruiser and her escort were embarking on a most honored duty. Aboard *Lang* sailors were often seen to pause and strain their eyes in the hopes of getting a glimpse of the individual for whom this voyage was taking place. At the very least they could see the blue banner which waved to them from high above *Tuscaloosa*, identifying the cruiser's passenger as their Commander in Chief, and the nation's leader, President Roosevelt.

Sharing in a presidential cruise was certainly an exciting way for any ship and crew to enhance the beginning of a career. Obviously, this was true for *Lang* and her crew. Being that this day was accented even further by its pristine beauty and peacefulness seemed only an added bonus.

Unfortunately, the excitement, the beauty, and the peacefulness of this departure was in vast contrast to the problems boiling around the world. Even at that very moment, in their distant realm of secrecy, German leaders were finalizing plans to a plot for their imminent invasion of Poland, an invasion destined to throw the world into a state of chaos. As a result, in the very near future beauty was to become rarer, excitement often unfriendly, and peacefulness nearly nonexistent.

Adolf Hitler was soon to apply the lessons of readiness to all. Certainly *Lang* and her crew were not ready, neither was Roosevelt, the U.S. Navy, nor any other U.S. branch of service. In fact, America was to learn the lessons slowly — and painfully.

In the meantime, Roosevelt, though very much aware of the rumblings in Europe and the threats coming from the western Pacific, continued to focus his greatest attention on the economic problems at home. Yet, even so, he often paused for a moment in allowance of some much needed relaxation. This latest cruise was an example of just such an opportunity for the president, and in one of his most favorite forms, sailing.

Having set their course northward, the cruiser and her proud escort sailed throughout the rest of that night and the next morning without any delays. But by afternoon of the second day, having just arrived off the Isles of Shoales, the two ships suddenly began to slow and were soon coming to a complete stop.

The reason for the pause could be seen a short distance away, where stood a small vessel having the silhouette of a mine sweeper. The vessel was in fact the converted submarine rescue ship *Falcon* (ASR-2), her crew performing some duty of obvious importance. Somewhere in the depths below lay the remains of the ill-fated submarine *Squalus* (SS-192), the focus of one of the most grueling salvage operations in Naval history.

The crew of *Lang* were well aware of *Squalus'* fate. Commissioned on 1 March, *Squalus* was nearly as new a vessel as was *Lang*. Yet, unlike *Lang*, her beginning was one of misfortune.

Having departed Portsmouth, New Hampshire, on 12 May for a series of test dives, *Squalus* had successfully completed her first 18 submergings when on 23 May she began another off the Isles of Shoales. It was then that disaster suddenly struck. A main induction valve failed during the attempt, causing the flooding of her after engine room. With the intake of water uncontrollable, the submarine quickly began to sink, her stern leading the way. Unable to remedy the problem, *Squalus'* desperate skipper had little alternative but order the after section sealed off, leaving 26 of his crew to their fate, while offering what seemed only slim hope to those who remained forward.

Trapped 60 fathoms (360 feet) below the surface within the confines of their sunken vessel, *Squalus'* remaining crew could only pray for deliverance. Above them, however, the process for their rescue was already begun. Precautions for just such an accident had been taken; a veteran of submarine rescue, *Falcon* had been stationed nearby and was soon on site to begin rescue operations.

Squalus's sister ship, *Sculpin* (SS-191), was first sent to locate the exact position of the sunken sub, which she did, establishing a communications link in the process. Then, using the newly developed McCann rescue chamber (an altered version of the diving bell), *Falcon* successfully reached down to the hull of the sunken sub and delivered the remaining 33 survivors to the safety of the surface. It was an amazing feat.

Afterwards, *Falcon* remained at the site, given the new task of raising the lifeless submarine from its watery grave. Further success, however, proved not so easy. Days had turned into weeks and weeks into months as the salvage operation struggled with technical difficulties and an often unabiding sea. But the operation was finally making progress. Cables had now been passed beneath the *Squalus'* hull and attached to pontoons to be filled with air for floatation. The salvage was very near completion.

From *Lang* and *Tuscaloosa* there was ample time for many sailors to observe the tedious work being performed. For two hours the two ships delayed their voyage, offering the president quality time to watch the operation, his keen interest sending encouragement to those men involved in the special task. Yet *Squalus* was not to appear this day, and so *Lang* and *Tuscaloosa* departed, proceeding on to their original destination.

The following day the two ships arrived at Campobello, but the stay was to prove to be short. Departing the ships for a period of rest and recreation ashore at his summer home, Mr. Roosevelt was gone for only a few hours before returning to *Tuscaloosa*. The ships then proceeded on for a visit to Sydney Harbor, Nova Scotia, where they arrived on the 16th.

The stay at Sydney Harbor was also short, but it was an enjoyable visit. Indeed, the people of Nova Scotia proved themselves an exceptionally kind lot, with seemingly unending hospitality. Some "farm boys" of *Lang*'s crew even had the opportunity to do some leg shaking at an old fashion barn dance before proceeding back to sea.

A very brief stop at Halifax then preceded the final leg of the trip, that of a return to New York. Noticeably, the recent visits had created a high spirit among the two crews. As a result, time passed quickly, and by 24 August the pleasurable presidential cruise had reached its conclusion.

Having returned to New York Harbor, *Lang* and *Tuscaloosa* stood off Sandy Hook, New Jersey, awaiting the voyage's final phase. Sea gulls hovered the two ships as they closed one another, while anticipation raced throughout *Lang*. The destroyer was about to receive a very special honor; President Roosevelt would transfer to her decks for transport to the Fort Hancock Landing.

Sailors aboard *Lang* turned out in ranks, their dress white uniforms brightened by glowing sunlight, while awaiting the president's arrival. Time, which had earlier passed by so quickly, suddenly slowed. Then he appeared, his notable figure standing out among a group of aides and bodyguards as from the cruiser he made his way to the destroyer's decks.

Making his way aboard slowly, the president's familiar smile was anxiously greeted by an extremely proud Captain Johnson. A boatswain sounded his pipe in welcome, and the presidential flag raised to its peak on the main truck at midship. At that instant *Lang* became the most important ship in the whole U.S. Fleet, and a wave of pride quickly spread throughout her crew. And though the journey to the landing was short, the honor it bestowed to the ship and crew would be treasured for a lifetime — and it was an honor destined to be received more than just this once.

The presidential cruise ended, yet *Lang*'s career continued forward, promising even greater excitement and challenge. Remaining based at New York, the next two and one half months *Lang* spent training along the New England coast. During this time, on 2 October, the destroyer sailed out of Boston Navy Yard en route to Rockland, Maine, for final sea trials. She carried aboard a special group of electrical, mechanical, and structural engineers, there to watch her performance closely. All ships and crews were needed in top condition and all new ship designs were needed to perform as were expected — the foretold war in Europe was now reality.

Under falsified pretense Hitler's Nazi Germany had invaded Poland on 1 September, and in response, on 3 September, England and France had declared that a state of war existed between themselves and the aggressor. President Roosevelt had declared the United States neutral, but it was apparent to many, especially to those in the armed services, that life was going to be much different. This was especially to be true for the men of the U.S. Navy, as off the United States all coastal water extending out 300 miles was declared off-limits to all the combatant's warshipping, requiring extensive patrolling for enforcement.

Circumstances as they were, change for *Lang* came quickly. On 13 November she was departing Newport, Rhode Island, for her new base at Galveston, Texas. Arriving there on the 18th, she joined her two sister ships, *Benham* (DD-397) and

Ellet (DD-398), for a two month tour of duty at neutrality patrol in the Gulf of Mexico and Caribbean Sea.

The neutrality patrols were truly something new to this young generation of sailors. At first they inspired a sense of suspense and excitement, but soon the dullness of the long patrols became a bore. Long days and nights at sea with repetitious routines, searching and policing but finding nothing abnormal, quickly set the men in bad humor. Each day space aboard the ship seemed to grow a little more confining. The crew were finally discovering the life of a sailor. Unlike the shakedown and presidential cruises, there were no exciting stops along the way. Instead, all that lay before them were miles and miles of water and hours upon hours of uninterrupted sailing.

After two weeks of uneventful patrolling *Lang* again returned to port, arriving at Corpus Christi, Texas, on the night of 3 December. Such opportunity was truly welcomed by the crew, as each man was more than ready to escape the ship's confinement for a refreshing visit ashore. Even as they arrived in port, however, disappointing news quickly struck its harsh blow; all liberties had been temporarily postponed.

Corpus Christi epitomized a problem that often confronted the fleet sailor, that of hospitality. Though some port cities welcomed sailors with open arms, others tended to be, in polite terms, anti-social. Upon entering the port of Corpus Christi, Captain Johnson had received a report of some recent violence against sailors within the city, a condition which he determined warranted his decision on liberties and some personal attention of his own. He was certainly aware of the need to allow his men their well deserved time ashore, widely evidenced by their obvious disappointment and decreasing morale. So on the following morning the captain departed his ship for his own personal visit to the city.

No greater amount of determination could any man have mustered; Captain Johnson walked into city hall prepared, literally, to make war. Confronting the mayor and chief-of-police head on, he bluntly stated that, despite the threats, he intended to allow his men ashore, and if city officials could not help ensure their safety, he would "send them ashore armed!" With his point well made, the captain returned to his ship without hesitation and allowed his men their leave.

This awesome display of devotion was to have an obvious impact on the crew, greatly impressing them and increasing an already growing respect for their captain. And, of course, the visit proceeded without further incident.

The stay a Corpus Christi lasted only four days, then after taking on supplies and fuel *Lang* shoved off to make the short trip back to her base at Galveston, arriving there on the night of 8 December.

At Galveston the crew received their pay and again liberty passes were handed out. Certainly the combination of a well paid crew just recently returned from long days at sea was to produce a night pitched toward the wild side. Visiting bars and clubs and "letting off steam" was common sailor practice, and this night was to be no exception. Yet the following morning's roll call disclosed no absentees among the crew, though there were several men who did visibly show the aftereffects of the previous night; one badly bruised and cut sailor had even tripped and fell face first on the sidewalk in his haste to return to the ship on time — or so he said.

By afternoon *Lang* was again back out to sea, steaming along through the gulf waters, headed south. Aboard her decks, however, were a few blurry eyed sailors who weren't sure which way they were heading or, for that matter, even caring. But this time the destroyer's destination was a patrol station just off Vera Cruz, Mexico, and its mission a little more direct.

Back in the month of September, when war in Europe had first been declared, all the major combatants found themselves with shipping parked in some of the many ports of the Americas. And, with the North Atlantic almost immediately becoming a major battleground, the task of retrieving those ships had become an extreme risk indeed.

For the Germans, one such vessel of importance was the luxury liner SS *Columbus* of the North-German Lloyd Line. Third largest and most luxurious of the German merchant fleet, she had remained moored in Vera Cruz Harbor ever since the outbreak of the war. Obviously, as long as the liner remained in the neutral port she was safe, but once she left and entered international waters she would become fair game. Considering the alternatives, the Germans seemed quite content with her remaining within the safety of the neutral port.

In the meantime, however, the Mexican Government, after having received some pressure of their own, had begun to pressure the Germans to get their vessel out. The U.S. Government (who no doubt had applied the initial pressure) watched the situation closely, and upon receiving news of the German liner's imminent departure, quickly dispatched *Lang* and *Benham* to Vera Cruz. There the two ships were to patrol just outside the Mexican port, wait for *Columbus* to depart (the date for which the Germans were keeping secret), and then trail her to keep track of her movements. Obviously, there was more to this mission than just keeping the peace.

Lang began the trip south alone, but later joined up with *Benham* on the evening of the 10th. Very early the next morning the two ships arrived on station, took up their separate positions and began their patrols.

For the first few days the patrols had no immediate results, returning the crew to a dull state of routines. Then, at 3:31 P.M. on the afternoon of the 14th, the liner suddenly appeared. She was at a distance of 12 miles and the *Benham* could be seen already on her trail.

Chapter 1 – 1939

From the bridge Captain Johnson directed his ship to close *Columbus* in preparation of their "shadowing" duty. From his position of observation, the captain gazed toward the vessel with great admiration. Her huge black painted hull boldly stood out along the horizon, while her white painted top half glistened in the sunlight. One could easily imagine her carrying her complement of wealthy passengers, her chefs serving the finest meals, and merry voyagers sipping on the best of champagne and wine. But on this day she carried no passengers; in fact, not a soul could be seen anywhere on the big ship. To others on *Lang*'s bridge the liner even seemed a bit ghostly in appearance, especially so as with the prevailing darkness her darkened outline became an eerie shadow.

In fact, the liner's outline was just a little too dark for Captain Johnson's liking, the liner's crew possibly hoping to elude the two watchful guardians. The only real evidence of the big ship's existence was a silver froth quietly created as she glided across the dimly moonlit sea, and this was at times very hard to detect. Signalling the liner, Captain Johnson insisted her crew switch on the ship's stern light as visual aide, or else he would order her illuminated by spotlight. *Columbus*'s stern light suddenly appeared, its solitary glow enlightening only a minute area of darkness, but to the captain's satisfaction.

The arrival of dawn produced no real change with the liner; she continued her eastward course and her decks remained vacant. *Lang* continued the observance, following the liner's every move. During the night *Benham* had been called away to search for another German ship, the freighter *Arauca*, but had since been replaced by the destroyer *Jouett* (DD-396). This new union was to continue trailing the liner as she proceeded quietly to cross the Gulf waters, drawing herself ever nearer the international waters of the Atlantic.

For *Lang* and *Jouett* trailing of the liner continued until shortly after daybreak of the 16th, but there it ended. Both ships were then relieved by *Schenck* (DD-159) and *Phillip* (DD-79), two old reactivated four piper destroyers now being used solely for neutrality patrol. Being released from the duty, Captain Johnson immediately turned *Lang* around and headed back for Galveston, arriving there the following morning. But the saga of *Columbus* was not yet over.

Lang's stay at Galveston was only to last about four days, but it was during this time the crew learned the true fate of the German liner. Following *Lang*'s departure *Columbus* had continued its eastward journey, safely passing through neutral waters; but, on the 19th, just after entering international waters 300 miles off the Virginia coast she was suddenly confronted headlong by a British destroyer. With certain capture imminent, the crew abandoned the liner, leaving her ablaze and sinking into the cold depths of the Atlantic.

Little doubt remained that the liner's every position had been secretly relayed to the British (one way American officials chose to help a friend while remaining able to claim neutrality). At any rate it was certain that *Columbus'* luxurious decks would no longer carry their complement of wealthy passengers on wonderful seafaring journeys, nor would they be used to ferry troops and supplies for the mighty Nazi onrush.

Lang departed Galveston on 21 December and headed back for Corpus Christi. The year was quickly coming to an end, but what a year indeed; few ships could boast such a beginning. What the future might hold remained speculative, but the war was certain to bring many more challenges.

In the meantime, focus remained on the present. Since most of the crew were from the East, a bit of homesickness was duly noted as the ship remained in a southern port during the Christmas season. Despite this, there was also noted new emotion among the crew, a real affection toward their new home. It was true, time and conditions were bringing about a new cohesiveness among the men and their ship.

With the crew complement being small, less than 200 at the time, nearly everyone knew everyone else by name. Consequently, the crew could fairly well be described as a large group of brothers. Though not all the brothers got along all the time (a few never), a new family type spirit was becoming prevalent.

The captain had become the father figure and, for better or worse, he had final say in matters related to the ship and crew. Not all captains would rate quite as high with their adopted brood as did Captain Johnson; his relationship with the crew could be said to be a little closer than his future counterparts, but it was not wartime and he could possibly afford to be so.

Lang was, of course, the mother figure; and she had so far earned a gold star in that regard. She had shown her boys some very special times, and some very special places, yet she had remained close to home, with mail and pay usually on time and fresh foods and water never lacking.

But times were changing, and quickly. The future was sure to bear darker moments. And though this newly found relationship and family spirit was destined to continue, the day was rapidly approaching when the recipe for it was to change.

Chapter 2

1940

The end of 1939 arrived and, aside from much heated rhetoric, had yet to produce the threatened land war in Europe. Beyond Germany's "lightening" defeat of Poland (Warsaw having surrendered on 28 September) and a few minor skirmishes along the French/German border, actual warfare on the European continent was yet to ignite. This otherwise inaction, though not intended as a slight to the very real and horrifying experiences of the Poles, gave reason for the media to label the declaration the "Phony War." Therefore, as the new year began, few people outside Europe gave serious regard to the conflict's true potential; and this was especially so in the United States.

In truth, however, neither England nor France had been fully prepared to fight such a full-scale war. Though both countries had potentially powerful militaries, each displayed early signs of weakness.

Whereas, Britain's Royal Navy was powerfully well established, her army was initially undermanned and ill-prepared, disallowing an immediate adequate defense of the homeland let alone establish a force powerful enough for a protracted war against Germany. Fortunately for the British the combination of the English Channel and the Royal Navy early on prevented Germany to threaten any meaningful assault against their island nation.

France, on the other hand, possessed an army and air force of formidable presence, more than adequate to protect itself from invasion. Yet the French leadership had mistakenly placed all their faith in an elaborate chain of fortified border defenses known as the "Maginot Line," boasting its impregnability. This overconfidence was to be costly as such faith was doomed to be shattered by German method and might.

Only at sea was there initial evidence of the declaration's reality. Though the land war may indeed have remained primarily a threatened campaign, this was not at all true in the North Atlantic. There warfare was very real and very deadly. At the start of hostilities Hitler had ordered his U-boats to attack all enemy shipping regardless of identity, the extent to which they were capable being characterized within the first 12 hours of conflict by the sinking of the British passenger liner *Athenia*, costing 112 lives, including those of innocent women and children.

From the outset, however, U.S. policy was determined to remain unchanged. Even the unforewarned and criminal attack on *Athenia* — with many Americans making up her passenger list — did little to persuade reevaluation of the war's true potential. The popular American isolation movement pushed harder than ever against any U.S. involvement in the European war. Most Americans ignorantly doubted Germany's ability to defeat both Britain and France. Those who warned of pending disaster and argued for an expanded role of America's military went largely unheard.

There was also the struggle between Japan and China to consider. This war also continued, but it too failed at alerting the American masses to its potential threat. Few ordinary people displayed any real concern to where this conflict might lead. China was distant and American interest there seemed minimal. Furthermore, the war in that region looked to be isolated and inconclusive; the Japanese might eventually control the territory but controlling the Chinese will to fight was considered by most a near hopeless proposition. Obviously, the fear that this war might lead to a direct attack against the United States was near nonexistent.

The fact remains that the clearly defined objectives of the antagonist's leadership were being ignored. As a result, the U.S., as a nation, in the government, the military and the civilian sector, was totally unprepared for the harsh reality of future events.

Despite most American's prevailing attitudes, however, 1940 was to hold many surprises and force many changes in thought and policy. That *Lang* and her crew were to experience several of those surprises as well as be included in the prerequisite of new policy seemed certain. Yet the true measure of turbulence the future was to bear remained a mystery.

As with all new ships of her time, *Lang*'s journey from infancy to maturity was destined to be a treacherous undertaking, and 1940 pointed the direction; war was to be unavoidable and would inevitably involve the United States. Just when and where that involvement would begin no one would know for sure. But the responsibility of growing up at a much accelerated pace would fall squarely on the shoulders of the armed services, and especially the Navy and newcomers such as *Lang*, of whom President Roosevelt had so much pride. Presently, however, it remained that the U.S. Navy's only authorized action was to be the patrolling of America's clearly defined neutral waters.

Chapter 2 – 1940

Lang yet remained in port at Corpus Christi on New Year's Day 1940. The destroyer had so far served nearly a full month of the neutrality patrols, and a readiness on behalf of her crew for a change from the monotonous rigors of their recent duty was most evident. Therefore, when news began to circulate that the ship would soon be departing for the east coast an immediate upsurge in morale was experienced. Even so, there was complete ignorance as to the event the move was to incorporate.

Just what intentions the move involved was of little concern to the crew; they were excited about the return, hoping the stay would be long enough for visits with family and friends. Such was not to be the case, however.

Arriving in port at Norfolk, Virginia, on 29 January, *Lang* was soon dockside and allowing men their liberty. But by 2 February the destroyer was again on the move, new orders in hand and steaming toward a new directive, Pensacola, Florida. There she was to return to patrolling the gulf, her new area of responsibility to extend all the way south to the Panama Canal.

Far from welcomed news, the voyage south had begun very somberly. Captain Johnson felt deeply his crew's disappointment at the renewal of patrol duty; he was not beyond the disappointment himself. Therefore, when just two days out to sea a new set of orders was received, redirecting the mission and promising an immediate lift in morale, no time was wasted in spreading the word. *Lang* was to continue to Pensacola, but rather than returning to the dull patrols as earlier prescribed, she would instead participate in a second presidential cruise.

A vigor not unlike that of her maiden experiences immediately returned to *Lang*. For the next several days the crew exhaustibly worked at preparing their ship for the presidential visit. The effort was so intense that some men even began to question if the president was worth all the fuss. Thoughts had returned to that time just prior to the first presidential cruise, when *Lang* was yet new, having therefore required little work in the preparations. Time had since had its effect; their ship was now showing evidence of her usage and requiring much greater effort at reestablishing her previous luster.

Obviously, several miles had been accumulated since that fateful day back in August of the previous year, though they had visibly manifested themselves ever so slightly. Yet the destroyer did show a few chips in her paint, some spots of rust here and there, a bit of tarnish to her brass fixtures, and a little excess of grease and oil on her machinery. These were to be expected as the salty sea takes its toll of all ships. Under any normal situation *Lang* would have been considered in "A-1" condition. But this was not a normal time. This upcoming voyage would require "spit and polish," a goal destined to keep the crew very busy throughout the next several days cleaning, and then cleaning some more. And, though many of ship's company would privately gripe about the extra work, theirs was an intent that *Lang* be the best looking ship afloat for the presidential cruise.

When indeed the destroyer sailed into the quaint southern port, arriving there on the 14th, she looked as if she had just "came off the assembly line." Everything on her shined, including her crew. Certainly the men had expended a great deal of energy during their labors, with several aching muscles as evidence, and when the opportunity came to display their ship before the people of Pensacola, they did so proudly.

Such effort had earned the crew a well deserved rest. That evening it was awarded, and most of the men found little difficulty in falling asleep. Watches remained alert and security was somewhat tighter, but otherwise there was little activity to disturb the surrounding peacefulness. Even the calm sheltered water of Pensacola Bay added its part to the tranquility of the night.

By early morning, however, *Lang* had again come to life. From within her bowels a full dressed crew rushed topside to take their places on deck. All preparations were now complete, with only the passage of time remaining till the moment of the president's arrival.

Anticipation weighed heavy upon the crew as they waited, though their suffering was not to be long. The presidential caravan arrived at the pier shortly after the crew's gathering, and Mr. Roosevelt appeared, closely shadowed by a group of aides, secret service men and reporters. Afterwards, the presidential entourage approached *Lang* and then moved up the gangway toward the main deck. A sudden high-pitched trill of a boatswain's pipe penetrated the air; and for a second time in the destroyer's short history the president's colors proceeded up to the peak of the main truck at midship.

With a proud and simultaneous effort, Captain Johnson saluted and greeted his Commander in Chief. In return, Mr. Roosevelt acknowledged the captain's welcome, again displaying his familiar smile, and then moved on to look over the ship and crew. Certainly his fondness for ships was made evident by his careful attention, and his nods of approval could have made the crew no prouder.

Following the quick inspection, the president and his entourage then proceeded to the forward section of the ship where a canvas canopy had been suspended around the forward most five-inch gun, or gun #1. From there Mr. Roosevelt was to enjoy the shelter as *Lang* taxied him into the bay and to his chosen transport, once again to be *Tuscaloosa*.

The transfer of the president went smoothly and, following the two ships being joined by the destroyer *Jouett*, the journey began. In the meantime, the small group of privileged press, consisting of George Durno (International News Service), Douglas Cornell (Associated Press), and Tom Reynolds (United Press), settled themselves aboard *Lang*, where they were to remain for the duration of the cruise. Obviously, the additional naval escort and the presence of the press greatly increased everyone's anticipation of the cruise. Yet it remained that no one but the president and his aides had true knowledge of their destination.

Such secrecy was bound to leave room for a considerable amount of speculation. Sailors were very good at speculation; they called it "scuttlebutt." Certainly many of *Lang*'s crew worked very hard to deliver a plausible story, yet it was the boys of the press who came up with the one story of most interest. Their conjecture determined the little convoy as headed for some grand conference at sea where the president would meet with envoys of the belligerent nations of Europe to discuss peace. But their effort, though sincere, proved mostly wishful thinking and far from the fact.

Some 48 hours out to sea the secrecy was finally dropped and the real reason for the voyage was given. It was then that Brigadier General Edwin M. Watson, the president's secretary and military aide, announced the destination to be the Panama Canal. There the president was to inspect defenses and confer with the commander of the Canal Zone, General Van Voorhis.

Though not as glamorous as hoped for, the mission was now established, and by noon on the 17th the convoy had reached a point in the journey just off the Nicaraguan coast. The weather this day was near picture perfect, with the sun shining brightly and the temperature in the eighties, bolstering enthusiasm among the crew to the uttermost.

That night the air cooled some and stars filled the heavens. An overwhelming sense of freshness and purity cast itself across the darkness with one continuous gentle breeze. Men who were off duty often made their way out upon the open decks to enjoy a moment of the serenity, refreshing both mind and spirit. This was another spectrum that was the life of a sailor. The solitude of such moments were to be shared by many, provoking a multitude of peaceful thoughts. Even during wartime there were to be moments like this. Clearly, however, war remained far outside the realm of thought on this night.

The pleasantries continued throughout the rest of the night and into the early morning hours, when at daybreak the ships arrived at the entrance to the Panama Canal. There the ships took a slight pause while Mr. Roosevelt disembarked his sea transport for shore. At Gatun Locks the president would begin his inspection, making the rest of the journey across the isthmus by train. Meanwhile, the convoy was to pass through the famous canal to meet up with the president at its opposite end.

For *Lang* this transit of the "Big Ditch" was a first, and therefore an exciting new experience for her crew. Transferring from lock to lock, sailors watched with amazement as water levels raised and lowered to the necessary depth for their ship to pass through, each movement being initiated by the tow of small electric locomotives.

Twelve such locks, each 1,000 feet in length and 110 feet in width, would require the process of passage be repeated by each ship of the convoy before all would finally reach their goal, the vast Pacific Ocean.

Here again, with an introduction to the world's largest body of water, *Lang* established another first in her aspiring career. In the future the Pacific was to hold many serious challenges for the destroyer, but such momentarily remained a mystery to her crew. For now, their entry was perceived as only an extension to the present cruise and the beginning of a new adventure.

The president had reboarded *Tuscaloosa* at Miraflores Locks in the late afternoon and shortly afterwards the journey had re-commenced. No time was wasted in heading to the convoy's next destination, a small isolated spot of land nestled in the Pacific some 400 miles south of Costa Rica known as Cocos Island. The purpose of the upcoming visit was to be purely recreational in nature, and was to allow the president some of his favorite pastime, fishing.

Arriving off the island on the 20th, the ships dropped anchor in the island's bay in preparation for their visit. A golden sky dotted by a number of smaller, fluffy clouds, each with a blue-gray body edged in silver, marked the beginning of the new day. Across a whitecapped ocean surface a golden trail formed, its origin a reflection of the sun which peeked above the horizon. The glowing trail seemed to lead directly to the island's sandy beach, where only the light crashing of small, foaming waves combined with the high-pitched call of a pair of seagulls to interrupt the surrounding tranquility. Dawn had arrived at Cocos Island.

Small boats were soon transporting various members of the crews to the island's shore, where a large congregation of sailors quickly formed. These men, their pant legs rolled in a manner of comfort, then broke off into small groups to investigate, beachcomb, wade, or just relax in some convenient shade.

A quick survey of the island proved it a small but alluring piece of Pacific real estate. Two large hills dominated the island's interior, while its surface was covered by a thick tropical forest and a carpet of thick green undergrowth. A few tropical flowers of bright yellow and red could be seen to boldly reflect their passion upon the background of foliage, while a most amazing variety of birds inhabited the trees. Ringing the forest at its border with the beach were many huge round stones, the surface of each having been worn smooth by many years of battering from both wind and sea. The beach itself glistened brightly, its surface providing spacious room for sandpipers their run, crystal clear tidal pools in which crabs could bathe, and enduring hiding places for a multitude of creatures who hurried to rebury themselves upon the receding of each foaming wave. And encircling the small land mass was the beautifully clear blue water of the Pacific, a water particularly well-known for its quality fishing.

Yellowtails, it was said, were so plentiful around the island one could catch them on "unbaited hooks." Once tiring of such simplistic sport, sailors could then use the yellowtails as bait for a more exciting game fish, sharks.

Indeed, it was during one of these fishing episodes that a young *Lang* sailor made what was called "a masterful catch." Using a light weight tackle outfit — one normally used for bass or trout fishing — he managed to hook a shark that was near ten feet in length. With considerable patience he carefully cranked, slowly drawing his catch alongside the ship, where it was at once hauled out of the water by use of the ship's boat winch.

Obviously, such a prize drew much attention; no one could quite figure out how a shark of such size could be hauled in with such light gear. But the mystery was soon solved as a sailor produced a knife and sliced deeply into the shark's belly. Not too surprising, from out of the bloody opening fell six to seven baby sharks, each about two feet in length, and each swimming away immediately upon hitting the water. The shark was a pregnant female that was just at the point of giving birth, making her far too weak to fight her captor.

Under similar circumstances, though on a different occasion, a giant manta ray was spotted investigating an area a short distance from the anchored ships; and in response a determined group of secret service agents and news men commandeered a 26 foot motor launch to give the creature chase. The manta, however, proved much wider than the motor launch was long. A real monster, the ray measured nearly 30 feet from wingtip to wingtip.

Undaunted by the creature's size, however, the determined launch crew continued their pursuit, and once they had gained the desired range they fired a harpoon into the monster manta's upper profile. The harpoon, which was attached to the launch by a half-inch manila line, quickly found its target and dug in firmly.

The manta's reaction was immediate; down it dove, deeper and deeper, and when the manila line ran out all its length down too went the launch. Uncontrollable laughter immediately erupted from everyone who witnessed the exhibition of foolishness. Cameras and equipment went flying through the air as the determined fishermen were sent on a premature swim. The wounded manta was not to be taken.

Unlike the previously caught shark the manta was not to allow any size line to hold its powerful mass. Taut to its extreme, the manila line snapped and, with almost complete unison to its outcast crew, the launch rebounded to the surface. Thus the show ended and the fishermen, their clothes thoroughly watersoaked and their spirits severely dampened, were safely recovered. And, despite their personal setback, the secret service agents and news men had successfully provided the sailors with a story destined to be told and retold throughout future years.

Time continued on its pace but allowed each member of the cruise to share in the spirit filled fun. From sunup to sundown — and so beautiful they were — everyone was to enjoy the serene surroundings of the secluded tropical island.

Each night a silver moon appeared to make a path across the sea, highlighting the whitecaps all around, while a warm sea breeze lazily flowed by those who would be out to enjoy the beautiful picture of peace. In the end, the only thing that could have made the sailors happier would have been the arrival of a shipload of beautiful girls to enhance their paradise found. But the girls never arrived, and all too soon the convoy was again on the move, retracing its path back to the states.

The convoy arrived back at Pensacola on 1 March. Obviously, the cruise had been very enjoyable, but the time had finally come for it to end. In so doing, President Roosevelt again made his way over to *Lang* in preparation for transport to the naval air station. And, with the presidential colors proudly flying once more, *Lang* completed her honored duty and returned the president to shore.

Later that same day *Lang* departed Pensacola and proceeded to her next destination. The journey would take her around the southern tip of Florida, up the southeastern coastline, and through the treacherous waters of Cape Hatterus to arrive back at the Virginia port of Norfolk on the fourth. There the destroyer spent ten days receiving a routine check-over and the crew spent time visiting with family and friends.

Lang's first full year of service was rapidly drawing to its close. Obviously, it had been a year that had brought with it considerable excitement and challenge. Yet, though uncertain in detail, the future promised even greater ventures and obstacles for both ship and crew. And a further hint to that future was to be provided by *Lang*'s next destination.

Despite American diplomatic efforts, Japan was continuing its territorial land grab in China, resulting in further escalation in an already ongoing war of words between the U.S. and Japanese governments. While both the threat the Japanese posed in the Pacific increased and the heated conflict in the North Atlantic intensified, changes in the makeup of the U.S. Navy were assured; as too were preparations for war. And for this reason Pearl Harbor, an otherwise obscure U.S. Navy Base on the Hawaiian island of Oahu, was to become the focal point of interest for both the U.S. and Japanese Navies.

Fleet problems, or exercises as more commonly known, had been conducted in the Pacific on several previous occasions, coming and going without any long lasting tribute. Fleet Problem XXI, however, was to be quite different, leading the U.S. Navy directly into a whole new aspect of attention toward both the Pacific and Japan.

Hawaii was picked for the fleet problems due that it was far enough west to be of some intimidation to the Japanese, yet far enough east of the International Dateline to safely prevent unwanted confrontation. That the Japanese would not react well to the

American display of power was to be of no surprise. Yet that Hawaii, and more specifically Pearl Harbor, was to evolve out of the exercise as the U.S. Navy's most important strategic center in the Pacific was not only surprising to many but highly controversial throughout the Naval leadership.

Indeed, Admiral James Richardson, then Commander in Chief United States Fleet, would emphatically argue the harbor was too small for his fleet, too distant for its proper resupply, and too primitive to sustain the necessary morale of its sailors. President Roosevelt, however, held the unyielding view of the base's strategic value as a deterrent to any future aggression by Japan. Therefore, Richardson was overruled; Pearl Harbor was to become home for the U.S. Fleet.

Per her orders, *Lang* had begun her move west across the Pacific in familiar stride. The course she sailed was an almost identical trace of the previous presidential cruise — obviously void the pomp and circumstance.

Nearly a non-stop voyage, Point Loma, San Diego, California, was to be the only layover for the ship and crew before proceeding onward to Hawaii. This pause lasted only a week, allowing for some well deserved rest and recreation (R&R). Then on 1 April the destroyer again weighed anchor and headed out to the open sea in continuance to her Hawaiian rendezvous.

So very quickly the western coastline faded, and many of the crew displayed an obvious sadness at the knowledge that their return would not be for some time. This, however, was just the first of many such departures. The sadness felt at this moment would only be compounded in the future. Even this day and month, which momentarily meant little more than a departure date and April Fool's Day, would a few eventful years in the future be the beginning of the darkest hours for *Lang* and her crew.

Despite a definite darkness in the future, the present had established itself in an explosion of bright sunshine. Each day of the quiet, calm journey westward began and ended with beautiful sunrises and sunsets, revealing the Pacific in its purest shade of blue. Such beauty combined with thoughts of new places to visit and venture upon kept the crew in high spirits. Even Captain Johnson found the journey to be uplifting — at least to a point.

His leadership at this point thoroughly established, having early on gained the respect of his crew, Captain Johnson had little to prove in keeping his authority intact. The pride he had in his ship and crew was never hidden, often displayed by his glowing face. The crew knew what he expected of them, and what to expect of him. This journey, however, the captain chose to do the unexpected, mystifying his men by calling for a special dress inspection, requiring "dress white uniforms with medals."

After being notified of the inspection, the crew looked at one another rather dumbfounded. "Medals, who in the world would have any medals at this time?" was the thought. The captain had obviously "flipped his lid."

Then, as to confound everyone the more, as some of the crew returned to their quarters they observed Kenneth R. Johnson, a third class gunner's mate, kicking the time out of his locker. As he kicked he yelled, "I'll be damned if I'll wear mine! He doesn't know I've got them!"

Gunner Johnson was considerably older than most of the rest of the crew, but otherwise no one knew him to be anything more or less than anybody else. He rarely spoke of his past and therefore his actions remained a mystery. But, once being bombarded with innumerable questions, he finally admitted to having served in the Army during the First World War. As it turned out, he was a hero, having a Silver Star, Bronze Star, three other American medals, three French medals, and a lanyard to be worn over the left shoulder.

Immediately upon learning the gunner's story, heads got together and plans began to formulate. A couple of men went to the ship's office to obtain a copy of Navy regulations to the order the medals should be worn. Meanwhile, the rest worked to convince the gunner of his need to follow orders, pausing in the debate only when the thought of seeing the captain's face caused an uncontrollable outburst of laughter.

Gunner Johnson, however, proved quite difficult to persuade. He just wasn't in favor of the idea at all, requiring several men great physical effort at just getting him dressed and on deck for the inspection. Fighting nearly every inch of the way, the gunner's boisterous resistance ceased only when on deck the division officer ordered him to fall in. Now he had little choice but to obey, and all that remained was for the captain to appear.

As the men waited, a warm tropical sun shone down and a continuous breeze of warm air flowed past their ranks. Seconds seemed to drag on and many of the men were finding it very difficult to keep a straight face. But then the captain appeared. With a slight smile on his face, he proudly approached wearing his own dress white uniform, and pinned to his chest hung a single medal. He hadn't even started the inspection when his eyes suddenly caught sight of the decorated sailor. One look at all the gunner's hardware was all it took. With a red face, the captain turned himself about and walked away. That ended that inspection, and never again was another held which called for medals. Obviously, the proud captain had been humbled by one rather humble gunner, and outmaneuvered by a crew much sharper than he ever expected.

The sailing lasted several more days. Then, one morning as sailors gazed forward a slight haze was spotted low on the horizon. As the ship drew closer, the bluish haze began to grow and take on a more visible form. Moving still closer, the bluish form turned a lush green and disclosed two dominate volcanic peaks, Mauna Kea and Mauna Loa. It was the "big island" of Hawaii.

Graceful flights of Seagulls began to fly around the ship as it proceeded on to the island of Maui and her destination of Lahaina Roads. All along the way the crew admired the beauty of this tropical paradise, a beauty so rich with color and enchantment that even the very existence of time was consumed.

At Lahaina an even greater sight greeted the crew. There before them in all its splendor stood the U.S. Fleet. It was an awesome display of power. Warship after warship dotted the channel, each alert, sharp, and invincible in appearance. And, as the sun shone down through gathering clouds, *Lang* proudly took her position among the grand assemblage, prepared to do her part.

Though originally never intended to be so long, the next two months *Lang* remained in Hawaiian waters participating in fleet problems. Challenge after challenge was presented the ships and crews, testing their abilities to perform the tasks for which they were designed. Each day had turned into a constant array of drills and practice, and for good reason; the land war in Europe had finally erupted with a vengeance, while relations with Japan were rapidly deteriorating to a point of no return.

At sea each dawn began in a soon to be familiar fashion. A loud "bong! bong! bong!" signaled general quarters, sending men hurrying to their assigned stations. Life preservers and helmets were hastily grabbed along the way of the rush. Phone systems cracked as each station reported "manned and ready!" Orders blared across the various loud speakers as *Lang* quickly began to pick up speed, slicing through the water in a sharp turn. Guns began to move up and down and around as the destroyer rocked beneath them. Then, just as suddenly as it had begun, it was over.

Obviously, such drills were to be a continuous exercise in training, preparing the men for what could be, and destined to be a never ending process that even war would not preclude. They were most definitely a considerable change of pace for the crew of *Lang*. With numerous anti-aircraft drills, anti-submarine drills, mock torpedo runs, and gunnery practices the challenges seemed never ending. And though somewhat exciting in the beginning, as months passed the rigorous training soon proved rather monotonous.

Finally, however, on 26 April *Lang* received a welcomed break in the training schedule to make her first entry into Pearl Harbor. There the crew found a base that was especially large, even though its waterways were momentarily congested with all the extra shipping. Intense construction of new facilities throughout different areas of the base did, however, disclose improvements for its future role. Yet to the crew of *Lang* Pearl seemed no more impressive (probably lesser so) than any other base they had previously visited. Places like Hickam Field (which had just been completed) Wheeler Field, and Ford Island left little to no impression upon their minds.

What was of much greater interest to the sailors stood just outside the confines of the base. Neighboring Honolulu, capital of Hawaii, was as modern as any small U.S. city, and therefore especially alluring to Pacific sailors. It boasted modern structures, bordered by wide streets of crushed lava pavement. Automobiles, street cars, and bicycles were in abundance and busily transporting the populous from one rendezvous to another along the business district, where after dark nightlife crowded the many bars and clubs. For those who longed for a more relaxed atmosphere, the city's ocean front boasted the crescent shaped beach of Waikiki, its background lined by tall coconut trees, luxurious foliage and near hidden structures of white and pink, highlighted by the famous pink Royal Hawaiian Hotel. Throughout the city's outskirts remained many reminders of the island's ancient past, including a great many occupied grass hut homes. And overshadowing all stood the mountainous peak of Diamond Head, Oahu's most famous natural landmark.

There was indeed much to explore and enjoy about the island. And, since Pearl was now home for the U.S. Fleet, it was certain that a great deal more time was destined to be spent visiting its sights.

Lang did, however, depart Pearl on 16 June for a rather quick return to the states. Her destination, by way of Puget Sound, Washington (where the crew received a well deserved five days of liberty), was San Diego, where she was to join destroyers *Somers* (DD-381) and *Wilson* (DD-408) in escorting the battleship *Maryland* (BB-46) back to Pearl.

This trip was routine and rather unremarkable. Occasional drills continued, especially on the return trip with *Maryland* in company, but nothing outside the ordinary occurred. And on the morning of 12 July Oahu was again sighted and Pearl was soon being revisited.

At her return, *Lang*'s first duty was to welcome aboard Commander D. P. Moon, Commodore of Destroyer Division 15. With the commodore's flag raised to the peak of the main truck at mid-ship, *Lang* assumed flagship for the division, which included destroyers *Sterett* (DD-407), *Benham*, and *Wilson*.

Destroyer Division 15 departed Pearl on the afternoon of 17 July to rejoin the still progressing fleet problems. This voyage was to take the division some distance to the south, stopping briefly at Lahaina Roads on the 19th and at Palmyra Island on the 22nd before proceeding further.

The uniqueness of this voyage was that at its climax the division was to cross the equator, which was to be yet another first for *Lang*. For sailors such occasion was very special, and Navy tradition dictated it be met with special ceremony.

Though a number of *Lang*'s crew had crossed the equator during previous service on other ships, a greater number had yet to meet the experience. Those who were veterans of previous crossings, the so-called "Shellbacks," were given charge of preparing a special series of initiation activities for the rest, the so-called "Pollywogs."

The spectacle was to begin on the evening of 23 July. It was then that a specter from the deep, Davy Jones, appeared on the deck of *Lang*. The apparition was actually one of the Shellbacks dressed as the devil of the sea, half naked, bearded and crowned with an authoritative chapeau. During this ceremonial visit he passed out subpoenas to the Pollywogs, requiring each to appear before the court of King Neptune.

Early the next morning the bluish bearded ruler of the sea made his grand appearance, again another of the Shellbacks in costume. With a crown sitting upon his head and a forked scepter in hand, he prepared to pass out judgements to the accused.

The first order of business, however, was the passing of command of *Lang* from Captain Johnson to the most powerful king. With a band of sea spirits at his side King Neptune received the captain, and in turn the captain relinquished command of *Lang* to him. Upon the exchange the Jolly Roger (the well-known skull and crossbones banner of black) glided to the peak of the main truck. Then, as the king and his court took their appropriate places, the lowly Pollywogs were each brought forth and the trials began.

One by one the Pollywogs had the charges — trumped up as they were — read to them. It was to be of no surprise that each one would be found guilty and sentenced to the extreme measure. All knew what to expect; all sentences were the same, a condemnation of enslavement to the dictates of the Shellbacks. Afterwards, his task all complete, King Neptune returned command of *Lang* back to Captain Johnson, and the ordeal began.

Large paddles prodded the Pollywogs along as the Shellbacks led them through a maze of misery. Forced to crawl around the ship on all fours, slide through canvas shoots filled with rotten garbage, do impossible chores, answer unanswerable questions, and endure enumerable other disgusting events, no Pollywog was to find his experience pleasant. In addition, nothing was ever to the satisfaction of the ruling Shellbacks, who wheeled their paddles to land on soon tenderized rear-ends of the Pollywogs for punishment. Very little mercy was shown anyone, and even officers, whose rank only meant the possibility of greater punishment, were not excused from the pain of transition from Pollywog to Shellback. Obviously, the memories of this day were destined to remain with those involved for some time. And, as the initiations thankfully ended, the new Shellbacks delighted in the day when they would be able to pass along the experience.

With a complete complement of Shellbacks, *Lang* arrived back at Pearl on 29 July. And almost immediately the destroyer returned to the old routine of patrolling and drilling. For the next four months *Lang* was destined to remain in the waters around Hawaii in near continuous training.

It was during this time, on 21 October, *Lang* and crew said farewell to a grand skipper. Lieutenant Commander Felix Johnson had served his ship and crew well, establishing and building upon a devotion to ship and duty. His tour aboard the destroyer now ended, he departed her decks one last time, directing his course to some future challenge in his naval career. Certainly Captain Johnson had been well liked by the crew, and they obviously hated to see him leave. More importantly, the crew dreaded his replacement, whose presence already graced the decks of *Lang*.

Lieutenant Commander John A. Waters, Jr., was a husky though seemingly quiet man. He had arrived aboard *Lang* to find himself in the awkward position of taking command of a ship where the captain before him was very well liked by his crew. As with every officer whoever takes a new command, he faced a crew who had considerable distrust in his leadership. Rarely, if ever, is any commander a carbon copy in personality and performance of his predecessor. Captain Waters was of no exception; he had a job to do, to set up his own command in his own way. This he would do and, as time progressed, his mild mannerisms would gain him the respect he so sought from his new crew.

Lang departed Pearl on 2 December. Captain Waters positioned himself upon the bridge and directed his new command on a course that would take them back to the states, the destination being San Diego. It was a welcomed transit for both captain and crew, overshadowing the recent change of command and lifting an otherwise shaky morale.

The trip proved to be pleasant, but the anticipation of the return caused time to pass by so very slowly. Yet, if only the crew could have been able to see into the future, just to know how precious this voyage eastward in the Pacific was to be. In many respects time was moving fast — so very fast indeed. The day was quickly approaching when many ships were to venture across the wide reaches of the Pacific and never return.

Finally, on 8 December, *Lang* arrived at her destination and settled in for a three week stay. During this time all hands received a week to ten days leave. Even while the crew remained aboard ship liberty was exceptional, with the crew being divided into sections, one aboard and two ashore.

The holidays were also exceptional. On Christmas Day the crew once again joined together as a family to share in the special occasion. In creating a little atmosphere for the event, a Christmas tree had been placed upon the ship's quarter deck. Obviously, since most of the crew were from the east, it was a little difficult in getting into the right mood without some snow, but this prevented no one from enjoying the feast created by the ship's cooks.

Indeed, Christmas dinner was a meal just "like mother used to cook," boasting roasted turkey, baked ham, oyster dressing, giblet gravy, cranberry sauce, sweet mixed gherkins, candied yams, buttered broccoli, celery and olives. For desert there were fruit cake, ice cream and hard candy. The drink was a good old sailor standby, coffee. And, added to all was a gift pack of cigarettes. Truly it was a special day — and no one could have known this was to be the last Christmas to be spent stateside by any crew of *Lang*.

Chapter 3

1941

While 1940 had been a good year for *Lang*, it had proven quite disastrous to the free world, and especially to those nations caught in the destructive whirlwind of the new European war. The blitzkrieg (lightening war) tactic adopted and utilized by the German Army had maximized its ability at defeating its adversaries, the scope and speed of such conquests stunning in proportions. By 10 May the Nazis had ran through Luxemburg. Four days later Holland had surrendered. 25 May had brought the first of many bombs to pound British soil. Three days later Belgium had surrendered. Two days after that the British Royal Navy had begun its near miraculous evacuation of hundreds of thousands of stranded British, French, Belgian, and Dutch troops from the shores of Dunkirk. On 10 June Italy had joined Germany by declaring war on France and England. Just four days later Paris fell. By 22 June France had surrendered. And in August Germany had begun a massive air offensive against the south of England that continued into the new year. Yet, despite near desperation, Britain alone stood.

In Washington D.C., President Roosevelt watched the situation carefully, exploring his options, knowing the United States could dire afford Britain's defeat. Yet American military intervention was clearly out of the question. The American public continued to want no part of the European war, making commitment of America's armed forces politically impossible. The best Roosevelt could manage was a "Short of War" policy which allowed the U.S. to assist in keeping Britain supplied with the war materials necessary to continue the fight. Hitler would have to cast the first stone if America's war machine was to get directly involved.

In addition to the chaos in Europe, Roosevelt also faced a situation where with Japan relations were growing increasingly worse. The Imperial Japanese Army continued its occupation of China and continued to seek ways of expanding its influence throughout eastern Asia. Hitler's successes in Europe only compounded the problem, as Japan saw the European weaknesses as opportunities for expansion into additional southeast Asian territories. The problem was compounded further when on 22 June Japan's somewhat moderate government was replaced by a militaristic one, positioning General Hideki Tojo as Minister of War.

War with Japan now looked completely unavoidable (in fact, Pearl Harbor had been warned to be on alert for attack as early as 7 June). Japan, however, remained vulnerable to American economic pressure, and in July access to several American markets had been denied her, including aviation materials and certain classes of scrap iron and steel. Thus Roosevelt hoped to slow Japanese aggression while forcing some type of diplomacy in avoidance of immediate warfare.

Obviously, the embargo of war materials was not well received by the Japanese, yet it did little to influence change in their behavior; by the end of August the Japanese Army had occupied northern Indochina, establishing advance airfields for future aggression. Then, on 27 September, in a deliberate display of their defiance the Japanese signed the Tripartite Pact, allying themselves with Nazi Germany and Fascist Italy. Three days later the U.S. government responded by tightening its embargo even further, halting all exports of steel and iron to the Japanese. And so tension continued on the incline and relations on the decline.

The beginning of 1941 brought no promise of immediate improvement in Europe's situation, but it certainly held some glimmer of hope. Europe remained under tight German control, yet Britain's steadfast opposition was proving a proverbial thorn in the Axis' side. Though Germany's bombing campaign of England had caused considerable death and destruction, British fortitude remained strong if not strengthened, and at great cost to the Luftwaffe. The Royal Navy also remained healthy, battling German U-boats in the Atlantic, stubbornly holding open sea lanes in the Mediterranean, and severely stinging the Italian Navy at its base in Taranto (a naval ariel torpedo attack due to be seriously studied and later copied by Japanese war planners for use at Pearl Harbor). Even the British Army was having success pushing the Italians back in North Africa, though such success was to be short-lived, the Italians soon to be re-enforced by Germany's newly formed Afrika Corp under the command of General Erwin Rommel.

In light of the reality of probable multiple confrontations in the near future, in July of 1940 the U.S. Congress had passed the "Two-Ocean Navy Bill." This bill allocated the funding for an increased building program of naval shipping for the creation of a new Atlantic Fleet, though actual building was to remain at peacetime levels. In the meantime, the U.S. Fleet remained almost entirely a Pacific Fleet, continuing its roll as intimidator to Japanese aggression, and so setting the stage for destiny to play its heavy hand.

Lang began the new year departing San Diego for a stint at the Mare Island Navy Yard, there to undergo two and one half months of yard overhaul. The British success at Taranto had not gone unnoticed by U.S. planners either who had seen the airplane's performances in the European and Asian conflicts as proof of the importance of providing ships a strong anti-aircraft defense. Therefore, six new gun stations for an increased battery of .50 caliber machine guns were to be provided the destroyer, these guns to be positioned on the starboard and port sides at forward (group I), midship (group II), and aft (group III). This increase in topside weight would also determine the necessity of removing the two after quadruple torpedo mounts, not only reducing the ship's offensive torpedo capacity to eight but testifying to the seriousness that versatility would play for warship survival in modern warfare.

Immediately following this overhaul, on 11 March, the destroyer and crew departed Mare Island to return to their Pacific home base in Hawaii. In the process, while in exit of San Francisco Bay, the ship passed beneath the monumental framework of the Golden Gate Bridge. The undeniable silhouette of this massive structure and the security provided by the West Coast were destined to become synonymous. For many a homesick Pacific sailor no sight would hold more promise or be more welcomed — and no sight would be more sadly gazed upon as it all too soon faded from the view of those who would depart to an unknown destiny.

Lang made a short trip back to San Diego and after a brief stay on 18 March departed for Pearl as a part of the screen for the carrier *Lexington* (CV-2). Though very much unknown to the crew of the destroyer, their new duty was only a preview of their future role. Obviously, carriers were to play a vital part in the upcoming Pacific campaign, yet just as vital to the carriers were their destroyer screens. The relationship between the two vessel types was destined to grow to one of endearment and mutual trust one for the other. Each was to serve as protectorate for the other, and though both were to prove very able to fight successfully in an independent manner, the security of having the other nearby was always to be welcomed.

Aside from the screening duties, the trip back to Pearl was otherwise unremarkable, the ships making their arrival on 25 March. Afterward, *Lang* reassumed the roll of flagship for Destroyer Division 15 and immediately returned to the routine of patrolling and drilling.

Under the circumstances, *Lang*'s crew had expected their stay at Pearl to be one of an indefinite period of time. Yet there had been some important changes during their absence, and destiny was again to direct their course.

The first group of changes had occurred while *Lang* had been going through her overhaul at Mare Island. On 1 February the United States Fleet had been renamed the Pacific Fleet and directed to be permanently stationed at Pearl (that same day Admiral Richardson, who had opposed the move, was relieved and replaced by Admiral Husband E. Kimmel). Meanwhile, the war in the Atlantic was spreading, Hitler's U-boats having moved into the central areas of those waters to take an even greater toll on merchant shipping. Also, new agreements between the U.S. and Britain had been made for the newly formed Atlantic Fleet to participate in escort-of-convoy as soon as possible. Thus the expanded threat to shipping and the new responsibilities of escort combined with ongoing neutrality patrols was placing a great strain on the limited resources of the small Atlantic surface fleet. And though new ships were being assembled, they were not keeping with demand.

U.S. Naval leaders debated the problem, and with reservation Admiral H. R. Stark, Chief of Naval Operations (CNO), finally ordered the transfer of one carrier, three battleships, four light cruisers and two destroyer squadrons from the Pacific to supplement the needy Atlantic Fleet. This change was to be initiated between the months of April and June, and on 14 May *Lang* departed Pearl to return to the East Coast for the new duty.

Obviously, the move was welcomed news to the destroyer's crew. Thoughts of being reunited with family and friends lifted their spirits to a new height. Yet, as *Lang* carried her jovial crew across the sea, the true outcome of the move remained veiled. Sailing in company of Battleship Division 1, which included the West Coast bound *Arizona* (BB-39) and *Nevada* (BB-36), who aboard could have known what fate had in store?

By 2 June *Lang* was once again transferring through the locks of the Panama Canal. It had been almost 14 months since she had last made this transit, and her crew was visibly anxious about getting through. After departing the canal at Balboa, however, the ship's course was diverted. New orders required the destroyer to spend a week of duty at Guantanamo Bay, Cuba, on anti-submarine patrol before continuing to the states.

Finally, on 11 June and in company of *Wilson*, *Lang* departed Guantanamo for the Philadelphia Navy Yard, arriving at the destination four days later. And there the happy crew were awarded a week of good liberty.

The visit at Philadelphia lasted till the 23rd. On this day, with *Wilson* still in their company, Captain Waters directed his ship back to sea and set a course to Boston, where they arrived on the next day. There, both destroyers joined the cruisers *Philadelphia* (CL-41) and *Savannah* (CL-42) — both also being recent transfers from the Pacific — to form Task Force 27. This force then departed Boston on the 25th for neutrality patrol on the ocean lanes leading to Bermuda.

During this new patrol the ships came in contact with a number of vessels. Several were stopped and investigated during the few days that the patrol lasted. Most of these were of little interest, but one vessel did bring to the crews of the American ships a bit of the Atlantic war's reality.

Stad Arnheim was an unarmed Dutch freighter, of little noteworthiness other than she had a few days earlier fished from the sea 15 survivors of the sunken German motor ship *Albert*. *Albert* had met her fate nearly a month earlier when bombed by British warplanes. Afterward, the survivors had clung to a single life raft, praying for rescue from their pitiful circumstance. Finally, 26 painful days later, they were spotted by the crew of *Stad Arnheim*. Obviously, the condition of the survivors was poor, with some suffering wounds from the initial bombing, and all suffering from exposure to the elements. *Stad Arnheim*, however, had no medical officer and could only provide basic aid. So it was, when the neutral American patrol was spotted, a call was given for medical assistance. In response, the American ships closed the freighter and the medical staff of one of the light cruisers were sent aboard. The survivors were then treated, and *Stad Arnheim* was then allowed to continue on her way. The fate suffered by the crew of *Albert* had, however, reminded the American sailors how perilous the war truly was, and just how cruel bad fortune could be.

The task force continued its otherwise unremarkable patrolling till 8 July, when it made entry into the beautiful coral group of the Bermudas. This visit was again to be another first for *Lang*'s crew, and one they would truly enjoy. The islands not only boasted natural beauty but also simplicity. Of the islands' more unusual features was its main forms of transportation, consisting primarily of bicycles and horse drawn carriages. The only exceptions to these were the few motor vehicles that belonged to the military high command. Yet these were used very discreetly, as the Bermudians were very displeased with their use on the islands. Indeed, the serenity of the islands was by far one of their greatest virtues.

Following nine wonderful days in the Bermudas *Lang* weighed anchor and began a journey to Charleston, South Carolina, where she arrived on the 19th. There she set in for a three week period of general overhaul work, which would again allow most of the crew a weeks leave.

Of the changes to be made to the destroyer, most again dealt with anti-aircraft defense. As an upgrade to her existing firepower, the .50 caliber machine guns were to be replaced by six new 20-millimeter Oerlikon guns. With their larger caliber, greater reliability and high rate of fire (450 rpm), these new guns would in the future prove worthy their investment over and over again.

In addition to these new weapons, another less visible but highly important addition was that of a new device, yet new in concept and early in its development, called radar (*Lang*'s initial version an air search (SA) type only). So new was the introduction of this device to ships that few men understood its method of operation, and few commanders were convinced of its usefulness. But, with further improvements, this new instrument of war was to later help tip the balance toward an Allied victory.

It was also during this stay that *Lang* received yet another change in her command. The quiet Lieutenant Commander John A. Waters, Jr., had not had a lengthy duty aboard the destroyer, yet his leadership was in every way successful. He had added to the ship's and crew's preparedness, and had, as his predecessor, done so while remaining on good terms with his crew. But though his role as skipper for *Lang* was ended, his career continued, taking him elsewhere in the service of his country.

As replacement for Waters there remained a short, slender Lieutenant Commander by the name of Erskine A. Seay (pronounced "Sea"). Obviously, there was again a considerable amount of apprehension toward the change on behalf of the crew. And this apprehension was not to be without warrant.

Captain Seay was strictly Navy; a by-the-book type who believed in procedure and the chain of command. He would deal with his men through his officers only, which would gain him no points with his new crew. Captain Seay, however, did not see his new job as a personality contest. It was not so important to him that his new crew liked him as it was that they respected his command. This they would certainly do in due time.

Lang departed Charleston on 12 August as a part of the screen for the carrier *Yorktown* (CV-5), destined for Norfolk. Arriving at Norfolk the following day, the destroyer remained in port for just two days before again departing, this time with a battleship/cruiser/destroyer task group headed for Casco Bay, Maine, to conduct maneuvers along the New England coast.

Arriving at Casco Bay on the 19th, the crew spent the next three weeks returning to the old routine of patrolling and drilling. Afterwards, on 12 September, Captain Seay directed his command back south, again in the company of *Wilson*, to begin a two and one half month tour of duty patrolling along the eastern seaboard between Casco Bay and Bermuda.

By the 17th *Lang* and *Wilson* had joined up with the cruiser *Nashville* (CL-43) for a three day series of exercises in anti-aircraft gunnery. The war in Europe and the threats from Japan were causing radical changes in military thinking and development, and the airplane was emerging at the forefront of concern, proving itself to be an extremely deadly and destructive foe as well as a highly effective aide in combat situations. Preparation of crews to meet this increased danger was given high priority. Yet friendly planes towing target sleeves (a giant-like orange shirt sleeve) on long cables some distance behind could only provide for practicing marksmanship against a speedy airborne target, not at all the type of death dueling experience of real combat. That experience could only be received the hard way.

Obviously, with her multi-purpose five-inch batteries, new 20-millimeter machine guns, and newly installed radar system (only a handful of ships had this devise by this early date), *Lang* was a very fortunate ship for her time. She was speedy, highly maneuverable, and well armed; all of which were needed in successful anti-air-defense. Despite her abilities, however, preparations in meeting the speedy developments of the combat airplane were to be never ending, with continuous improvements to be an ongoing challenge for both ship and crew.

Lang ended her latest patrol duty returning to Casco Bay on 28 November. There she remained for only two days before again departing, accompanying the *Yorktown* to Norfolk, where they arrived on 2 December.

By this time most everyone realized that war for the United States was just around the corner. The crew of *Lang*, like most other servicemen, had known the probabilities for some time. They had been spending month after month for the past year and a half preparing for its likelihood. They were also aware of who the enemies would likely be. But, like everyone else, they remained ignorant to exactly how, when or where it would begin. Very soon they, along with everyone else, were to learn the answer.

Japanese plans to attack and destroy the U.S. Pacific Fleet at Pearl Harbor had originated in the astute mind of Fleet Admiral Isoroku Yamamoto. Having lived in the United States for a time while obtaining a portion of his education (a student at Harvard and a naval attaché to Washington), Yamamoto learned much about the American way of life, culture, and industrial might. Those high-ranking American officials who had dealt with him greatly respected his intelligence and shrewdness. When playing such challenging games as chess and poker, he studied carefully each of his opponents and always played to win. As Fleet Admiral he had applied such special traits and knowledge to his office to great advantage. And, knowing Japan was determined to expand her influence throughout the Far East, provoking both the U.S. and Britain toward war, he quickly begin studying how best to meet his future adversaries, and especially how to deal with America's powerful Pacific Fleet.

In January 1941 Yamamoto had secretly ordered his staff to begin assessing his plan to attack Pearl Harbor. On 1 February he had secretly forwarded his plan to Rear Admiral Takijiro Onishi, Chief of Staff of the Eleventh Air Fleet, for further study. And from there the plan was handed over to Commander Minoru Genda, the Imperial Navy's brilliant long-range fighter operations innovator.

Obviously, Yamamoto's plan was risky, even to the point of playing with disaster, but Genda agreed it was possible.

Defeating the United States in war, however, was never a question for Yamamoto; he knew well America's present and potential power. A successful attack against Pearl Harbor, hopefully destroying the U.S. Pacific Fleet's short-term ability to interfere, was to allow the Imperial Navy and Army free reign to establish a fortress in the Pacific so powerful as to make American intervention too costly in lives and money for the American society to stand. Yamamoto knew any war with the U.S. that could not be forced to terms within two years Japan would lose. Therefore, a bold and massive blow must be used in the outset, and Pearl Harbor was to be the key recipient.

Throughout the first half of 1941 Yamamoto's Pearl Harbor attack plans remained his own carefully guarded secret. Then, on 25 July, Japan announced to the U.S. its agreement with Vichy France for Japanese military occupation of French Indochina as a co-protectorate of the French colony. This occupation constituted an ominous threat against the U.S. territory of the Philippines and American reaction was prompt; the very next day Roosevelt ordered the freezing of all Japanese assets in the U.S., effectively choking off all Japanese trade with the west and especially that for oil.

The Japanese economy would not long be able to stand such drastic measures and her military would not long move without oil. The ball was now in Japan's court, so to speak, and the Japanese government could either give up ground or go to war with the United States. The door was opened, and the following month Yamamoto took the opportunity to present his bold plan at striking at America first to the rest of his naval commanders.

Yamamoto's plan received careful attention, and much criticism, but in the end was accepted. Planning began in earnest in September with the official order for the operation given on 5 November. Admiral Kimmel had made a habit of bringing his fleet to port every Sunday, and Yamamoto knew this, therefore the attack was planned for 8 December (7 December Hawaiian time). On 10 November the Imperial Fleet began the first of its departures en route to the predesignated rendezvous points. Then on the 25th Yamamoto issued the order sending the fleet toward destiny and the sleepy, unsuspecting Navy base at Pearl Harbor.

Lang was moored in berth "One" at Norfolk Navy Yard on the morning of 7 December. Security on the base, as with other bases, was watchful, but mostly for acts of sabotage. Security patrols from each ship in port had been on watch every night during the time *Lang* had been in port. Yet, there were few restrictions and several of the crew were able to get two to four days leave. No one suspected this day to become a "day of infamy."

It was mid-afternoon when word first arrived of the attack on Pearl. As with most everyone else, the news was quite shocking to the crew of *Lang*. It only seemed like yesterday that they had been a part of the Pacific Fleet stationed at the now devastated base. They had made many friends there. The battleships *Arizona* and *Nevada*, with whom they had made their way back to the states, were now sitting on the harbor's muddy bottom. Many of the men who had stood upon the decks of those mighty ships back during those days in May were now dead, entombed within the hulls of their sunken vessels. It was hard to believe, and had not fate intervened *Lang* could have just as easily been a part of it.

As evening arrived security became much tighter. On the *Lang* a skeleton gun crew was stationed at the rear most five-inch gun, or gun #4, as beacons from searchlights reached out here and there. In a near blink of the eye their world had been changed, and there was much confusion as how to approach the new situation. War, for all intent and purposes, was now reality. The following day the president and congress made it official. Three days later Germany and Italy declared their unity with Japan in war against the United States. Now came the real test. No longer was war to be out of sight and distant.

Due to the unsettling circumstances of the newly declared war, a certain amount of paranoia and confusion had everyone on edge. The key to civility and order seemed to be in keeping everyone occupied, and in the Navy that meant drills. For the next two days alerts were frequent and drills near constant.

At 11:15 A.M. on the morning of the 9th Captain Seay put his crew through a fire drill exercise. The fire drill had hardly ended when at 2:45 P.M. the crew was called to general quarters on a base alert. One hour later fire crews were once again called to duty — but this was no drill.

During the earlier alert, as men had rushed to their general quarters stations, someone from the ship's galley had in their haste failed to extinguish the fires on the galley ranges where were left two pans of grease. About an hour later the forgotten grease ignited and smoke came billowing from the galley. As fate would have it, however, the freshness of the day's previously held fire-fighting exercise assisted the crew to quickly react to confining and fighting the fire. Yet, despite their quick effort, heavy smoke and toxic fumes hampered each attempt at squelching the blaze. The stubborn flames refused to die, and some 35 minutes later the Navy Yard Fire Department arrived to give welcomed assistance to the tiring crew. Even so, it took another 20 minutes before the flames were finally extinguished.

The fire had caused a considerable amount of damage to the electrical cables, paintwork, sheathing, and fresh water lines, but it could have been much worse. Fortunately, Captain Seay had picked a good day for a fire fighting exercise, no doubt allowing the crew their quick response and preventing a great deal more damage.

The fire damage was quickly repaired and *Lang* went back to sea on 21 December. In the company of the carrier *Ranger* (CV-4) and destroyer *Rhind* (DD-404), she was once again headed south to patrol the South Atlantic shipping lanes just out of Bermuda. It was somewhat like old times, but unlike the past this time they were in a state of war, and clearly this experience was to be a bit unsettling and filled with anxiety.

The waters where they now sailed were stalked by several of Germany's menacing U-boats. Many times these silent underwater hunters had proven themselves highly effective and deadly in the Atlantic, striking swiftly without warning, and the United States Navy could dire afford any more major losses. So with watches at their stations and periodic sound and radar searches, the ships of the carrier task force cautiously maneuvered back and forth from a base (straight-line) to a zigzag course. As evening arrived the ships were darkened as watches continued their searches. Obviously, no contact was to be ignored.

Having kept their vigil constant, the ships found their way unhampered, safely arriving at Murray's Anchorage, Bermuda, on the 23rd. Remaining in the safety of the anchorage throughout the night, the task force headed for open sea the following morning. Complemented by the addition of the cruiser *Savannah*, the force set its course for the island of Martinique.

Many of *Lang*'s crew remembered well this island from back in the days of the shakedown cruise. A part of the Lesser Antilles, the 385 square mile island was just one of a small group of island colonies belonging to France. It was here that Napoleon's wife Josephine was born. And here, in 1902, that the once beautiful city of Saint Pierre was totally destroyed by the volcanic eruptions of Mount Pele, killing nearly 40,000 people.

Now Martinique was under the control of the Vichy French government, a puppet of Nazi Germany. Relations between the United States and the Vichy French were momentarily under great strain. At issue was the knowledge that sitting within the harbor of the island's capital, Fort-de-France, were some French warships, which included the aircraft carrier *Bearn*, cruiser *Emile Bertin*, and six new tankers. American officials feared, with the U.S. Navy having been so severely weakened at Pearl Harbor, that in taking advantage of the situation an effort might be made to get those ships into the hands of the Axis. The *Ranger* Task Force was being sent to see that that did not happen, and the stage was set for conflict. But by the next day word was received that "all was well" and for the ships to return to Bermuda. Diplomacy had averted this crises.

Though it had proven to be only a necessary show of strength, *Lang* had participated in her first serious effort of the war. It was only the beginning of many efforts. And, with her return to Bermuda being on the 25th, she was to spend her first Christmas away from the states. It, too, was only the beginning — the beginning of many lonely holidays away from home.

Lang departed Bermuda on 17 January in the company of two other destroyers as escort for the newly built British battleship HMS *Duke Of York*. The trip would again take the destroyers a considerable distance across the deadly U-boat infested Atlantic.

Yet, despite the obvious dangers, four days later the ships had safely completed the initial crossing, rendezvousing with three British destroyers at a pre-arranged point some 800 miles from the British Isles. Afterwards, the ships turned about for the return trip to Bermuda.

Even as the ships had reached the rendezvous point, the weather was noted to be quickly changing for the worse. After turning back toward Bermuda each passing minute saw sailing conditions deteriorate further. The sea began to toss violently as swells grew bigger and bigger and winds increased to near hurricane strength. For the next three days the ships were given a tremendous beating. One minute they would be riding a swell high into the air, and then the next minute they would drop with a sickening thud as the swell rolled out from beneath them. Then a second swell would send tons of water across their decks, making it totally impossible for any member of their crews to venture outside.

Inside *Lang*, men would gather in groups to try to story the time away. Several men would make their way to the ship's mess to try to drink a cup of coffee, there to listen to the ship's thin hull pop from outside pressure and watch as previously spilt coffee ran back and forth across the deck. Then, as the ship would suddenly make a violent roll to one side, each one nervously awaited it to right itself — which it always did.

In the engine rooms, while holding on to keep from falling into the machinery, hard working sailors kept the engines turning at an rpm that would have normally moved the ship along at a speed of 11 knots. But now, with the screws spending about as much time out of the water as in, six knots were the best that could be achieved.

The terrible battering of the ships continued till the early hours of the 24th, when finally the sea began to settle. *Lang*'s crew were just beginning to feel able to relax when at 4:08 A.M. an urgent distress call from the British freighter SS *Empire Wildebeeste* was picked up by the destroyer's radioman: "SOS, SOS, SOS — Torpedoed; 39°30' N, 59°54' W." Though low on fuel and remaining in hostile territory, Captain Seay immediately directed the destroyer to begin a high-speed run to give aid to the stricken vessel and her crew. Later, in the early afternoon, *Lang* arrived at the freighter's last known position and began searching a 240 mile area, a task destined to last into and throughout the night.

When morning arrived lookouts were still searching the sea, as yet without success. Visibility was excellent, but with the sea swells still quite large a small boat could easily be missed.

Though the destroyer's fuel supply was reaching a critical point, Captain Seay determined to continue the search. Using estimates made on the wind and current drift factors, he directed his ship to move to a position farther north.

Finally, at 1:10 P.M., one of the lookouts shouted a sighting; he had momentarily spotted what looked to be a pair of yellow trousers lashed to an oar at a distance of about four miles. The ship began to close and the makeshift distress signal continued to bob in and out of sight as the swells continued their raising and lowering.

Moving yet closer, two small boats could be seen lashed together. Within the two boats were contained 34 surviving crewmen of the sunken *Empire Wildebeeste*. They had drifted with the current to a latitude of 39°55' N and a longitude of 59°02' W, a position some 47 miles from the original site of their vessel's sinking.

By 1:25 P.M. all of the survivors had been brought aboard. Included in their number were the freighter's captain, nine other officers, and the wireless operator who had sent out the original distress call. All of the survivors were in surprisingly good shape despite their harrowing ordeal. The only one to even show any wounds was the wireless operator, who had suffered some minor bruises and a cut lip, which received prompt medical treatment aboard *Lang*. And soon all the survivors were in dry clothes and receiving a good warm meal.

Meanwhile, the story of what had happened to *Empire Wildebeeste* began to be told. As related by her crew, the freighter had departed Hull, England, 20 days earlier to begin her fateful journey to the southwest. By the early morning hours of the 24th, after having successfully transited what was considered the worst of the journey, they had reached an area considered to be relatively safe. Suddenly and without warning their ship rocked from the impact of a torpedo.

The hit was fatal, and the freighter's captain immediately ordered preparations for abandoning ship. No more had he issued the order when a second torpedo ripped into the already doomed ship's hull, sending additional torrents of water gushing into her inner compartments. Fortunately, however, neither blast had caused any initial casualties among the freighter's complement, and all her crew managed to take to boats in time to escape their fast sinking vessel. Then began their 34 hour ordeal in the open sea in wait of rescue.

That evening the crude signal rig was made with the yellow trousers and hoisted on a makeshift mast. The following morning they were sighted by a passing plane of the Royal Canadian Air Force. The pilot circled his craft, dropped some flares and a note asking their condition and needs, and then departed. It was only a few hours later that *Lang* appeared and snatched them to safety.

Unfortunately, another boatload of survivors was still missing. Captain Seay continued to search the area far into the next day. But, after nearly exhausting *Lang*'s fuel supply, the search was finally called off with no more survivors having been located.

The operation had emptied *Lang*'s fuel tanks to the point she could no longer make Bermuda. Captain Seay had no choice but ask for the assistance of the Navy tanker *Sapelo* (AO-11) in refueling at sea. Obviously, this attempt would be dangerous, especially considering a German U-boat was known to be operating in the area. Yet, despite some very tense moments, the refueling was a success. And afterwards the two ships returned to Bermuda, where *Lang* transferred her grateful *Empire Wildebeeste* survivors to the care of port authorities.

On 17 March, After having spent most of the past month and half patrolling around Bermuda, *Lang* departed for Norfolk. Two days later she safely arrived at her destination, where she spent an additional four days receiving some slight modifications and alterations.

Besides welcoming aboard several additional personnel, the destroyer also received some important changes. Her two after five-inch guns, #3 and #4, which were originally open mounts, were covered by temporary steel shields and canvas tops, and the railing around each of the new 20-millimeter machine guns were also canvas covered, simulating a type of gun tub for each. These improvements, though seemingly slight, caused a certain amount of inquiry from the crew as to their meaning, and soon proved to be a mere hint of things to come.

With all modifications complete, by the 23rd the ship and crew were once again heading out to open sea. In the process, just as *Lang* reached Point Prep off Norfolk, she accidentally struck a buoy and fouled her starboard screw. The damage to the screw caused a terrible vibration throughout the ship, and the next day Captain Seay directed his ship into Boston Navy Yard for hurried voyage repairs. Within eight hours *Lang* was once again underway, her damaged screw completely replaced.

On the next morning *Lang* reached her newest destination, pulling into port at Casco Bay. Upon her entry she passed several other warships congregated there; and it was apparent to most of the crew that the number of warships was unusual. Scuttlebutt was soon travelling throughout the ship that something was up, with each man putting forth his idea as to the meaning of the gathering. Fuel was added to the conversation when all the commanding officers were called ashore for a conference. Shortly after, *Lang* had her fuel tanks topped off with fuel and extra provisions were brought aboard. Little doubt remained that something serious was in the making.

Lang's crew were not unlike the many other untested servicemen that were preparing for war. With immense confidence in themselves and their ship, they eagerly awaited the opportunity to prove their worth in combat. The ship was in top condition and the crew well drilled. They gave little consideration to the abilities of the enemy. What had happened in the Pacific had been a "sucker punch." Next time it would be different. "Just wait till we get our shot at 'em," was the prevalent thought.

Truth was that the enemy was well prepared to meet the challenge, also being well equipped and well trained. More importantly, the enemy was made up of tough veterans. The Japanese seemed unstoppable in the Pacific, and the Germans were in tight control in Europe. So far news was far from being promising. America's war was just beginning, and it was to be long and bitter. Many young lives would be lost and many families would shed a great many tears before it would be over. There was to be more than enough war for everyone, and *Lang*'s crew was destined to receive more than their share. However, at this early stage, they had yet to truly experience the fear that real warfare brings. *Lang* had yet to meet the enemy or fire a shot in anger. No bombs, torpedoes, shells, or bullets had been flung at her in a hostile manner. But this was all about to change. *Lang* was about to sail on her first major mission of the war, and from it to one combat situation after another till the war's end.

Chapter 4

Malta

By their own declaration of war on the United States, Hitler and Mussolini had done both President Roosevelt and Prime Minister Winston Churchill a great favor. The Japanese bombing of Pearl Harbor had enraged the American populous and rallied them behind Roosevelt's war declaration against the Japanese nation, but it remains highly doubtful they would have supported any effort by Roosevelt to also join the European conflict. Therefore, had not the two Axis leaders made their declarations, Roosevelt's hands would have likely remained tied to his "Short of War" policy of aiding England despite her desperate need for America's full support. Indeed, Churchill had prayed, even begged for America's entry into the war against Germany and Italy; that his enemies had succeeded in doing what he had been unable to do had given him great reason to be jubilant — he now knew the war could be won.

Hitler's ambitions combined with the ease of his early successes were finally proving to be costly. On 22 June 1941, he had decided to further expand his conquests by breaking his non-aggression pledge with Stalin and sent his army invading the Russian homeland. Initially, Hitler's panzers had little difficulty in their push eastward, soon threatening to capture the Soviet capital, Moscow. But by December the Germans were not only fighting against growing resistance but also against lengthy supply lines and the bitter Russian winter.

With his eastern campaign stalled and in trouble, Hitler saw Japan's crippling first blow and war declaration against the United States as an opportunity to be made to his advantage. By honoring the Tripartite Pact and declaring war on the United States, Hitler expected in return that Japan would declare war on the Soviet Union, thus drawing away some of the Russian troops concentrated before his army and sending them toward the Manchurian border where were amassed Japan's mighty Kwantung Army. Instead, Japan's leadership reneged and signed their own non-aggression pact with Stalin, leaving a very angry Hitler facing not only Russia's full might in the east but also, through his own dubious declaration, an eventual second front in the west, facing the combined powers of Britain and the United States. Such was to be his demise.

Momentarily, however, Britain and the United States were of no immediate threat. They remained on the defensive, both at war with all three Axis powers and both losing considerable ground in their initial united struggle.

Japanese forces had mounted a blitzkrieg action throughout the Far Eastern and Pacific regions ever bit as profound as the Germans had first done in Europe. Just one day following their devastating attack on Pearl Harbor, Japanese forces struck at British controlled Malaya, successfully landing troops north of Kota Bharu. In the course of the attack Japanese planes caught the British battleships *Prince Of Wales* and *Repulse* in the open sea and without air defense, sinking both ships and successfully crippling British sea power in the region.

Two days later Japanese forces successfully landed on American held Luzon in the Philippines and by 22 December were landing 100,000 additional troops in an all out effort for control of the strategic islands. On that same late December date Japanese forces also received the surrender of the lightly manned American naval base at Wake Island. And on the 25th, Japanese forces accepted the surrender of the British crown colony of Hong Kong.

Throughout January Japanese forces continued their advance through the Philippines, pushing General Douglas MacArthur's beleaguered defenders farther and farther south. On 20 January the Japanese struck into Burma. And on the night of the 30th, British forces evacuated Malaya to make their final stand on Singapore Island.

By 15 February the British naval base and bastion of Singapore had fell to the Japanese Army. And in Burma the Japanese continued their advance.

March continued to add to the woes of the Allies as the Japanese began the month by capturing Rangoon, capital of Burma. And in the Philippines, General MacArthur was evacuated to Australia, leaving General Jonathan Wainwright to fight a doomed defense on the Bataan Peninsula till finally forced to surrender his exhausted army on 9 April.

But not all was bad news for the Allies. On a more positive note, at the Russian front the Soviet Army had launched a December counter-offensive which, aided by a bitterly cruel winter, had sent the German Army in mass retreat from Moscow. This struggle, however, remained far from over and was destined to be long and bloody, Stalin desperately needing what the U.S. and Britain were yet unable to deliver — a second front.

Yet, despite their bitter losses in the Pacific, both the U.S. and British leadership understood their priority to win back Europe. The Allies had long determined that Germany was the more serious threat, and therefore must receive the greatest attention. But by just which route and what timetable was to be best at opening the second European front was to be a matter of serious contention. Obviously, Russia requested the second front to start immediately. But such a task at this point of time was physically and materially impossible for the U.S. and Britain. They would have to begin their campaign where opportunity and the chance to win already existed, and momentarily only in North Africa and the Mediterranean Sea was that a possibility.

Prior to the Pearl Harbor attack, on 18 November, the British 8th Army had launched a full-scale offensive from Egypt against Rommel's Afrika Corp in Libya. After Pearl Harbor the British attack became even more aggressive as it was thought this might be the last chance for British forces to gain a major victory before American forces joined the fray. By 17 January the push had resulted in the expulsion of nearly all German and Italian forces from Libya, dealing them considerable losses in equipment and manpower. It was indeed a victory but the battle was to prove far from over. Keeping supply routes to Egypt open became a major concern and stopping resupply of Rommel's forces a major challenge. One important key to both of these efforts was the small British held island fortress of Malta.

Momentarily, Malta was the only base the Allies had remaining in the Mediterranean. From the island British planes and submarines had effectively operated to take their toll of German supply efforts to Rommel's forces in North Africa, aiding in the success of the British 8th Army's offensive across Libya. But Malta was totally surrounded by a number of Axis air bases, having no less than 600 German and Italian planes within its range, and having long been the target of heavy aerial bombardments. In February these bombardments increased and threatened to make the island's air capability ineffective and allow German resupply of Rommel go unopposed. Such would undoubtedly put the recent British victories in Libya at peril. But with no bases close enough to the island to fly fighters in direct, and with risks to precious cargo ships too great to chance a relief convoy, the only possible answer was in the use of carriers to deliver the goods. Only problem was the Royal Navy was already overextended and could not readily supply the ships necessary for such a task; so came the call for American assistance.

In a series of correspondence to Roosevelt, Churchill informed the president of the desperate situation. He pointed out that following their capture of Singapore the Japanese were in an obvious position to seize Madagascar from the Vichy French which would in effect make passage in the Indian Ocean near impossible and block the back-door supply route to the Mediterranean. To prevent this from happening Churchill needed to send a naval force to deliver a Free-French expeditionary force to seize and hold the island in the name of General Charles de Gaulle. The only ships available, however, were in the western Mediterranean, and their departure would leave the sea lanes around Gibraltar very vulnerable. This would require diverting other warships of Her Majesty's Fleet presently patrolling in key areas of the North Sea to the Mediterranean. And to complicate the situation even further for the Royal Navy, there remained the problem of resupply for Malta.

In the past the British had used their carrier *Eagle* to shuttle Spitfire fighters to the island, launching them at sea at their maximum flight range. This had worked well, but *Eagle* was now laid up for a month of repairs. Even if she had been available, her normal Spitfire capacity was only 16, certainly not enough for Malta's immediate need. The British carrier *Argus* was too small and too slow to meet the task. And the carrier *Victorious* could not carry Spitfires due to her lifts being too small. But Churchill had a solution; he now had an ally to call to his aid.

The British prime minister did not hesitate to request American help. Though he knew the U.S. Navy's critical situation in the Pacific, he boldly requested American warships to help in filling the gap in the North Sea patrol areas. And he asked Roosevelt for the loan of the carrier *Wasp* to help in ferrying Spitfires to Malta.

Obviously, Roosevelt understood what was at stake. Malta was key to the Allied effort in the Mediterranean, and had to remain in operation. The choice was clear; the president gave his approval. Time had come for the U.S. Navy to make a major showing in the European conflict, thus to lead to the formation of Task Force 39 and *Lang*'s first major wartime experience.

The morning hours of 26 March found the newly formed task force neatly tucked within the safety of Casco Bay, awaiting its eminent departure. Dawn's light had exposed thousands of sailors feverishly going over last minute details in preparation of their vessels to take to sea. Finally, boilers were lit and turbines began to come to life. And with fuel tanks topped, extra provisions stored, hatches battened down and sea details at their stations, one by one the ships began to slip through the channel and into the Atlantic.

The first group to depart was made up of eight destroyers, of which *Lang* was a part. Upon reaching the mouth of the channel, the destroyers began to disperse and take up their stations for sweeping the area for any possible enemy submarines before the larger, capital ships made their exit. Once these searches were complete and the "all clear" was given, the next ship made its appearance.

USS *Washington* (BB-56) was the U.S. Navy's newest battleship. She was 35,000 tons of pure power, carrying nine 16-inch guns, twenty 5-inch guns and numerous additional anti-aircraft guns. Obviously, she could've been a great boost to the ailing Pacific Fleet, but Roosevelt had elected to keep her in the Atlantic. She would now serve as flagship for Task Force 39, Rear Admiral John W. Wilcox, Jr., commanding.

Following behind *Washington* were two heavy cruisers, *Wichita* (CA-45) and *Tuscaloosa*. At seeing the familiar silhouette of *Tuscaloosa*, many of *Lang*'s crew were reminded of those great times on the presidential cruises; cruises that were peaceful and full of expectation. Now, as they headed to an unknown destination, the crew expected an entirely different type of cruise; one filled with danger and uncertainty.

Then from the channel came looming forth the ship which would play the greatest role in the coming operation, the 15,000 ton aircraft carrier *Wasp* (CV-7). Though unknown to the crew of *Lang* at the time, she was also to play a great part in their destiny for the next several months. In fact, so close were to be *Lang* and *Wasp* that the crew was to adopt the slogan, "whither *Wasp* go'eth, so go'eth *Lang*."

It seemed only fitting that these two ships were destined to serve so close together. John Lang, the seaman for whom *Lang* had been named, was born in Curacao, Netherlands West Indies, on 17 June 1794. He later became a citizen of New Brunswick, New Jersey. By the age of 18 he was already an accomplished seaman and was serving in the then young United States Navy aboard an 18-gun ship — the first *Wasp*. At that time the United States was involved in the War of 1812 against Britain. On 18 October of that year *Wasp* engaged the British sloop-of-war *Frolic* in deadly combat. With both ships being badly damaged in the ensuing battle, it finally reverted to a contest of hand-to-hand combat. *Wasp* crossed *Frolic*'s bow and at this opportune moment John Lang — having once been impressed into service on a British warship and wanting to settle the score — jumped to the enemy ship's bowsprit and onto her deck. His fearlessness so stirred the rest of the crew that they followed suit and soon had *Frolic*'s crew overwhelmed. It was a victorious moment in history for *Wasp* and Lang against an old foe, Britain. Now, in quite the irony to the past, *Wasp* and *Lang* were going to Britain's aid.

The task force quickly assembled and the screening destroyers took their stations. Quietly the ships began their journey across the choppy waters of the U-boat infested Atlantic. To this point the destination remained a secret. But once well out to sea the secrecy was finally dropped, all crews being informed they were headed to Scapa Flow, Scotland, there to join up with the British Home Fleet for some special missions in an Allied effort to hamper the enemies' advance.

Momentarily, however, it was the advance of Task Force 39 that was being hampered. Almost immediately the ships had ran into foul weather, with waves so high as to wash across the flight deck of *Wasp*. Obviously, this was not the way sailors preferred their sailing, though it did provide the luxury of pretty much eliminating any threat of German U-boats.

The bothersome rough weather continued throughout the night and into the next morning. Then at 10:31 A.M., as an even further hampering of the voyage, the "man overboard" alarm sounded aboard *Washington*. While an immediate muster was being taken aboard the battleship, *Lang* and the other destroyers quickly began an extensive search of the area. Shockingly, the muster revealed the only person missing was Admiral Wilcox. With this revelation the search intensified. Lookouts strained their eyes searching the heavy sea for any sign of the overboard admiral, but their effort proved in vain. *Wasp* sent up a plane in one last desperate attempt but the plane crashed and the pilot lost. Determining further searching useless, the admiral was listed as lost at sea (the circumstances as to Admiral Wilcox's loss were never fully determined) and the ships continued on their way. Rear Admiral Robert C. Giffen assumed the command.

As the weather began to calm, the ships began to alternate from a base to a zigzag course. Soundmen kept alert to the sound of any possible U-boats and radarmen kept track of every blip that might possibly be one of Germany's deadly long-range Condor bombers. But by 3 April, having made no enemy contacts, the force successfully met their guide for the rest of the journey, the British cruiser *Edinburgh*. And by 8:00 A.M. the following morning they were all safely within the harbor at Scapa Flow.

Upon their arrival at the British naval base *Lang* crew were quick to begin a careful visual inspection of the area, curious of their new home port's facilities. What they found was anything but impressive. Unlike the many places they had had the pleasure of visiting in the past, this place was dull in appearance. It had no trees, no grass, and no excitement. The only things seemingly to be found there in great abundance were rocks, mud, and other servicemen. To their bitter disappointment, the crew quickly learned there were more reasons to stay aboard ship than there were to go ashore. And it was just as well, as visiting the sites was not on the immediate schedule.

Indeed, for the next few days *Lang*'s crew was kept quite busy preparing the destroyer for further travel. Fuel tanks were once again topped off and ammunition was given routine daily inspections.

On the second day Captain Seay directed his ship and crew outside the harbor to check the working order of the destroyer's degaussing equipment. This important machinery was used to set up a neutralizing magnetic field for protecting the ship from magnetic-action mines, a real threat in their new theater of operations.

Despite the hectic schedule, however, the crew still managed several opportunities at meeting and getting acquainted with their new comrades-at-arms. Upon each meeting, inquisitive *Lang* sailors were to question their British counterparts about their ships, women, and the war. When their work disallowed any visitation, they would often pause to watch as British ships moved in and out of the harbor, noting that many bore the scars of battle. Obviously, such scenes testified to the reality of the many dangers of their own upcoming mission into enemy territory, creating a multitude of solemn thoughts among the crew.

The expected departure from Scapa Flow finally came on the morning of 9 April. At 7:16 A.M., and with an ominous sounding "Good luck mates!" from their British counterparts, *Lang* joined destroyers *Madison* (DD-425) and HMS *Echo* in escorting *Wasp* out to sea. The carrier group, now designated Force W, was then to set sail for the Scottish seaport of Greenock, there to pick up the cargo designated for Malta.

Once outside the harbor *Lang* and the other destroyers took up their screening positions with the carrier, cautiously beginning the journey with continuous searches of both sea and sky. As their journey south proceeded, the ships most often traveled an alternating zigzag and base course as defense against torpedo attacks. But at 1:00 P.M., as they arrived to enter the northern stretches of water between Scotland and Ireland known as the minches, the ships deviated to turn windward. The minches were known to be mined and quite commonly stalked by menacing U-boats, and the move allowed *Wasp* to launch some of her stubby Wildcat fighters for extra protection before proceeding further.

To this point the journey had proceeded quietly and without interruption, and transit of the minches did not see this change. And some 24 hours after having departed Scapa flow, Force W was safely passing through the sub nets at the mouth of the Clyde River and proceeding toward port at Greenock.

As the American ships navigated up the Clyde, their crews were to be overwhelmed by the unexpected reception they were to experience. All along the river's banks crowds of people had gathered to cheer their arrival. Small British and American flags were waved energetically as Britons welcomed the aid of their newest ally. Such fanfare was of obvious inspiration to the American crews. Never before had they received a personal welcome so intense, and they could hardly wait to get ashore to put it to the test.

But visits to Greenock were not to be on the agenda. Other than shore and security patrols, the crews were restricted to their ships. Obviously, such restriction did not set well; however, the mission was far too important to risk some loose-lipped sailor allowing information to fall into the wrong hands. Yet, despite this order, several of *Lang*'s crew decided the beckoning of the sensual seaport city was just too great to ignore and a rash of AWOLs occurred. Even though every violator was to knowingly face court martial upon his return — and all did return — it did little to restrain them: youthful sailors facing an uncertain future were dogmatic in their efforts to experience every pleasure of life, and only in rare instances were the rules breakers disciplined beyond monetary fines and/or loss of future liberty. American sailors, as with all American servicemen, were always to find it difficult to conform to the restraints of war. The additional loss to freedom brought on by war made them angry and, in the long run, added to their incentive to defeat the enemy.

Preparations for the continuation of the journey were near non-stop during the stay at Greenock. Fuel tanks were once again topped off while every piece of equipment was checked and double checked. Of most importance, of course, was the loading of the precious cargo of Spitfire fighters, a total of 47, carefully positioned on *Wasp*'s flight deck for transport to their Mediterranean launch point. The mission then resumed on the morning of the 14th, the ships withdrawing from their berthings to head back to sea. Force W now included the addition of the British destroyers *Inglefield*, *Ithuriel*, and *Partridge*, and the British battlecruiser *Renown*. Obviously, by this time the Axis powers expected some attempt from the Allies to send relief Malta's way. With so few options available, it would not be difficult for the enemy to determine the method. Since the arrival of the American vessels was certainly known, even keeping secret those ships to be used in the attempt would be near impossible. Only timetables and routes could be effectively used in keeping the enemy guessing as to where best to place their submarines and to send searching reconnaissance aircraft. Indeed, getting to the launch point and returning without enemy detection would be extremely difficult, and the entire operation would be very risky.

As was routine, once out to sea the destroyers set up an anti-submarine screen for the protection of the two larger ships. Afterwards, Force W proceeded on an alternating zigzag and base course to the south, sailing at a speed of 18 knots.

The first day out of Greenock proceeded without incident. As night arrived all ships were darkened and the voyage continued undisturbed.

Early the next morning the ships switched on their degaussing equipment and began constant sound sweeps of their areas. Speeds remained constant and course changes were often as the force remained alert to every possible enemy threat.

As dawn arrived so too did a massive amount of fog. Visibility decreased to less than 500 feet, greatly increasing the hazard of collision among the ships. Yet, despite the danger, speed did not decrease as extra lookouts were posted to aid in the watch. And by 10:00 A.M. the fog had lifted without incident, the ships immediately commencing a zigzag course as they continued their southward heading.

That evening, as the sun began to near the horizon, the ships slowed some and turned into the wind. *Wasp* became the center of activity as planes began warming their engines in preparation to take their patrols into the sky above. Various ones of *Lang* crew watched as the Wildcat fighters slowly lifted off their floating platform of steel to soar off into the pale sky above. Few of the onlookers, however, truly understood the importance of the cover being offered. They had yet to face the challenge of the enemy air machine, or had they even witnessed the destruction thereof. The procedure being displayed on this evening fascinated them, but the respect that they would later gain for such friendly air cover would be an earned application. With it there would be security; without it they would be vulnerable to fearful swarms of enemy planes and their lashing of deadly fire and steel.

The second day had went well and nearly ended without incident when at 8:20 P.M. *Partridge* suddenly picked up a definite submarine contact on her sonar. In response, the formation made an immediate emergency 90 degree turn to port, away from the contact point. Meanwhile, *Partridge* broke away to make a depth-charge attack against the prey. A canister rolled from the destroyer into the sea and within seconds a deep underwater explosion was pronounced, the concussion strongly felt by all the other ships as they sped to a safe distance. For an additional 20 minutes *Partridge* searched for and attacked the unseen enemy. Results of the attack were listed as "unknown," but at the very least the sub had been denied its own opportunity of attack.

For the rest of the darkened hours the ships progressed without any further incident. But at 7:37 A.M. the next morning the soundman aboard *Lang* called out "contact, dead ahead, sir!" Captain Seay immediately sent a warning to the rest of the force and then prepared for action. His crew was already at general quarters stations as a standard precaution against dawn air attacks, so when he gave the order to "drop depth-charge" little hesitation was given. Within a second of the order a single 600 pound canister rolled from its rack on the destroyer's stern and into the sea.

Just a very few seconds passed, then the whole ocean seemed to jar, and with a horrendous explosion a huge geyser of foaming water gushed high into the air. *Lang* began to circle the area, her soundman listening intently to relocate the contact. For 30 minutes the searching continued but to no avail. *Lang*'s first attack of the war may have been against nothing more than a school of fish, yet no chances could be taken with any possible contact; better to kill fish than let some well positioned enemy submarine get off some well placed shots.

Afterwards, *Lang* rejoined the force and continued her screening duties. The rest of the third day and all of the fourth proceeded without any additional incidents. As the ships passed along the Spanish coast they intentionally sailed out of sight of known Axis coast watchers. Then, at 5:18 A.M. on 18 April, the ships identified Saint Vincent's Point on the Spanish coast and prepared for the run to the British fortress of Gibraltar and gateway to the Mediterranean.

At 1:05 P.M., having entered the Straits of Gibraltar, the silhouette of Gibraltar, most commonly called "The Rock," was sighted at a distance of ten miles. The ships of Force W formed a column and proceeded to enter the Mediterranean before entering the mighty fortress' harbor. As a result, she being the lead U.S. warship of the formation, *Lang* was awarded the distinction of being the first U.S. man-of-war to re-enter the Mediterranean since America's declared entry into the now truly global conflict.

By 2:00 P.M. all the ships of Force W were safely within the confines of the harbor of the British base. Base personnel quickly began refueling and reprovisioning of each of the vessels in preparations for the continuance of their mission. And by 9:00 P.M. the ships of Force W were again on the move, using the darkness as cover for their departure. As had been feared, the Axis was indeed aware of Force W and its mission. German radio broadcasts promised the destruction of the entire force, and the threat was not to be taken lightly.

The operation was quickly drawing to its most critical stage. As the ships proceeded, sharp-eyed lookouts carefully searched the darkness for any sign of the enemy. Their eyes strained to focus on distant points of momentary attention. The heart of one raced as he momentarily caught a glimpse of something unusual. A second, closer look was taken, the lookout's voice ready to pierce the air with alarm, only to lose sight of the object in question or find it a trick of the sea. Day and night the routine continued; watching, trying to anticipate, but seeing nothing.

Caution remained paramount, and at 5:34 A.M. on the 20th it reached its peak. The force had finally reached fighter distance of the island of Malta; the launching point for their precious cargo of Spitfire fighters. Speed now became of the utmost importance. They must complete their task as quickly as possible and get out before being located by the enemy.

Turning into the wind, the carrier quickly came to life. Air crews rushed to move the planes into launching positions. Pilots were settled into their cockpits. Props began to turn and engines began to fire, as telltale puffs of exhaust smoke signaled each ignition. Within seconds the first takeoff signal was given and the first of 11 Wildcat fighters began to lift from the deck, the rest to follow in close order.

As the Wildcats gathered overhead, flying cover for the operation, air crews worked at a heated pace preparing the Spitfires for their launch. Within minutes the first of the sleek British fighters was airborne. One after the other the Spitfires lifted into the wind till all of the first group were successfully away.

As air crews hastily prepared the second group for launching the first group, now in formation, flew low over the ships in a farewell salute before proceeding on to Malta. When their darkened forms passed through the paleness overhead, their blue exhaust flames plainly visible, sailors waved and cheered.

Minutes later the second flight of Spitfires followed their comrades into the air, also to salute the ships of Force W upon their departure. And by 7:30 A.M. all of the Spitfires were successfully on their way to Malta, the drone of their powerful Rolls Royce engines fading off into the distance.

The main task now complete, *Wasp* recovered her Wildcats and Force W quickly turned for home. Many dangers still remained, however, and great caution would be required in retracing their steps back to the protection of Scapa Flow. There was destined to be additional sound contacts (most of unknown determination) and some rain to contend with, but otherwise the return trip was rather unremarkable. And, after having faced headlong the German threat of destruction, by 4:00 P.M. of the 26th, Force W was once again within the safety of the Scottish port from which they began.

Meanwhile, the fate of the Spitfire fighters had not fared as well. Initially, all the fighters arrived at Malta safely. But before ground crews were able to refuel the new arrivals a wave of enemy bombers appeared and successfully destroyed several of the parked planes. By the end of the month 23 of the original 47 Spitfires delivered by *Wasp* were scrap, with several additional heavily damaged, making Malta's situation as desperate as ever. It was clearly evident that another effort at reinforcing the island would be needed if the fortress was to survive.

Lang had made the return to Scapa Flow with the rest of Force W, but there would be little time for the destroyer and her crew to rest. By the afternoon of the 29th she was again at sea as escort for *Wasp*. Joined by the U.S. destroyer *Sterett* and the British destroyer *Blackmoor*, the ships were again destined for Greenock in preparation for another mission to the Mediterranean.

Arriving at Greenock the following afternoon, little time was wasted in loading 47 additional Spitfires aboard the American carrier, again for delivery to Malta. Afterward, *Wasp* again headed out to sea, escorted by *Lang*, *Sterett*, and the British destroyers *Echo* and *Intrepid*, all passing out through the submarine net at the mouth of the Clyde on the morning of 3 May.

This trip south proceeded pretty much as the first, with periodic launchings of air cover and a similar alternating zigzag and base course. And the first day passed without incident.

It was not till near noon of the second day that the ships were first forced to take evasive action, when *Intrepid* made a possible sub contact. A thorough search for the suspected intruder was made but the contact was lost.

At 7:38 P.M., *Echo* made a second contact. Once again the other ships took evasive action, turning hard to port. *Echo* circled to make a depth-charge attack on the target but the results were negative, the contact again being lost.

No worthwhile incidents were encountered on the third day. The only tense moment came at near noon when *Wasp* picked up an unidentified plane on radar. The plane, however, never came close to the ships and was soon off screen.

The fourth day started out just as smoothly as had the previous, but at 10:07 A.M. *Lang*'s soundman picked up a definite sub contact just 750 yards off her port beam. General quarters alarms sounded, the P. A. system cracked with orders, and men quickly manned the depth-charge racks. While the rest of the force took evasive action, *Lang* went hard to port, leaning from the tightness of the turn as she went on the offensive.

As the turn progressed one of *Lang*'s Y-guns cracked to send its lethal charge arching high into the air. The canister hit the water and sank in the area of where the intruding sub was thought to be. A couple of seconds passed and the sea jarred, bubbled, and gushed as the charge detonated below. Two additional charges were fired, each duplicating the volatile eruption of the first, and then there was a pause.

The soundman listened, and almost immediately he picked up propeller noise from the fleeing sub. New fixes were made on the enemy's position and *Lang* bore down on the location, letting fly with a pattern of nine additional lethal depth-charges.

Once the water had settled from the last deep explosion, *Lang*'s soundman again listened for the sub. Nothing was heard. Captain Seay kept his destroyer in the area for another ten minutes searching but making no additional contacts. A small oil slick was spotted but nothing more was found to confirm a kill. Nevertheless, the destroyer's crew was jubilant, confident they had sunk or at the very least mortally wounded an enemy sub. And, despite its questionability, Captain Seay would say nothing to squelch his crew's enthusiasm; for he was proud of his crew's performance and the possibility of a sinking was indeed real.

Afterward, *Lang* rejoined the other ships, and the rest of the trip to Gibraltar proceeded without further incident, arriving at the southern gate on the afternoon of the 7th. At Gibraltar the ships were all quickly refueled and by midnight were again sailing into the Mediterranean.

The original force that had left Greenock was now expanded to include the British destroyers *Partridge*, *Ithuriel*, *Georgetown*, *Salisbury*, *Vidette*, and *Charybdis*, the battlecruiser *Renown*, and the carrier *Eagle* which was carrying 17 additional Spitfires for Malta.

Once again the ships of Force W navigated the treacherous waters eastward successfully, reaching the launching point for the Spitfires at 6:32 A.M. on the second morning without incident. As both *Wasp* and *Eagle* turned into the wind their crews turned to the task before them. *Wasp* began the mission by again sending up a flight of her stubby Wildcat fighters for extra cover, to be closely followed into the air by the Spitfires from both carriers. And again, under threat from attack from both air and sea, a speedy execution of the operation became paramount.

The carrier crews gave a superb performance in precision air launch procedures, and in just a little over an hour had all the Spitfires airborne and Wildcats recovered. The only glitch to the operation had come when one of Spitfires inadvertently lost its belly fuel tank, forcing it to return to *Wasp*, its pilot masterfully setting his fighter on the flight deck with apparent ease. Though truly deserving of his chance to rejoin his comrades in their mission to Malta, the disappointed pilot was denied the opportunity; the ships could not risk the delay required for the launching of the single plane, and were quickly turned westward for passage back to safer waters.

The ships arrived back at Gibraltar at 12:25 A.M. the following morning, mooring there only long enough for refueling. And within five hours they were back at sea, cautiously retracing their path back to Scapa Flow.

By noon the ships of Force W were well on their way back to safety, and news of their success was already ahead them. So happy was Britain's prime minister that he sent his congratulations while they were yet at sea, sending a message which read: "Many Thanks To You All For Timely Help. 'Who Said A Wasp Couldn't Sting Twice?' (signed) Winston Churchill." It was truly an honored moment, with copies of the message made and given out to everyone of the crews.

Indeed, this second mission had been a great success. All 63 Spitfires launched by Force W safely arrived at their intended destination in time to be refueled and back in the air to meet headlong a large flight of enemy bombers. The surprised enemy planes were quickly scattered, many being destroyed, greatly impeding the enemy's ability at future attacks. The day was to mark the turning point in Malta's present situation and help guarantee her survival as an Allied fortress in the eastern Mediterranean.

Force W's mission was now complete, and at 8:25 A.M. on the 15th, six days following their departure from Gibraltar, the ships were all safely returned to Scapa Flow. With only some rain and a couple of false sonar contacts taken into account, their final return passage had been the most uneventful of all.

With their services momentarily no longer required, it was finally time for the American vessels to return to the states. *Lang* refueled and brought aboard fresh water and provisions, and by the morning of her second day in port was again heading out to sea. In the company of four additional U.S. destroyers and the cruiser *Brooklyn* (CL-40) she joined in the escort of *Wasp* back across the Atlantic for home, destination: Norfolk.

Along the way the ships took their usual precautions of periodic air cover and alternating course changes. Additionally, periodic drills were ordered in keeping the crews alert and sharp. During this time *Lang*'s crew was once again given an opportunity to sight in their weapons on one of the war's more evasive targets. To this point enemy fighters or bombers had yet to threaten the destroyer in any real way. Still, it was obvious that contact with these deadly weapons could not be avoided forever in this war. Therefore, planes from *Wasp* took to the air towing target sleeves, and as the target came into range gunners opened fire, splitting the air with high-velocity steel in their effort to get a direct hit. The day was quickly approaching when accurate gunnery might well mean the difference between the crew's life and death, and every opportunity to gain experience was taken seriously.

Meanwhile, the journey westward proceeded pretty much at an unremarkable pace. On the night of the 24th the ships did run into a thick layer of fog. Visibility was reduced to as little as 200 yards. The blindness increased the chances of collision among the ships, yet they continued on a dangerous zigzag course at a speed of 15 knots. The following morning, however, the fog began to lift and without incident to the ships. Soon the sky was clear and Wildcats were sent airborne for their extra protection.

Though there remained reason for caution, an air of confidence and satisfaction began to consume the crew of *Lang*. They were a happy lot, as the taste of success and the anticipation of returning home sent morale soaring. Their latest mission of the war had yet to impress upon them the reality of warfare itself. At this point in time they had little reason to display any real fear of the suffering war was to bring their way. Yet, whether the men of the present crew were to remain with *Lang* or move on to some other ship, all would soon learn the harshness and bitterness that real warfare brings.

The long journey back home finally ended on the morning of the 27th. With many miles of treacherous travel behind them, *Lang*'s crew was happy to see welcoming flocks of sea gulls as in the distance the hazy outline of the eastern coastline of the United States made its appearance. Home was such a wonderful sight. How often they had thought of it, and how much more often they would think of it in the future. Each moment to be spent there was to be precious, and each opportunity to return there would be hard fought for. At Norfolk several *Lang* sailors were to receive six days leave, rewarding most with the long awaited chance to visit with family and friends. And the moment was truly well deserved.

The U.S. Navy's first venture into the Mediterranean since entering the war had been met with success. Though not in time to prevent the reinforcement of Rommel, allowing him the ability to strike a deadly counter-offensive against the British in Libya, the Malta mission ensured the Afrika Corp's eventual demise. And the joint mission with Britain also proved both navys' ability to work well together, sending a strong signal to all adversaries.

Not only had *Lang* been a part of this successful operation, but she had been the only U.S. warship to accompany *Wasp* on both missions, and the only other ship, British or American, to make the complete voyage from Scapa Flow to the Mediterranean and back with *Wasp* twice. Obviously, no real battle had taken place, yet she had earned her first battle star and had taken credit for her first kill. By the time of her return to Norfolk a small silhouette of a submarine along with an Italian flag (determination of nationality is unclear with the exception that Italian submarines were known to be in the general area of the attack; and no Axis submarines have been confirmed sunk that day) were proudly painted on the wing of the bridge, designating "the one they got" while going to the aid of Malta.

Certainly *Lang* had served her country well in the Atlantic, but this latest mission was to be her last in that campaign of the war. At Norfolk the temporary canvas shields that had covered the two after five-inch guns were removed to make guns #3 and #4 open mounts once more, and the two after 20-millimeter guns were removed and replaced by two new twin 40-millimeter anti-aircraft guns. Additionally, two new radar types were added to the ship, that of surface search (SG) and fire control (FC).

These new changes gave the destroyer added punch to her offensive capability while in turn increasing her ability at self-defense, characteristics the crew would soon greatly appreciate. For *Lang* was now destined to enter a whole new theater and face an entirely different type of enemy, one highly skilled and deadly effective in open sea combat. She and her crew were soon to face the extreme test of survival, where one's ability and skill, laced with a touch of luck, made warriors victors and, more importantly, survivors.

Chapter 5

Guadalcanal

W hile *Lang* and *Wasp* had been serving with the British in the Mediter-
ranean, elsewhere the war had shown a great many new developments.
The news was a mixture of good with the bad but showed promise of the
Allies' ability at punching back, and decidedly so.

In the Philippines, on 9 April the last desperate defenders of the Bataan Peninsula
finally surrendered to the Japanese invaders, whereupon thousands of American and
Filipino prisoners began their horrendous ordeal to be known as the "Bataan death
march." The island fortress of Corregidor, however, was to hold out nearly another
month, costing the Japanese nearly 60,000 additional casualties, but to the same end.
As the result, the Japanese gained complete control of the former U.S. possession.
Obviously, this was not good news, but the sacrifice the defenders had made had
bought the Allies valuable time in preparing for future actions.

The more electrifying moment at this early stage of the war came when President
Roosevelt announced to the world that on 18 April American pilots launched from
"Shangri-La" had successfully bombed military targets on Japan proper. Indeed, in a
daringly unconventional raid, Lieutenant Colonel James H. Doolittle had led sixteen
B-25 medium bombers from the flight deck of the carrier *Hornet* to bomb sites within
the Japanese cities of Tokyo, Nagoya, Osaka, and Kobe. Though the actual results of
the attack were of minimal consequence to the Japanese war effort, its success raised
American morale and greatly embarrassed the Japanese military leadership.

Of the 80 pilots and crew that had flown in Doolittle's Tokyo raid 71 made it to
safety, most to friendly areas in China. But the China-Burma theater was to prove no
haven for security. Japan held a tight grip on China, and by the end of May powerful

Japanese forces would successfully push British, American, and Chinese defenders out of Burma and into India before being held. This again was not good news, but in the process of its conquests the Japanese Army had stretched its supply lines to the extreme limits, a weakness the Allies would later exploit.

In another Allied success, however, and being of one reason for *Lang* and *Wasp* having been in the Mediterranean, on 5 May a British and Free-French expeditionary force was successfully landed on Madagascar. Within two days this strategic island was fully secured, denying the Japanese any easy opportunity at adding its naval facilities to their growing list of conquests.

And just as Madagascar was being secured, in the Coral Sea region of the South Pacific the first carrier battle between the Imperial Japanese and U.S. Navies was beginning. At the end of the two day air engagement the Japanese had lost the light carrier *Shoho*, one destroyer and several smaller craft sunk, with considerable damage to the fleet carrier *Shokaku* and massive plane and pilot loss for the carrier *Zuikaku*. American losses were the oiler *Neosho*, destroyer *Sims*, and the fleet carrier *Lexington* sunk, with light damage to the carrier *Yorktown*. A tactical loss for the U.S., this engagement, by denying the Japanese short-term use of two key carriers, was soon to prove to be a strategic loss for the Japanese.

Still, at this point in time the Pacific remained mostly Japanese domain. The Japanese had set up an elaborate chain of island defenses with a perimeter of defense that stretched as far east as the Ellice Islands, some 4,000 miles southeast of Tokyo. Included in their perimeter of defense was the island of Wake, only some 2,400 miles west of Honolulu. Each island had become an intricate part of the Japanese offense and defense, providing a platform for air defense, stations for resupply of their navy, and staging areas for further offensive moves. Allied resistance had so far ranged anywhere from none to heavy, and had completely failed at stopping the Japanese advance.

Such news made the future look rather bleak to the crew of *Lang*. They had spent ten days at Norfolk but by 7 June were again slowly beginning to make their move back to the open sea. At their departure different ones of the men paused to gaze back toward the pier area, sadly waving one more good-bye to the small group of family that had gathered there. Such departures had always been sad, but even more so during wartime, when the ship was headed for "God knows where." Under the circumstances, while remaining in the company of *Wasp* and with the Pacific Fleet having lost a carrier, it was not too difficult for the crew to suspect their destination to be the Pacific, yet wherever they were headed there was sure to be trouble.

Incredibly, just at about the very time that *Lang* was making her departure from Norfolk, the final act of a major U.S. victory in the Pacific was taking place; as the crew of the Japanese carrier *Hiryu* had just scuttled their ship. The battle at Midway was ended, changing the course of the Pacific war. With the loss of four carriers (*Akage*, *Soryu*, *Kaga*, and *Hiryu*), two heavy cruisers and three destroyers, and damage to two battleships, three heavy cruisers, and one light cruiser, the Imperial Japanese Navy had been dealt a serious blow from which it would not recover. U.S. losses amounted to the carrier *Yorktown* and destroyer *Hammon* being sunk. Finally, with this single engagement the Japanese advance in the Pacific was stopped and the two navies were more equalized in strength, though the battles to win the war were just beginning. Time was right that the U.S. could now go on the offensive.

As ordered, *Wasp* carrier task force moved south, whereby its passage was to be all too familiar to the veteran *Lang* crew. Entering the warm Caribbean, many of the men were reminded of their many ventures in these waters in a far more peaceful time. Time had now turned these waters, along with nearly every other body of water in the world, into a battleground. Blood stained its surface, and the blood of those who would preserve freedom as well as those who would fight to oppress it was destined to continue to flow into its depths for many more months to come.

The voyage proceeded quietly, and by 9 June the ships had made their arrival at the Panama Canal. As was suspected, the ships made the passage through the locks to enter into the blue Pacific. Afterwards, they continued on a course, by way of San Diego, departing there on the 30th, to proceed on into the hostile South Pacific, as yet unaware of their intended destination.

Obviously, their journey toward enemy territory warranted considerable caution. Each evening the ships were darkened, and around the clock posted lookouts, radarmen, and soundmen shared in the search for intruders. It was a different ocean, a different campaign, and a different enemy, but the dangers remained relatively the same. The Japanese I-boat was just as cunning and deadly as their German counterpart, and the Japanese surface fleet, though severely weakened, remained the superior navy in the Pacific. The risks were indeed high, and those men on duty remained diligent in their watch. Each one hoped not to see or hear anything that might be hostile, but at the same time, if it was out there, they hoped to see or hear it in time.

The night also brought with it the warm night air, its currents often rushing across the destroyer's deck, causing a continuous whistling in her stays as she glided along. Men would sometimes slip out on the destroyer's open deck and just relax at some cozy spot, smelling the fresh air and taking in a moment of quiet as stars twinkled in the darkness above. The tranquility of such moments would motivate many peaceful thoughts; happy thoughts of home and the future. The reality of where they were or of what might happen tomorrow was most often placed far outside their young minds.

As daylight appeared, so too did the resurrection of old routines. Men who wandered about the outer decks while semi-consumed with their daily chores, sometimes paused to look out at the other ships that accompanied them in their travel. Dotted about were some of America's finest warriors of the sea, each duly prepared to give their all for their country. The sight of such power brought a great sense of security to the crew as they sailed farther south and west, ever closer to the many dangers the Japanese posed throughout the Pacific.

The sailing proceeded without interruption, with only the slightest pause on the morning of 6 July while all the ships passed across the equator. This, a second crossing for *Lang*, allowed veteran Shellbacks to again lead lowly Pollywogs through the traditional ceremonies, including the ruthless episodes of humiliation and pain. On this occasion, however, circumstances would promote some isolated cases of compassion unseen in the initial crossing.

On the 17th, following continued unremarkable sailing, the ships successfully crossed the international dateline. Proceeding on a southwesterly course, the following day they safely arrived at the island of Tonga Tapu, Tonga Islands. There *Wasp* and her escorts joined with other ships to form Rear Admiral Richmond K. Turner's Task Force 62.

After having spent only a couple days at this rendezvous area, the force departed on the 21st. But just prior to this departure *Lang* once again had a change in her command. The sharp Lieutenant Commander Erskine A. Seay, who had so successfully established a well-organized command structure and while instilling preparedness among the crew, departed *Lang* for a new command elsewhere. He and his impersonal techniques had remained unpopular with the crew, yet he had, as personally hoped for, earned their respect and trust as a leader. Unfortunately, he would be denied the opportunity to share in their fast approaching test of courage and skill, a test that in their success he should rightly be included with some of the credit.

Seay's replacement was to be a real firebrand, a Lieutenant Commander by the name of John L. Wilfong. The crew was soon to find their new Captain to be a man with an extremely short fuse, his temperament oftentimes making him extremely comical to watch. Despite his obvious lack of emotional control, Wilfong knew well what it took to command a ship, and was ready and willing to meet any challenge that might be forthcoming, including that of gaining the trust of his new crew.

The upcoming challenges, however, soon appeared to be far greater than Wilfong or his officers and crew had so far imagined. Arriving in the Fiji Islands on the 26th, they found themselves being greeted by another complete task force. Such assemblage of shipping was awesome to behold, with various members of the crew temporarily transfixed by the sight of its size and potential power. Numerous troop-laden transports and cargo ships burdened with supplies and materials stood within an outer circle of warships. Carriers *Saratoga* and *Enterprise* were joined by *Wasp*, a group as a whole capable of carrying 250 combat aircraft. In the distance a single battleship, *North Carolina* (BB-55) the only battleship then available to the U.S. Navy in the Pacific, stood proudly with its big 16-inch guns bristling. And circled entirely about were a multitude of strongly armed cruisers and destroyers. The additional ships were those of Rear Admiral Frank J. Fletcher's Task Force 61. And together the two task forces were to spend the next few days off the island of Koro, there to rehearse air attacks, shore bombardments, and troop landing operations. Obviously, this was no playful gathering; something serious was in the making.

Scuttlebutt traveled wildly throughout the ships, as sailors eagerly gave great effort at figuring out just where they might be headed. That they would soon be taking a serious challenge to the enemy was of little doubt; but where? The following day they were told. They were headed for the Solomon Islands, there to make landings on the Japanese held islands of Tulagi, Gavutu, Tanambogo, Florida, and Guadalcanal.

Situated just a few hundred miles east of New Guinea, the Solomons were made up of seven large and numerous medium and smaller sized islands. Prior to the war these islands were of little interest to anyone. They were primitive, secluded, steamy, hot, and malaria infested. Even as the war neared, none of the future combatants seemed to give the islands any strategic value. The Australian government had established a small seaplane base in Gavutu Harbor, but their interest in and knowledge of the rest of the Solomons area remained minimal.

Though the Solomons seemingly demanded little respect, the same did not hold true for the Australian seaplane base, which the Japanese quickly determined warranted their attention, their planes beginning bombing operations against the site early in January 1942. In May, during the Coral Sea episode, and as the small Australian force on Gavutu became threatened by the Japanese build-up, the site was ordered evacuated. In turn, the Japanese quickly sent in a small force to occupy the island of Tulagi. One month later the Japanese returned again to the islands, this time with a sizable force to land on Guadalcanal there to prepare defensive positions and begin construction of a forward air strip. And it was this effort which was to set the stage for one of the bloodiest struggles of the war.

Just a short distance west of the Solomons' western most point stood the powerful Japanese island fortress of Rabaul. With elimination of this base foremost in his mind, Admiral Ernest King had as early as February determined that the Solomons would make a good starting point from which offensive efforts against the Japanese could begin. Forward bases were quickly established in the New Hebrides and New Caledonia as support of the landing operation, should it be given the green light, which King had initially targeted for Tulagi to begin on 1 August. But, when in July a routine reconnaissance flight sighted the construction on Guadalcanal, bringing fears of its future threat against the Navy's newly established forward bases and its ultimate aim, the elimination of Rabaul, King determined capture of Guadalcanal a priority.

Obviously, there was little time for planning the operation, and little information on the islands' terrain and enemy defenses to help with the planning. The First Marine Division had been chosen for the ground assault, but the Navy had the task of getting them there and providing for their support, and neither branch was prepared for such venture. Therefore, the date for the assault was pushed back to 7 August, which helped with some of the preparations, but equipment shortages and lack of training continued to plague the operation.

Indeed, the landing rehearsals undertaken at Koro were a complete flop; bombers missed their targets, ships fired inaccurately, and several of the landing craft suffered mechanical failures and or got hung up on reefs. Yet, despite these problems, on the morning of the 31st the two task forces began their move to the Solomons. And they certainly needed no additional discouragement at this point, but nature's message seemed all too clear; at their departure a large red sunburst displayed itself upon the distant horizon, tempting many sailors to interpret the sight as a bad omen for the operation's success.

Understandably, tension among the crews was great and grew steadily with each completed mile. The U.S. Navy had not attempted a wartime amphibious assault since America's war with Spain in 1898, and never to such a scale nor since the introduction of the combat airplane. Intelligence on the layouts of the targeted islands and of the enemy deployments there remained minimal which, in addition to the poor rehearsals, gave good reasons for some questioning of the sanity of the operation. Despite these shortcomings, however, crews remained in good spirits and morale was high.

For *Lang*'s crew the operation so far seemed rather business as usual, much like their experience in the Mediterranean. Their destroyer's initial duty placed her as part of the screen for Carrier Task Force 18. Once reaching the Solomons area, and following the invasion force's departure for its positions off the targeted islands, she would then move to take up a plane guarding station. Not too surprising she was to remain close to *Wasp*, providing anti-aircraft and anti-submarine protection as well as providing for rescue of any downed pilots and overseeing their transfer back to the carrier.

In the meantime, the entire task force proceeded cautiously toward their rendezvous with the Solomons. Throughout the daylight hours carrier planes lifted from their host flight decks to patrol the skies above and search the sea below for any sign of the enemy. When darkness ended the air searches, radarmen, and lookouts increased their vigils, having inherited sole responsibility of spotting hostile intruders.

These searches were around the clock, and throughout these tense hours general quarters was called with great frequency.

During one of these calls to general quarters, on 3 August, *Lang*'s crew was given opportunity to test fire some of the ship's ammunition. The result of the test was less than encouraging. Of the ten rounds fired, seven failed to explode. If the count was any accurate indication, some 70 percent of the destroyer's ammunition supply could be considered defective. Certainly this was not the ideal way to be heading into a potential battle.

On Guadalcanal, however, the approximate 2,000 Japanese troops (made up mostly of engineers and laborers for the airfield construction) were completely unaware of the approaching task forces. It mattered very little, as defenses on the island were nearly non-existent. The Japanese had since occupied the abandoned Australian seaplane base at Gavutu, providing for some local air defense, but a false sense of security had led this base to be lax in its preparedness. The Japanese command simply did not expect the U.S. capable of such an offensive operation so soon.

Fully prepared or not, the American task forces on the morning of the 7th began their attacks. Having successfully reached their objective without enemy detection, the carriers and their support ships moved to their pre-assigned stations, and at 5:22 A.M. had established positions 100 miles south of Guadalcanal.

While the troop transports and their screens moved on to their positions just off the islands' shores, the carriers and their screens turned into the wind in preparation of the launching of air strikes against pre-arranged enemy targets. With clockwork precision carrier crews performed to quickly send swarms of fighters and bombers airborne, their droning engines soon to fade to the north. At this point there was nothing left to do but wait.

Aboard *Lang*, sailors stood at their battle stations ready for action, nervously anticipating a warning of certain Japanese counterattack and expecting swarms of incoming enemy planes at any moment. The radarman watched his screen. The soundman listened to his phones. The radioman listened and the signalman watched for any incoming messages. Men manning the open mounted guns also helped in searching the sky. Men in the closed mounted guns could be seen frequently peeking out through open hatches to get a glimpse of the outside. Below decks, sailors were secluded in their own little world, their only touch with the outside through those men who wore headphones and relayed orders and news from topside. On the bridge, Captain Wilfong stood quietly, fully prepared to direct his crew into mortal combat. Yet, despite all the careful preparations, the expected attack never materialized.

The only planes to be seen this day were friendly, and as these initial flights returned they brought news of what was transpiring. Soon the news was traveling from ship to ship; the first flight had caught the enemy completely by surprise, destroying nine Zero float fighters and four Kawanishi flying boats at Gavutu and without a single loss to themselves. Later flights brought news that the landings at Lunga on Guadalcanal were progressing with no beach opposition remaining. Such welcomed news provided all crews with reassurance, as the whole operation was going much smoother than ever anticipated. Yet, obviously, this fight was far from finished.

The powerful Japanese base of Rabaul was within striking distance, and quick word of the American attack would warrant its quick response. By early afternoon P. E. Mason, an Australian coastwatcher on southern Bougainville, was reporting a flight of enemy bombers heading east toward the Guadalcanal area, estimating their time of arrival between 1:00 and 3:00 P.M.

Planes from *Wasp*, their presence in the air having been nearly non-stop since the invasion's beginning, quickly flew off to meet the enemy challenge. Meanwhile, ships and crews once again braced themselves for action. But, once again, the attack failed to materialize. Within an hour the planes were returning to the carrier's deck, bringing with them claims of having downed four enemy bombers while having scattered the rest.

This defensive effort had overextended some of the plane's fuel capacity, however, and it was for this reason that *Lang*'s crew had their first opportunity at displaying their skill for pilot rescue. While most of the planes landed safely, one pilot, his Wildcat sucking on empty fuel tanks and unable to reach the carrier, purposely guided his craft to crash land the water near the destroyer's area of patrol. Hardly had the spraying water settled before *Lang* was closing the sinking plane's position. Within seconds the destroyer had reached the crash site, pinpointed the buoyant pilot — his plane now completely submerged — and was sending two swimmers over the side to his rescue. In a very short time the pilot, Lieutenant Wilson Wright, was retrieved and brought safely aboard ship, where he gratefully received dry clothes and minor medical attention in preparation of his transfer back to *Wasp*.

There would be no more excitement this day. The rest of the afternoon went by without any additional challenges from the enemy and ended quietly. And that evening, as general quarters were routinely secured and watches methodically returned to their posts, off-duty sailors smartly took the opportunity to catch up on needed rest, almost assured that morning light would be the beginning of another long and restless day.

As expected, sunrise brought almost immediate warnings of confrontation. From a second Australian coastwatcher, Jack Read, stationed on northern Bougainville, an urgent report was received warning of 40 heavy bombers flying southeast from

Rabaul. Once again flights of Wildcat fighters lifted off the carrier in an effort to intercept the attackers.

This time, however, the bombers took an unusual route and managed to evade the Wildcats, able to reach the American transport area and attack in full strength. Reports of the attack quickly reached the carriers and the fighters were immediately redirected. In the meantime, the transports and their screens had to fend for themselves, which they did with deadly accurate anti-aircraft gunnery, downing seven of the Betty bombers and driving the rest away. The fleeing enemy bombers then ran straight into the redirected flights of Wildcats and suffered nearly total annihilation, with only one lone attacker able to return to its base.

Lang's radioman continued to keep Captain Wilfong updated as each report of the action came in. Initial information reported up to four transports having received some damage during the air attack. But later reports indicated only two ships having received serious injury: the transport *George F. Elliot* (AP-13) was set afire by one of the downed bombers which crashed into her deck and exploded, leaving her disabled and sinking; and the destroyer *Jarvis* (DD-393) was struck by a torpedo, leaving a 50 feet gash in her starboard side, though she remained able to sail off for repairs.

Later that afternoon *Lang*, along with all other ships of the air support group, received direct orders from Admiral Fletcher to move from their present position of 120 miles south of the transport area to a position farther southeast, strangely beyond his carrier planes' range of support for Turner's transports. Some commanders questioned the reasoning of the sudden departure, leaving the vulnerable transports at a time when enemy air attacks were increasing. Yet, despite some frustration with the order, the carriers and their escorts turned away from Guadalcanal, making 15 knots.

For the ships of the air support group the night of the 8th to 9th was quiet, with only the usual amount of precautions. Back in Savo Sound, off Guadalcanal, however, disaster was to strike with surprising fury.

Vice Admiral Gunichi Mikawa, Commander of the Imperial Japanese Navy's Eighth Fleet at Rabaul, had learned of the American landings shortly after they had started. And by late that afternoon he had gathered up five heavy cruisers, two light cruisers, and one destroyer and begun making his way toward Savo Sound.

Several early sightings of Mikawa's fleet were made by both submarine and planes, but the proximity of the ships to the Japanese naval bases (along with mis-identification of their types) led the American commanders to disregard their threat. At the moment it was the threat of enemy air attacks, even more so after the departure of the carriers, that was of the most concern.

For more than 24 hours Mikawa's fleet sailed unmolested, quickly closing the unsuspecting American transports and their covering screen off Savo Island. There

Rear Admiral V. A. C. Crutchley (RN), commanding the eight cruisers and the destroyer screen comprising support for Turner's transports, had on the evening of the 8th dispersed his ships into three sectors, unwittingly setting himself and his ships up for tragedy. The battle lasted barely 35 minutes. By morning Mikawa was safely sailing back to Rabaul having served the U.S. Navy the greatest defeat of its history.

Lang first received word of the defeat, as did the rest of Fletcher's force by radio early the morning of the 9th. First came reports of a night engagement with enemy surface ships off Savo Island. Next came the sad news that the cruisers *Astoria* (CA-34), *Quincy* (CA-71), and *Vincennes* (CA-44) had been sunk. A third report stated that in correction *Astoria* was not sunk and might possibly be saved. Yet this semi-good news did not hold true; as, despite hours of giving every possible effort to keep the mortally wounded cruiser afloat, she finally died and slipped below the surface to her final resting place. Additionally, the heavily damaged Australian cruiser *Canberra* had to be scuttled, and the cruiser *Chicago* (CA-29) was damaged so badly as to spend the rest of the year out of action. And *Jarvis* was missing (not till after the war was it learned that *Jarvis* was also a casualty of the Savo Sound disaster, possibly having received additional damage from both enemy and friendly fire while having inadvertently sailed through the battle area, but definitely spotted and misidentified as a damaged cruiser to Rabaul, where from enemy planes were directed to her position at dawn, sinking her with all hands).

The news sent an unimposed hush throughout *Lang*. As the ships of Fletcher's force continued to sail their southeasterly course, their now jittery crews suddenly became much more serious about their duties. Nothing was overlooked; and nothing was sometimes turned into something. Not far from *Lang* gunfire erupted from the cruiser *Salt Lake City* (CA-25) to startle the shaken crew, the cruiser reporting her gunfire directed at an unidentified submarine close aboard. It was later determined that her edgy gunners had killed only a fish.

Following the tragedy at Savo Sound, Turner quickly unloaded the transports and removed his remaining ships to the safety of Noumea, New Caledonia. The next few weeks that followed *Lang* remained with Carrier Task Force 18, continuing her screening duties. During this time *Wasp*'s group made no additional direct contacts with the enemy; however, on the 25th and while some 300 miles southeast of Guadalcanal, the group did receive a report of action between Japanese carriers and *Saratoga* and *Enterprise*. This report claimed an enemy light carrier *(Ryujo)* sunk and 71 (the actual number was closer to 90) enemy planes shot down. But the victories had not come without cost. Also reported was news of the *Enterprise* having been heavily damaged by three bomb hits and having lost eight of her pilots. Indeed, casualties were mounting fast on both sides, and the battle for the Solomons had just begun.

Lang had so far spent 45 straight days at sea and served with *Wasp* since 27 March. But on 4 September *Lang* finally departed the carrier to proceed to Noumea for a needed rest. As she departed the carrier's side the destroyer *O'Brien* (DD-415) arrived to fill her vacancy in the screen.

Lang's trip to Noumea was cautious but unhampered. Once there, the crew spent a couple of days in port but the stay was disappointingly short. New orders sent the destroyer on a series of missions escorting fleet oilers from various Australian ports to rendezvous with task forces in the open sea and also escorting between the island ports of New Hebrides and New Caledonea. These rather unremarkable duties were to consume the rest of the month.

It was during this time, however, the men of *Lang* again received very distressing news. On 20 September a message was received that *Wasp*, the ship that had so affected their own past, had been sunk by some well placed torpedoes from an enemy submarine. In an additional twist of fate, *Wasp's* gunnery officer, Lieutenant Commander George Knuepfer, whose gallant leadership was credited with helping to save many of the carrier crews' lives, had previously served as *Lang's* executive officer while under the command of Lieutenant Commander Waters. But what was even more haunting to *Lang's* crew was news that in the same attack the destroyer *O'Brien*, their own replacement, had also suffered a serious torpedo hit.

Three days later *Lang* departed Brisbane, Australia, on her last of the series of escort missions. This time she escorted the two U.S. submarines S-37 and S-41 to Noumea, whereupon her arrival she met the torpedo damaged *O'Brien* taking on repairs.

For the next several days *Lang* was destined to remain in port. But, on 10 October she departed Noumea as escort for the fleet oiler *Cimarron* (AO-22) and the partially repaired *O'Brien*. The group was to proceed to Suva, Fiji Islands, and then on to Pearl Harbor, where *O'Brien* would receive a full structural overhaul.

The journey to Suva was accomplished without incident, all three ships arriving safely in port on the 13th. After an additional three days layover, the group recommenced the voyage toward Pearl. But *O'Brien* was in trouble.

Even as the ships were departing Suva, *O'Brien* was experiencing considerable problems with leakage. With each nautical mile the leakage for *O'Brien* became increasingly worse. Under such conditions, it easily became evident that the crippled destroyer would not reach her intended destination without further repairs to her hull. It was decided that the ships should change course for the port of Pago Pago, Tutuila Island. In the meantime, the crew of *O'Brien* began tossing all loose gear overboard, lightening their ship's weight in the attempt to keep her afloat.

Still hoping to reach port, *O'Brien*'s crew continued to nurse their crippled ship along. They had brought her 3,000 miles from where she had first received her wound, and did not intend to give her up now. But, at 6:00 A.M. on 19 October, just off Samoa the destroyer suddenly hesitated with a jerk, her keel snapping and her hull beginning to break up near her quarterdeck.

A half-hour later her disheartened crew — with the exception of a salvage party — began to abandon ship. In orderly fashion, her crew made their way to waiting boats for transport to *Cimarron*. Within another half-hour the salvage party, they too unable to do anything more for the dying ship, were also removed from the vessel. And soon all members of *O'Brien* crew were safely aboard *Cimarron*, having suffered no casualties.

Obviously, the death of a ship was an experience few sailors could ever forget. From *Cimarron* and *Lang* sailors watched and listened as *O'Brien* began to shudder and vibrate with a sickening noise. Her metal groaned and moaned and cried out as her seams split and her structuring began to pull apart. The crews stood helplessly in their observation as the destroyer quickly began to settle amidship, her bow and fantail simultaneously rising into the air to form a "V" on her way down. By 8:00 A.M. it was all over; *O'Brien*, her final exhale of air consumed in a gurgle, disappeared below a pool of debris cluttered foam.

Throughout the sad episode various *Lang* crew could hardly help but ponder *O'Brien*'s fate, and contemplate just how close they had been from their own brush with disaster. How fortunate *Lang* had been; how unlucky *O'Brien*. Of all the time *Lang* had spent with *Wasp*, her likely death had been separated from her by only two weeks. Had not fate intervened on their behalf, it likely would have been their own destroyer they just witnessed slide beneath the sea.

With *O'Brien* gone, *Lang*, and *Cimarron* recommenced a course to Pearl Harbor, where they safely arrived five days later. This was *Lang*'s first visit back at Pearl since the attack, yet evidence of that disastrous day still remained for the crew to view. Though much of the damage had been repaired and most of those ships severely damaged or sunk during the attack had since been resurrected to sail again, there still remained the sunken capsized hulls of *Utah* (BB-31) and *Oklahoma* (BB-37). And, of course, there lay *Arizona*, her flag still waving proudly, wherein her sunken hull were entombed 1,103 of her crew. These sad sights, added to their recent experience with *O'Brien*, served to reinforce the crew's desire to defeat the enemy. And, obviously, Captain Wilfong appreciated his crew's enhanced warrior spirit, knowing such spirit was to be as much a weapon as was any gun in his destroyer's arsenal.

While at Pearl *Lang* underwent some repairs of her own before returning to active duty. Afterwards, however, she still did not immediately return to where the action was the hottest, spending most of the next month in training around the Hawaiian area. Finally, on 1 December, the destroyer headed back for the war torn region of the Solomons, serving as escort for the aviation tenders *Wright* (AV-1) and *Hammonsport* (AKV-2), which were carrying Marine scouting/bombing squadrons to Espiritu Santo, New Hebrides Islands, where they arrived on the 12th. There she would spend an additional ten days conducting battle rehearsals with a cruiser task force before being sent back to Guadalcanal.

Meanwhile, during *Lang*'s absence, fighting on and around Guadalcanal had been fierce and costly for both sides. The Japanese were determined not to lose the island, using every option at their disposal at reinforcing its garrison and at striking at the blockading American navy. By the time of *Lang*'s return, so many ships from both navies had been sunk in Savo Sound, it had now inherited the new name "Iron Bottom Bay." The carrier *Hornet* (CV-8) had died there, so too had the cruisers *Atlanta* (CL-51), *Juneau* (CL-52), and *Northampton* (CL-26), and no less than ten American destroyers (including *Lang*'s sister ship *Benham*). Thousands of men from both sides had perished in the savage land and sea battles to secure the island that in the beginning neither side had believed essential to their overall strategies — and the battles for it yet raged.

Departing Espiritu Santo on 22 December, *Lang* sailed in the screen for transports bound back to embattled Guadalcanal, where she was to spend much of the next several months in helping with resupply and reinforcement efforts. It was during this time that the final American push to secure the island began.

With the arrival of the new year the battle for the island was finally nearing its conclusion. And, on 22 January, *Lang* departed Tulagi Harbor to make the short trip over to the Guadalcanal coastline to join in the effort to secure the island once and for all.

As the destroyer moved along the island's shoreline, different ones of the crew stared out at the land where so much heavy fighting had taken place, the air around them thick with the stench of rotting jungle and death. By this time the battle for the island was all but over, but there remained some heavy pockets of resistance to be mopped up.

On this day Marine spotters, having located a large group of Japanese northwest of Kokumbona village, called for fire support from *Lang*. The coordinates were given and the destroyer's gunners went to work as the five-inch guns were brought to bear. Suddenly, there was a loud boom, jarring every inch of the ship as her batteries sent forth a message of death to the enemy ashore. Following this initial blast the guns paused, awaiting word from the Marines for any corrections. Then, following only slight adjustments, the guns resumed their cannonade, firing for effect.

73

During the thunderous gunnery, a lone *Lang* sailor stared through the destroyer's optics to witness the massive carnage ashore. Through smoke and flying debris he could see the enemy soldiers scampering in an effort to find cover, their panic divulged by their disarray, only to disappear as a violent eruption marked the end of their earthly existence.

The onslaught was short but effective. Later, reports confirmed the accuracy of *Lang*'s guns. The destroyer's batteries had destroyed an enemy supply dump and a battalion headquarters, in the process wiping out an entire battalion of enemy troops.

Two days later *Lang* would once again give fire support to the Marines. On that afternoon her five-inch guns again delivered death to four more enemy troop concentrations while destroying yet another supply dump as well as a group of crude shelters.

Lang spent the next four days protecting unloading transports and supply ships off Guadalcanal, and afterwards joined the screen for some small escort carriers that were guarding convoys traveling from between the Fiji Islands and different areas of the Solomons. These rather unremarkable duties were to last up through July.

It was during this time, however, on 27 June, that *Lang* arrived in Havannah Harbor, Efate, New Hebrides Islands, with a very excited crew. News had come that Destroyer Division 12, of which *Lang* was presently a part, was going to New Zealand for some long-awaited rest and recreation. As the news spread, chatter intensified among the men. Each sailor began to share his plans with the others for the upcoming visit, most plans including pubs and women. Soon though, their excitement turn to disappointment — all of the division, except for *Lang*, were making the journey.

Instead, *Lang* was to receive the "honor" of having the division commander come aboard to take charge of a group of destroyers that would be screening for escort carriers that, in turn, would be guarding a convoy of merchant ships and transports headed for Guadalcanal. And on the following day the destroyer departed in the company of the escort carrier *Sangamon* (CVE-26), her embittered crew cursing their misfortune.

Obviously, the majority of the crew were pretty frustrated, but for at least one *Lang* sailor the ride turned out to be pretty fortunate. Quartermaster Eldon Coward had originally been assigned to the attack transport *McCawley* (APA-4); that had been some 35 days earlier when he had first made his arrival in the South Pacific at Noumea. Coward, a Texan used to hard work, spent much of his time on the island helping a "Seabee" construction battalion build quonset huts on the other side of the town. Unfortunately, it was during one of these work details that *McCawley* came into port, where she remained only a short time and then made a quick departure, causing

Coward to miss his assignment. Obviously, he was upset when he learned that *McCawley* had left without him, but command quickly reassigned him to another ship, the destroyer *Lang*.

Coward then began a series of shuttle rides that eventually got him to Havannah Harbor. There he met *Lang*, officially joining her crew's ranks just one day before her departure with *Sangamon* to Guadalcanal. Three days later he received word that *McCawley* had been sunk just off the island of Rendova, having first been hit by a torpedo from an enemy torpedo plane and then mistakenly hit by a second torpedo from poorly informed American torpedo boats. Coward suddenly remembered how disappointed he had been when he had missed that very ship back in Noumea; now he took pause to be thankful he had ended up on *Lang* instead.

Following her unwanted and uneventful escort duties, *Lang* again returned to Havannah Harbor. But on 13 July she departed again, this time in the company of the destroyer *Stack* (DD-406) and the destroyer minesweeper *Southard* (DMS-10) for a return to Tulagi.

By this time the battle for Guadalcanal had long ended. On 18 April, Admiral Yamamoto, while flying to Bougainville to help in bolstering his troop's sagging morale, had been shot down and killed, adding further to the American victory. Still, the battle for the rest of the Solomons continued its rage. And the fierce contest between the two opposing sides was destined to cost many more lives before its conclusion.

For *Lang*, however, the real battles had not even begun. To this point the destroyer had managed to steer clear of major trouble — or possibly providence had just guarded her path. Yet, with a war of such magnitude, trouble was sure to find her. And, sure enough, the moment had finally come for *Lang* to step into the ring.

Chapter 6

Vella Gulf

After six bitter months of bloody fighting the battle for Guadalcanal had finally ended. The Japanese had been determined to regain its control but had failed. They had poured men and materials onto the island in the great effort to push the Americans off, only to be frustrated by a blockading American navy and beaten back by a stubborn group of U.S. Marines and Army troops. They had sent their bombers on perilous long-range missions, beyond the range of valuable fighter escort, to strike the Americans on both land and sea, only to lose most of the flights before they had a chance to release their deadly cargoes. And they had sent their navy to battle the U.S. ships offshore and bombard the U.S. positions on shore, successfully using their proficient night-engagement skills to deal death to several American men-of-war, but it was not enough. The real estate of Guadalcanal had become far too costly for the Japanese, and in the first week of February 1943 the island was evacuated.

That the Japanese were able to hold out on Guadalcanal as long as they had could be attributed primarily to one individual, that of Rear Admiral Raizo Tanaka. Using fast destroyers and submarines to navigate a direct route from Rabaul and through the Solomon Islands to be known as "The Slot," Tanaka successfully delivered reinforcements and supplies to the beleaguered island garrison. Tanaka's supply train, most notably referred to as the "Tokyo Express," met with great resistance, however, and its increasingly alarming losses of precious destroyers was key to the Japanese determination that Guadalcanal was to be given up. Yet before the end Tanaka's destroyers were to play one final role, pulling off one of war's greatest escapes, when from 1–9 February they successfully evacuated over 11,000 Japanese troops from Guadalcanal and escaped to safety without the Americans' knowledge till days after its occurrence.

Nevertheless, Guadalcanal had been wrenched from the grips of the Japanese Empire. This was the first real battlefield victory for purely American land forces, and its importance was to be celebrated. It proved that the seemingly invincible Japanese war machine could be solidly defeated. And though the effort had indeed been costly, many important lessons had been learned which would save lives in the battles yet to come. Guadalcanal marked the beginning of America's march to Tokyo, and the eventual end of the Pacific War.

Lang's part in the Guadalcanal victory was obviously minimal, but she had participated and had accomplished every duty asked of her and her officers and crew throughout the campaign. Of all ship types involved in the battles around Guadalcanal, destroyers had suffered the greatest losses, with the Japanese having lost 11 and the Americans having lost a total of 14. These losses put a great strain on both navies, yet even more so for the U.S. whose destroyer fleet was divided among two ocean campaigns. *Lang* remained among the surviving destroyers active in the Solomons. The battles for this chain of islands was far from over, and under the circumstances it was certain that the destroyer's role was to increase.

Escorting and screening for the larger ships had so far dominated most of *Lang*'s past. Her duties had up to this point of the war been with the carriers, where she had fortunately kept clear of any direct enemy contact. Not that she had never been in danger of such contact; every day in the South Pacific had been and continued to be dreadfully dangerous. Enemy submarines were a constant threat to all shipping, especially carrier fleets, which they already had tallied a deadly score. Planes too, were a constant menace, having brought their own brand of death and destruction to several ships around the Solomons. And Japanese surface warships had proven themselves very deadly opponents, especially when engaged in night action.

As *Lang*'s crew began settling into their new base of operations at Tulagi, a small island that set within the confines of Purvis Bay, Florida Island, morale was basically high. In fact, the men were eager for some action. Other than the dropping of depth-charges on submarine contacts during the Malta operation and the shelling of enemy positions on Guadalcanal, they had yet to really tangle with the enemy. More importantly, they had yet to have the enemy return fire, causing many of the crew to be somewhat overconfident and complacent toward the threat of death. But this was soon to change.

On 3 June Admiral William Halsey issued the order for the next step of the Solomon's campaign, the invasion of New Georgia Island. Preliminary landings by small units of Marine and Army raiders began on the 21st, while the main landings began on the 30th, taking the American war machine one step closer toward Rabaul.

Again, the Japanese navy sent the Tokyo Express to help in reinforcing New Georgia and its neighboring islands with troops and supplies, culminating in the battles of Kula Gulf (6 July) and Kolombangara (12–13 July). And, again, the Japanese displayed their proficiency at night engagement against a superior force, their Long Lance torpedoes sinking the cruiser *Helena* (CL-50) and destroyer *Gwinn* (DD-433) while severely damaging the New Zealand cruiser *Leander* and the American cruisers *Honolulu* (CL-48) and *St. Louis* (CL-46). Japanese losses amounted to the cruiser *Jintsu* and destroyers *Niizuki* and *Nagatsuki*; their remaining ships escaping with only minor damage. And the Japanese had not been deterred from landing 1,200 troop reinforcements on Kolombangara. So the campaign continued, the Solomons' real estate destined to cost much more men and material before its end.

Lang joined the New Georgia operation on the 17th, departing Purvis Bay with a few other destroyers to help cover six high-speed destroyer transports (APDs) that were en route to the invasion landings at Enogai Inlet. At a speed of 27 knots, these ships traveled across the waters of "the Slot" to arrive at their destination at near midnight. From there *Lang* and the other screening destroyers began to maneuver in northern Kula Gulf to afford cover to the unloading transports.

Just as the operation was getting into full swing and about an hour into the destroyers' patrol, word was received of three approaching enemy destroyers having been spotted by a "Black Cat" (a radar equipped Catalina) patrol plane. As the American ships were already at general quarters, only a warning of the contact and the direction of the enemy approach was issued.

Lang's lookouts stared silently across the darkness, searching out every shadow while anticipating eminent sighting of the enemy vessels. At 1:36 A.M. a visual was made, the enemy moving on a northward heading. The anticipation was suddenly replaced by nervous excitement. From *Lang*'s bridge Captain Wilfong called out the order, "Stand-by to attack with guns and torpedoes!" Gun crews prepared their weapons to throw devastation toward the unsuspecting destroyers, anxiously awaiting the order. Throughout the rest of the ship men stood in silence, expecting the firing to begin at any moment and unsure what to expect afterward. Then, with confident exclamation, Captain Wilfong shouted, "Main batteries, fire!" And the five-inch guns responded with a violent boom, each volley echoed by the five-inch guns of the other American destroyers.

Through the darkness the five-inch projectiles sped toward their targets. Time suddenly seemed to pause with the race of each sailor's pulse. For a second the darkness yielded nothing; then a small flash was noted — then another and another till the distant darkness began to dance with light. The American gunners had found their targets and hits were quickly observed on all three enemy ships. Wilfong reported across the TBS (talk between ships) that the "leading ship (was) definitely hit by our salvos."

79

(Previously classified information was released in 1972 that divulged the "three Japanese destroyers," as reported by the patrolling Catalina, to have been American patrol torpedo boats. This mistaken identity and resulting "friendly fire" caused no casualties to any of the vessels involved, and it was later surmised that the "hits" reported were overshots that struck the shore of Kolombangara.)

Seemingly caught off guard, the surprised enemy frantically turned their ships about and began to belch out clouds of chemical white smoke to hide themselves while making a hasty, high-speed retreat. In the meantime, after making a short chase, during which *Lang* fired a total of 67 rounds of five-inch ammunition at the fleeing enemy, the firing abruptly ended, allowing the enemy their escape. The initial mission of the American destroyers would not allow them to finish the job; the safety of the unloading transports was their main concern for the moment.

The group of destroyers turned to head back to their original stations, their battle seemingly over. *Lang* was just beginning her turn, her crew feeling confident and beginning to relax some, when suddenly the ship was jolted by a violent underwater explosion. The destroyer jarred and the crew staggered from the shock of the high-explosive bomb. Dazed for just a moment, *Lang*'s crew quickly recovered and immediately prepared for battle. Gun crews scoured the sky for a target while the radarman began a desperate search for the high-flying menace; but the culprit had already made its escape, the bomber's form no longer accessible to the radar's span of vision.

Enemy planes had indeed located the patrol, yet the destroyers continued to cover the landing operations. Within the hour the gunners twice opened fire on attacking bombers. During the second attack a bomber planted four bombs directly ahead of the destroyer *Pringle* (DD-477), showering her with sparks but causing no damage. And though the attack did come dangerously close for comfort, all the ships safely returned to Purvis Bay, arriving there at dawn.

Three days later *Lang* once again departed Tulagi in escort of APDs to New Georgia Island. This time the mission was completed with no major contact with the enemy.

After returning to base, *Lang* was soon on the move again, departing on the 22nd as escort for the damaged New Zealand cruiser *Leander*. *Leander* had been struck by a torpedo some ten days earlier during the battle of Kolombangara, inflicting some serious structural damage and killing 28 of her crew. She had since made temporary repairs and was ready for departure to some safe port where further repairs could be made. *Lang* was to escort her as far as Espiritu Santo, where both ships safely arrived the following day. Afterwards, *Lang* returned to Tulagi, and there her crew was allowed a few days of rest.

In the meantime, the New Georgia campaign continued but progress was slow. Reinforcements were needed for a final push, and on 31 July *Lang* departed Tulagi for

Kakum Beach, Guadalcanal, to resume helping with the task. There she was to join up with destroyers *Sterett* and *Stack* to escort five tank landing ships (LSTs), each loaded with troops, to the Onaiavisi Entrance, New Georgia Island.

The ships departed Kakum under the cover of darkness, each ready to meet whatever challenge might lay before them. *Lang*'s crew prepared for action, trying to show no fear though somewhat less convincing as on previous assignments, their eagerness dampened some since the action at Enogai. In addition, anticipation, nervous energy and the sultry heat combined to allow them little rest, which promoted further thought of their future fate — a result which only time could reveal.

Near daybreak of the following morning the ships safely reached their destination and landing operations were begun. As a bright morning sun announced the new day soldiers climbed into their landing craft for their journey to the black sandy shore. The mugginess of the morning was made evident by the steam rising from within the island's jungled interior. Perspiration covered every man as the operation commenced. Then, just as the troops were making their way to the beach, from out of the blinding sun suddenly appeared six enemy Val (Aichi D3A) dive-bombers screaming down on the landing force.

Bombs went whirling toward the landing craft and the troops they were dispersing. In desperation, anti-aircraft fire immediately erupted in a wild effort to thwart the attack. Radar had failed to see the approaching enemy, and so quickly had the planes appeared that not all guns were fully manned. In addition, various men had their attention momentarily diverted and were transfixed when within their clear view body parts and debris flew through the air from a direct hit on one of the landing craft. Combine the rattle and boom of the gunfire with the thud of the bombs and the roar of the planes and all became a deafening rumble, which added even greater confusion to the minds of the men. Eyes tried to keep up with the movements of the planes, but it was impossible. Orders and information were yelled through the phone systems, trying to direct the crew, while men on the receiving headphones passed on the communication to others, many times using hand signals to overcome the intense noise.

Then, with little warning one of the Vals peeled away from the others into a 65 degree dive and headed straight for *Lang*. Five-inch guns began pounding at the target but were totally ineffective. Gunner's Mate Robert Allbritton had been near one of the mid-ship 20-millimeters when the attack had started. He quickly grabbed the gun and began firing without critical aim, watching the gun's tracer rounds as aid for targeting. Perspiration stung his eyes as he kept up the guns staccato rhythm throughout the plane's approach.

Yet the plane continued, screaming by and releasing its deadly cargo which impacted and exploded barely 100 feet off the destroyer's port bow. Sailors ducked for cover as spraying shrapnel went sizzling through the air. Holes were torn in the stack, a life raft, and the outer casing of a ready ammunition box. One good sized piece of shrapnel pierced a two-inch hole through the ship's skin on the port bow about three feet above the main deck. Several other smaller fragments landed on the main and superstructure decks, but luckily none of the crew were killed or injured.

Chief Machinist Mate Robert Glass found himself staring down at a four-inch bomb fragment that had hit the superstructure near the machine shop and had dropped near the forward engine room hatch where he was standing. He carefully scooped up the warm and weighty piece of steel, a fragment that just moments before had the potential of making a real mess of a man's flesh and bones, and sent it to the bridge.

Meanwhile, the action continued. Captain Wilfong called out for a damage report as he and others on the bridge watched the duel to its conclusion. Below them Allbritton's tracers continued to blaze a trail toward the target. Then, a sudden burst of flame appeared at the side of the plane and a portion of the left wing disintegrated. Flinging wildly out of control, the doomed bomber plummeted down through the air to crash and burn within the island jungle, a black pillar of smoke marking its end. Throughout the destroyer there erupted cheers; Allbritton's gun handling had scored *Lang* her first definite kill of the war.

From the beginning of *Lang*'s first gun shot to her last a mere 18 seconds had expired. During that time the five-inch guns had only managed to release seven rounds, while Allbritton's fast firing 20-millimeter had spit out a total of forty. Indeed, almost as suddenly as the planes had appeared and the action begun, it was over. The remaining enemy planes had since retired to safety. And, as smoke from the gunfire still hung in the air, there was nothing left for the crew to do but begin to check for damage and study the scars that had been acquired.

Meanwhile, now that the action was ended, Signalman Scott McIntyre had slowly come to his feet. When the action first began he had been standing at his general quarters at the after steering station with orders to take over the steering should the bridge receive a hit and be knocked out. The after steering station was located on the after deckhouse just slightly aft and between the two twin 40-millimeters. As those two guns had followed the path of the plane, their gun crews trying desperately to get him in their sights, the port forty had traversed around to point directly across the deckhouse and right into McIntyre's face. Though the signalman knew that cam stops on the gun would not permit it to fire upon reaching that point, he took no chances. Having suddenly come face to face with the inside of the barrels, now looking five times their normal size, he did the only logical thing and flung himself down upon the hard steel deck. The bruising he received, however, had been truly unnecessary as the forties had been unable to get off a single shot at the speedy bomber. Yet through all the noise and confusion he was far from the only one to dive for cover.

Truly, *Lang*'s latest experience had been frightening, to say the least. This action, as had no other to date, testified to the crew just how serious this war was and just how vulnerable their human lives could be. They had beat this "Jap," but he had come very close at getting them first, and at this stage the "road to Tokyo" was to be "a long ole road to haul." No doubt they would run into many more relatives of that Japanese pilot before this war was to be over.

On the following morning *Lang* was back within the safety of Tulagi Harbor. Yet, with possession of the Solomons remaining a heated contest, no *Lang* sailor expected to remain there long. And indeed they would not.

American ground forces were close to finishing the New Georgia campaign but continued to be slowed up by the Japanese ability to get in reinforcements and supplies, a fact which American ground commanders rightly questioned the U.S. Navy. Rear Admiral Theodore S. Wilkinson had just taken over command of the Third Amphibious Force from Admiral Kelly Turner, and it was he who was now receiving all the complaints. He decided the Tokyo Express had been a thorn in the Navy's side quite long enough, and determined to put an end to its nightly runs once and for all.

Wilkinson's choice to complete the task at hand was a young, talented Commander by the name of Frederick Moosbrugger. And just how Moosbrugger was to accomplish the feat was completely up to his own discretion — just so long as the job was done.

Moosbrugger was commander of Task Group 31.2, a force which consisted of eight destroyers, of which *Lang* was one. Rarely had destroyers been given such opportunity. For the past year and a half screening and escorting the larger ships had seemed the destroyer's sole purpose in the war effort. To have the chance to lead destroyers, alone, into action was every destroyer commander's dream, and a dream that Moosbrugger had just been given access.

Obviously, Moosbrugger accepted the challenge given him most energetically, feeling very confident in the abilities of his destroyers and their officers and crews. Consisting of two destroyer divisions, his command was made up of the fastest, most reliable and most fully weapons capable destroyers in the U.S. Fleet. Destroyer Division (DesDiv) 12, under Moosbrugger's personal command, included the destroyers *Gridley* (DD-380), *Maury* (DD-401), *Craven* (DD-382), and *Dunlap* (DD-384), the latter being Moosbrugger's flagship. Destroyer Division 15, under the command of Commander Rodger W. Simpson, included *Wilson*, *Sterett*, *Stack*, and *Lang*, *Lang* being Simpson's flagship.

Moosbrugger's division still retained their original allotment of 16 torpedo tubes, now integrating new flash hiders for greater cover when firing at night. Simpson's division, on the other hand, while having less torpedo capacity, had greater gunfire capability with the addition of their powerful twin 40-millimeter mounts. And both divisions were radar equipped.

Certainly capability and readiness were important factors for success, but a plan of action was also needed. On 5 August Moosbrugger met with Simpson to work on the operational details. But before the meeting was ended it was interrupted by a message from Wilkinson, directing Moosbrugger to depart Tulagi at 12:30 P.M. the following afternoon with his two divisions (less *Gridley* and *Wilson*, which were to remain behind) and proceed to Vella Gulf, south of the Russells and Rendova, and sweep the area for enemy traffic. Wilkinson had received intelligence which seemed to predict a possible run of the Tokyo Express through that area sometime after midnight. As Wilkinson had no cruisers to spare, and his motor torpedo boats (PTs) were licking wounds from a previous engagement three nights before (an action which had seen the loss of Lieutenant John F. Kennedy's PT-109), it was totally up to Moosbrugger's destroyers to meet and stop the suspected Japanese reinforcement effort.

Early the next morning Moosbrugger again met with Simpson to finalize their plans. Afterwards, the rest of the destroyer commanders were gathered together and informed of the mission and familiarized with all pertinent intelligence. Moosbrugger was clear on emphasizing several critical pieces of information. One, it was suspected the Japanese may use a cruiser in addition to destroyers in the sortie, threatening potential heavier, longer ranged main batteries with which to contend. Two, this was potentially to be a night torpedo and gunnery action, which the Japanese had so far had tremendous success. Furthermore, he pointed out, if his commanders were to have success, they must take advantage of the element of surprise, hit hard and fast, and coordinate their attacks.

Moosbrugger's plan sounded simple enough — although its execution would surely prove more difficult than mere words could make it seem. In effect, after entering Vella Gulf, the two divisions would divide into two columns. Moosbrugger's division would be the lead column, while Simpson's would form some distance to the right behind Moosbrugger's. There would be a reduction in speed to reduce the visibility of their wakes, and they would stay close to the shoreline to make it more difficult for the enemy to detect them, either visually or with radar.

If enemy destroyers were encountered, Moosbrugger's division would make the initial attack with torpedoes. Immediately afterward, Simpson's division would follow up with gunnery and torpedoes. If, however, after a complete search of the area the anticipated Japanese destroyers were not located, the divisions would concentrate on any barge traffic found. If nothing could be located by 2:00 A.M. (a predetermined time set by Wilkinson) the two divisions would return to their base.

By 11:30 A.M. the meeting was over and all the commanders were back aboard their respective ships and sailing out of Purvis Bay (one hour ahead of schedule due to *Maury* having an engineering problem which limited her speed). While proceeding through Iron Bottom Sound the ships maneuvered to make an "S" turn in salute of the many sailors and ships that had died there. Initialized by Simpson, the salute also served to remind those sailors of the task group of just what the Japanese were capable of doing, especially during night action. Each sailor must remain alert and perform their specific duties well — or else the fate of those they had just saluted could become their own.

Even as Moosbrugger's ships were leaving Tulagi, Captain Kaju Sugiura, aboard his flagship destroyer *Hagikaze*, was leading a squadron of four destroyers that were carrying 900 soldiers and 50 tons of supplies destined for the island of Kolombangara. At 11:30 A.M. his Tokyo Express was located north of Bougainville heading southeast at high speed.

Hagikaze and sister ship *Arashi* were leading Sugiura's column. They were both of the Kagero Class, being the newest and best destroyers in the Imperial Japanese Navy, each boasting a length of 388 feet and a displacement of more than 2,000 tons; yet they carried no radar. Destroyers *Kawakaze* and *Shigure* made up the rest of the column. They were both of the older Shiratsuyu Class, being nearly identical in size and capability as Moosbrugger's destroyers, though they too carried no radar. And only *Shigure* was unburdened with the extra weight of troops and supplies.

Having sailed various headings at a speed of 27 knots, the American destroyers by 4:00 P.M. had reached a point just south of the Russell Islands. It was at this time that Moosbrugger received a report of the Japanese destroyers having been sighted by a Black Cat patrol plane just north of Buka Island, the column moving on a south by west heading.

Continuing on their planned course, the American destroyers at a little before 8:00 P.M. suddenly ran into a violent rainsquall. They were just passing the south shore of Rendova Island, but with the sheets of rain blasting against their portlights the shoreline became totally blotted from view. Still, determined to meet his schedule, Moosbrugger pressed his ships forward at speed, utilizing radar and soundings as eyes.

Once having passed through the squall all crews were called to general quarters; and at 10:00 P.M., while passing through Gizo Strait and entering Vella Gulf, the ships were slowed to 15 knots. By this time the sky had cleared but the darkness was pitch black. Visibility was between 3,000 to 4,000 yards. The sea was icy smooth which, combined with their slow speed, created very little visible wake from the ships. Conditions at this point were perfect.

As the men aboard *Lang* manned their battle stations, those who could looked out across the darkness, straining their eyes for any sign of the enemy. Other than the known destroyer threat, there were several other menaces to watch for. The Japanese quite often used heavily armed barges (Daihatsus) and submarines to make their nightly supply and reinforcement runs not to mention the constant threat of enemy planes. It would be crucial that they locate the enemy first, in whatever form he appeared, and be able to pass on the critical information speedily.

Since all of Moosbrugger's destroyers had been built before the introduction of radar, none had been constructed with a designated area for a Combat Information Center (CIC). One of the valuable lessons learned from the previous engagements in the Solomons was the importance of speedy information gathering. The CIC had proven its worth, offering commanders the luxury of almost immediate access to most the information needed to execute a combat operation often saving them valuable time in making decisions which could ultimately have grave effect upon the outcome. So, to accommodate this valuable asset, on each of Moosbrugger's destroyers a makeshift CIC was placed within the captain's emergency cabin located just behind the bridge.

On *Lang* the CIC was already a focus of attention for both Commodore Simpson and Captain Wilfong. There, Lieutenant Pemberton Southard, *Lang*'s Executive and CIC Officer, and a radarman, a soundman and an assistant were strenuously working in the cramped quarters. Staring over details of a chart that was laid out on a makeshift chart table suspended above the captain's bunk, Southard kept Simpson and Wilfong informed of chart readings, soundings and radar searches, while in turn Simpson tried to keep his ships as close to shore as possible to evade detection by the enemy. This and more information became even more important as it was learned that the Black Cats, which were to have helped in keeping track of the enemy, had been grounded by foul weather.

As the American destroyers continued to move along in a two column battle formation along the Kolombangara shoreline, their radars continued to search out through the eerie darkness for the enemy. Suddenly, at 11:18 P.M. *Dunlap* reported a surface contact at 90 degrees true and at a range of 4,060 yards. The moment turned tense as lookouts strained their eyes to make a sighting through the dense black that lay before them. But five minutes later the contact was determined to be false.

After another ten minutes *Lang* once again received a reported contact from *Dunlap*. This time the target was bearing 359 degrees true, at a range of 23,000 yards. Three minutes later *Craven* verified the contact. With this verification, Moosbrugger reported to Simpson that his lead division was preparing to fire full port torpedoes broadside. As the contact closed to within 15,000 yards four very distinct targets were now shown on the radar screen, and the apprehension began to mount as seconds drug slowly by.

With the two opposing destroyer columns closing one another at a combined speed of 50 knots, the distance between the two reduced quickly. At 11:40 P.M., the torpedo officer aboard *Dunlap* announced the track angle at 290, the desired angle for

86

firing torpedoes, and Moosbrugger gave the order to "execute." One minute later, his DesDiv 12 fired 24 torpedoes at a range of between 4,820 to 4,300 yards to the target. Immediately afterwards Moosbrugger took his division hard to starboard.

From the moment that Moosbrugger had given the order to his division to fire, *Lang*'s bridge had remained silent. Three minutes passed; then the radio's tactical circuit cracked as Moosbrugger reported a spread of 24 torpedoes successfully launched. In response, Simpson ordered his division hard to port and to "stand-by to fire."

Visibility was still under 4,000 yards and no lookouts from either division had yet sighted the enemy ships. Nerves began to wrench as lookouts and gunners peered desperately through the darkness.

Meanwhile, the Japanese had remained ignorant of Moosbrugger's destroyers. A lookout on *Hagikaze* first spotted the American destroyers just as Moosbrugger's division was swinging his ships starboard. His report sent the Japanese crews on a flurry of confused preparation for battle, but it was too late.

Back on the American destroyers men waited in silent agony, counting the seconds. With the passing of what seemed too much time, men began to fear failure. Then suddenly, three terrific explosions were observed, quickly followed by ten more violent explosions. As best as could be initially determined three ships had been hit. One, a large ship thought to be a cruiser (actually *Arashi*), burst into a violent inferno, lighting the entire area around it.

Aboard *Lang*, sailors stared with amazement as a second enemy ship (*Kawakaze*) suddenly slipped right up next to the brightly burning "cruiser," silhouetting herself and presenting the perfect target.

Taking full advantage of such good fortune, Simpson quickly ordered his division to open fire. With deadly accuracy the five-inch guns of his three destroyers erupted with violent unity. Hit after hit was observed as the ship began to burn. Then *Stack* fired four torpedoes into the target, putting the finishing touches to the already doomed ship. No more was needed, and the firing ended. The enemy ship had slipped below the surface and from the view of those who watched. Only four minutes had been required for Simpson's division to complete their first action.

One minute later Moosbrugger's division, having now returned to take part in the surface onslaught, began firing on a second enemy destroyer (*Shigure*) that also was passing near the burning ship. Simpson quickly ordered his division to open fire on the same target. Just as quickly, the enemy destroyer began taking evasive action as she began belching out chemical white smoke while moving out at a high-rate of speed. Determined to thwart the escape, the American destroyers took chase as they continued to lob five-inch projectiles the enemy's way. At the same time, the enemy gunners made a feeble effort to return the fire, which was very inaccurate. Then, after having observed several hits on the fleeing enemy, the ship disappeared from the radar screen. Determining this ship sunk (actually only sustaining minor damage, *Shigure* escaped to continue in the struggle for the Pacific, meeting her end on 24 January 1945 when torpedoed by the American submarine *Blackfin* (SS-322) off Kota Bharu), the American destroyers returned to the area of the burning "cruiser."

Upon their return, both divisions recommenced firing intermittent rounds into the midst of the burning remains of the enemy ship. Suddenly, at 12:10 A.M., a terrific explosion erupted from her which sent a tremendous burst of fire high into the air. The explosion was deafening but the burning hulk stubbornly remained afloat.

Shortly after this explosion Simpson's division spotted yet another enemy destroyer (*Hagikaze*) silhouetted by the flames. Ordering his gunners to open fire, Simpson watched as their accurate rapid fire obliterated the topside of the targeted ship from forward to aft. On board the *Lang* the gun barrels of the five-inch batteries became so hot from the intensity of the fire they began to glow red. Then *Sterett* discharged one final volley from which immediately followed a blinding flash of the enemy destroyer's exploding magazines, and within seconds she was gone.

With no other targets being picked up on radar, at 12:20 A.M. Simpson informed Moosbrugger that his division was going to fire six torpedoes into the remains of the burning "cruiser." As soon as Moosbrugger reported his division clear, Simpson ordered *Lang* to fire her "fish." Five minutes later the radar screen was clear of all enemy ships. Forty-three minutes after Moosbrugger's division had first begun the attack, it was all over.

Afterwards, the task group circled the area where the action had just taken place and the crews stared out at an awesome sight. Nothing could have come any closer to the Biblical description of the "lake of fire." Giant patches of orange flame still covered the water as clouds of black smoke smothered other areas. The putrid smell of burning oil and lingering sulfur from the gunfire filled the nostrils of those who observed. The eerie sight was enhanced by the sounds of hundreds of men screaming, crying and groaning as the ships churned through a sea full of living and dead bodies. It was a vision of hell, a full exposure of the horrors of war.

Following the short observance the ships departed the area together and headed to make their retirement down "The Slot." Though, after having traveled some distance from the sight, Moosbrugger decided Simpson should return to the area to pick up one survivor for intelligence gathering.

As Simpson returned, the water was still flaming from the burning oil. *Lang* moved quietly through the area as cries and screams again rose up out of the darkness. All hands were ordered to keep quiet, in hopes the survivors would think they were a Japanese ship coming to their rescue. The Japanese sailor had proven himself in the past to be just as stubborn about surrender as his army counterpart — and also just as dangerous. With their suicidal nature, no Japanese survivor could be trusted, thus the reason for Moosbrugger's order to only pick up one.

As extra precaution, a group of armed sailors were then ordered to one station at midship to pick up the survivor. No where else on the ship were survivors to be allowed to come aboard.

Hardly had the destroyer slowed when one survivor began to crawl aboard at the screw guard, at the ship's stern. He quickly met a violent rejection. As he began to pull himself out of the water, a sailor on the fantail picked up an empty five-inch shell casing and gave it a mighty toss. The casing whizzed through the air to slam the surprised survivor squarely in the face, driving him back into the water, never to be seen again.

Other survivors could be seen at some distance from the ship. One could even be heard shouting "banzai" in a manner that ironically suggested victory. But none of the survivors came close enough to the station at midship to be picked up. Finally, one *Lang* sailor became impatient and shouted, "Get over here you son-of-a-bitch." Upon hearing the English speaking voice, someone from out among the darkness blew a whistle, and then every voice became silent. There were no more cries, no more groans, only an eerie, ghostly quiet.

By 2:00 A.M. it was obviously clear to Simpson that no survivor was to be taken captive, and so he ordered Wilfong to turn the ship and move out at a speed of 30 knots to catch up with Moosbrugger and the other ships.

As they made their return trip, sailors aboard *Lang* began to reflect upon their part in the great victory. They had whipped the enemy at their own best game, a night torpedo action. It almost seemed too easy. As far as they knew they had sunk four enemy ships, one thought to be a cruiser, sending many Japanese sailors and soldiers (numbering 1,210) to the spirit world. To make it more outstanding, though one sailor aboard *Lang* had been injured, not one American life had been lost in the action.

The only casualty, Seaman First Class Mitchell Sang, had been at his general quarters station in the handling room for the #3 five-inch gun. As the shell loader he placed the heavy five-inch projectiles on a hoist to be taken up to the gun for firing. Sometime during the course of the battle he had made the mistake of getting his hand into the loading slot just as the hoist came down, mashing it good. Still, numbed by the shock and excitement, he had managed to remain at his station for the duration of the battle, reporting his injury only afterward.

As *Lang* reentered Purvis Bay with the other ships, it was truly a proud moment for the crew. They had taken part in what they knew to be a very outstanding victory. On the way back to the base some of the crew had fashioned four little Japanese flags to represent the four enemy ships they claimed, which along with a broom (representing a clean sweep), now hung from the yardarm. Obviously, for each crewmember the memory of this day would remain for a lifetime, and for Mitchell Sang the memory would always be close at hand, his physical scarring being permanent.

Glorying over their victory was to be short, however, as on 9 August *Lang* again departed Purvis Bay as part of Moosbrugger's task group, headed back to Vella Gulf. This time *Gridley* and *Wilson* would take part, as *Maury* and *Stack* remained behind.

Following the same course and using the same battle plan as before, the ships reentered Vella Gulf at 10:58 P.M. Moosbrugger had hopes of catching another Tokyo Express run and repeating his success. Little did he know that due to that success the Imperial Japanese Navy had suspended all future Tokyo Express runs, the very results Wilkinson had so hoped for.

Despite the Japanese Navy's unwillingness to chance a meeting with Moosbrugger's destroyers again, the American ships would not be without targets. Sixteen minutes after entering the gulf, the ships made their first contact. The target was thought to be a small barge moving at a speed of seven knots along the shoreline of Liapari Island. Yet it was decided not to pursue the barge in hopes of finding "bigger game."

After making sweeps of the reefs around Gizo Island and Blackett Strait, the ships began a sweep of the western shoreline of Kolombangara at 11:45 P.M. Two minutes later they made a second radar contact of a barge bearing 100 degrees true, at a distance of 6,200 yards. Once again the target was passed up and the ships continued their search of the gulf.

No additional contacts were made till 12:04 A.M. when *Dunlap* picked up a contact bearing 43 degrees true, at a distance of 6,420 yards. Two minutes later *Lang* picked up three contacts bearing 13 degrees true, at a distance of 5,310 yards. Within another minute *Dunlap* picked up a second contact close to the first and this time a lookout spotted the barge. Since the gulf had now been thoroughly searched, Moosbrugger ordered Simpson's division to open fire on the targets while he kept his own ships in reserve, just in case the Tokyo Express should suddenly appear.

By 12:20 A.M. lookouts on *Lang* had the three enemy barges spotted, and having now moved within 1,000 yards of the targets Simpson gave the order to open fire. Suddenly, the five-inch guns boomed to life, being directed by radar, sending round after round toward the doomed barges. At the same time the barges opened fire on *Lang* with light caliber machine guns, causing exposed sailors to duck for cover as the small rounds ricocheted off the ship's steel plating along the bridge and the starboard side of the hull. But *Lang*'s accurate fire quickly silenced the enemy gunners and within 12 minutes two of the barges disappeared, probably sunk, with the third probably escaping with minor damage.

Within the next hour and a half *Lang* fired on at least three more targets, one thought to be the same barge that had been the second passed up contact of earlier in the night. Two more of these barges also disappeared and were believed sunk.

As this action drew to its conclusion, Moosbrugger ordered the retirement of his task group, departing Vella Gulf at a speed of 30 knots to safely return to Tulagi later that morning. Again, success accompanied the destroyers, and again Wilkinson was pleased. Ten days later ground fighting on New Georgia ended; the Japanese had lost again.

In the meantime *Lang* had returned to her old escorting duties, though with a great deal more respect. This time she escorted the escort carrier *Sangamon* while guarding the sea approaches to the Solomons. And afterwards, on 21 August, she departed with *Sangamon* for Samoa, and thence on to San Francisco. She was to return a hero of the Pacific campaign, and the crew could hardly wait for the well-deserved visit home.

It was obviously refreshing to be headed east for a change. And Shipfitter Denver Fleming took this opportunity to reflect upon the great victory of the past month. While he passed the time, he penned the following poem to express his own pride in the Lang and her accomplishments:

"The Mighty *Lang*"

Twas on the night of August six,
And the morn of August seven,
We fought the Japs at Vella Gulf
And sent them to their Heaven.

The odds were all against us,
They had a cruiser and three cans,
But we struck at them with fury,
And then we took it on the lam.

But leaving soon was not to be,
The Dunlap said return,
To pick up Jap survivors,
From the Jap ships that did burn.

After it was all over,
And the Lang did steam away,
We all felt kind of proud inside,
As we steamed in Purvis Bay.

The flags were at the yardarm,
The whistle it did blow,
The Mighty Lang had scored again,
And we let the whole fleet know.

But now that it is over,
And the battle is forgot,
We're heading for Frisco Bay,
And bearings are getting hot.

Yes, she's getting kind of tired,
But you seem to hear her say,
"You can treat me like a Bastard,
But I was a hero for a day."

In our way we all felt sorry,
As the victory song we sang,
We know she's stood a pounding,
And she's still "The Mighty Lang."

And if the fleet should ever,
Steam into the Devil's lair,
You can bet your last plugged nickel,
That the Lang will lead them there.

Chapter 7

Gilberts and Marshalls

On 4 September (1943) *Lang*'s approach to the safety of San Francisco Bay was nearing its end, and there was no mistaking the crew's elation. More than a year had passed since the destroyer's last visit to the West Coast, and that seemed a lifetime ago. Now, as the Golden Gate welcomed their victorious return, their relief and joy were clearly evident. Obviously, they understood well their good fortune. For a while, at least, their feet would once again be established on the solid, secure ground of home. Indeed, they had been lucky; of the great numbers of men recently shipped into the perilous South Pacific, many had found fate much less generous.

Certainly *Lang*'s crew was anxious about their long anticipated visit ashore. Yet the destroyer's need for an overhaul would first require their attention at getting their ship into dry-dock at the Mare Island Naval Yard. Operations in the Pacific were sure to be in need of the destroyer again, and little time could be wasted in getting her prepared to return to the effort. Yard workers would do their part to see the fleet did not come up wanting; Mare Island's crews were now working around the clock to complete jobs in weeks or even days that used to require months. And, despite a bit of impatience with the task, the crew did not fail at seeing their ship's appointment met.

Afterward, the crew finally received the liberties they had so long sought, with most of the men awarded a 19 day leave, beginning on the 6th. Doubtlessly, few of the crew were to waste such precious opportunity. For those of the crew who were married, there were emotional reunions with wives and children, many spouses having moved to the West Coast in wait of just such an occasion. Others of the crew departed on trains to skate across the country for a special visit with family and friends in the region of their native homes. While still others remained in San Francisco, visiting such familiar areas as Market Street or Vellejo, content at patronizing the many bars and clubs while readjusting themselves to the sights and sounds of real civilization — and, of course, always telling a tale or two of their South Pacific exploits in the process.

Indeed, the war was never far from the minds of any of *Lang*'s crew. They knew what they had left behind, a job unfinished and far from any conclusion. Every corner newsstand, every movie house newsreel, and every other serviceman continually reminded them of the desperate struggle, and its beckoning for their return. Yet such news was not all bad. The past year had also produced many encouraging reports.

While *Lang* had been serving her time in the Solomons, doing her part in the victories at Guadalcanal and New Georgia, elsewhere other positive gains by the Allies had also been made. In other areas of the Pacific, American and Australian troops had pushed back a Japanese attempt at capturing Port Morseby, Papua, New Guinea, while far to the north American Army troops recaptured the Aleutian islands of Attu and Kiska. In the North Atlantic, improved convoy methods combined with greater numbers of screening destroyers were beginning to take a heavy toll on German U-boats. Over Northern Europe, Allied air power was playing havoc with the German Luftwaffe, German industry and Germany itself. In Russia, the Germans had ended the summer of 1942 with initial success at pushing deep into Russian territory, threatening to consume the industrial city of Stalingrad; but by late November a Russian counter-offensive had sent the Germans on a hard retreat which progressively continued into the new year. In North Africa, the British Eighth Army in Egypt had in late October launched an offensive against Rommel's forces in Tunisia. By the middle of November American forces had landed and occupied Algeria and Morocco. When spring 1943 arrived the two Allied armies began a united effort at ending the North African campaign once and for all, finally defeating the much daunted Afrika Corp in mid-May. Still, much more fighting lay ahead.

For *Lang*, however, it was her past fighting which continued to occupy most discussions during the stateside visit. Her story as a victorious warrior of the South Pacific campaign was of curiosity to the public, and it was this foreseen opportunity at publicity that had earlier led to an episode of heated controversy.

It was during the second presidential cruise that President Roosevelt had presented a signed photo of himself to the ship and crew. That photo had long since occupied an honored spot mounted to the bulkhead of the destroyer's wardroom. During the height of the battle of Vella Gulf, however, the continuous shock of the rapid firing five-inch guns had jarred the photo loose to fall to the deck, busting its frame and shattering its glass.

A young war correspondent of the International News Service by the name of Pat Robinson had been aboard *Lang* throughout the engagement, being witness to the entire action of that night. The story he recorded was most descriptive and accurate, yet when he learned of the fallen photo of the president he delighted in the possibility of incorporating the event in the article for his readers. In his enthusiasm, he approached Commodore Rodger Simpson, the division commander aboard *Lang*, with a very special idea for the photo, and there the controversy began.

It seems the ambitious Simpson and the high strung Captain Wilfong were of clashing personalities, often placing them at odds. Though of no obvious intent, the commodore had often managed to push Wilfong's volatile temperament to its very edge. It appeared that Simpson's over-zealous methods were at the forefront of their differences. The commodore was a pleasant man and obviously a daring leader, yet it was said of him that "he simply didn't have enough to do, sometimes causing him to interfere with the duties of *Lang*'s junior officers." Wilfong strongly resented such intrusions into his command, especially when the proper chain was bypassed, as Simpson so often did. The captain's anger reflected in his fiery eyes, but he had so far managed to control his often explosive tongue — that is until the ordeal of the damaged photo.

Robinson's idea was merely a suggestion that Simpson send the damaged photo, on behalf the ship and crew, back to Roosevelt as a souvenir, asking in return for a new one as a replacement. It was a simple plan but required some special cooperation and, evidently, one vital tweak. Simpson, however, approved the plan, obviously finding its potential publicity very appealing.

With little delay, Simpson then commissioned a member of the crew to create a 24 by 30 inch white parchment scroll. On the scroll was attached the damaged photo, torn in a "V," bordered on the right by silhouettes of one light cruiser and three destroyers, on the left by four Japanese flags, and underneath by an American eagle bracketed with furled American flags. And, finishing out the document was the following inscription:

"On the night of 6–7 August, USS *Lang* with Task Group 31.2 intercepted in Vella Gulf a Japanese force consisting of one cruiser and three destroyers rushing troops to their sorely pressed forces in New Georgia. With a well-executed gun and torpedo attack the Japanese force was destroyed and sunk. The U.S. force achieved no damage to ships or personnel. Except, the shock of gunfire tore this picture from its moorings and damaged the inscription. The Officers of USS *Lang* respectfully request of their Commander in Chief a replacement. (Signed) Cmdr. Rodger W. Simpson, U.S.N., division commander and Cmdr. John L. Wilfong, U.S.N., commanding."

The latter signature, however, was not to be an easy acquisition. When Simpson and Robinson first approached Wilfong with the scroll and their idea for it, the heretofore controlled captain suddenly erupted with overt anger. Though the photo had indeed fallen, busting the frame and glass plate, Wilfong had seen the photo afterward and knew it to have otherwise been undamaged. Incensed at their obvious scheme, he directly accused both Simpson and Robinson of intentionally damaging his ship's property for a publicity stunt, and initially refused to add his signature.

A heated argument erupted which Simpson, determined to win, gave no ground. Yet Wilfong's stubbornness also refused to allow Simpson a quick victory. The debate was lengthy and volatile, but finally the captain tired and begrudgingly consented to fully endorse the scroll as earlier requested. As a result, Robinson did get his story, Simpson did receive his publicity, and later the ship was awarded a replacement photo from a very grateful president.

Being of no known connection to the photo incident, it was just a short time later, on 6 October, that *Lang* and crew bid a fond farewell to the ardent Commander John L. Wilfong. His command had successfully seen the destroyer and her sailors through their baptism of fire in the South Pacific and brought them safely back home. Such success had gained him the crew's admiration and respect. But, as with *Lang*'s previous captains, his time had come to move on. And in his place a new commander would stand, destined to lead the destroyer and crew back to the fire from whence they came.

Lang's newest leader, Commander Harold Payson, Jr., was a tall, slender man, being very handsome in appearance. Unlike his most previous predecessor, his mannerisms were calm and easygoing. The crew were soon to find, to their obvious liking, this man one with whom they could deal on a personal level. Indeed, Captain Payson was to prove to be a "sailor's captain," a popular type of leader, rarely found in the usual rigid structure of a wartime navy.

In the beginning, however, the crew still showed their usual distrust in their new, untested leader. With the most recent experiences in the Pacific conflict clearly in the forefront of their minds, *Lang*'s veteran sailors had good reason to be wary of such unproven leadership. Despite this, Payson had by 30 October settled into his new role most completely, proudly positioned on the ship's bridge to shepherd his new command back to sea — and back to the war.

For the crew this departure was the most difficult so far experienced. Sadly gazing back toward the pier, a few sailors gave one final farewell wave before returning to their duties. A blanket of strange silence had draped itself across the ship as the men were consumed by their innermost thoughts. The depression at the reality of their leaving home again, unsure of a return, had a most solemn effect on every individual. With each passing moment they knew the security provided by home waters was lessening. The disappearance of the Golden Gate and the fading of the American coastline only compounded their misery. And when *Lang* was suddenly alone, sailing independently toward some unknown destiny, morale fell to its lowest ebb.

The initial sadness was indeed profound. But, as had been exemplified on previous departures, after the passing of a couple of days the crew began to rebound from their depressed state. Their work aboard ship was addressed with more vigor. They began to tell jokes and spread wild tales, reintroducing laughter among their ranks. And life again returned to a normal routine, or at least as normal as life was possible on a ship the size of *Lang*.

By the end of the 5th day most woes were completely set aside. The sailing had been great and they had reached their first destination, Pearl Harbor, as planned and without difficulty. Soon the crew was again being awarded time ashore.

It was rather obvious to most *Lang* sailors that this stay would be short, and that they should take full advantage of this last visit with civilization before their assured return to the war. The veteran *Lang* crew had no misconceptions of the future; opportunities to escape the confinement of the ship were doubtlessly to be fewer and fewer, confrontations with the enemy were almost certain, and the chances of a safe return would be lessened with each advance toward the Japanese homeland.

During *Lang*'s absence the South Pacific conflict had continued at a heated pace. Despite several sound American victories, the Japanese continued to strongly resist every advance against them. In fact, in the Bougainville region of the Solomon Islands, fighting for final American control still continued. The struggle for the Solomons had lasted more than a year, but this bloody campaign was finally nearing its end. And, as a result, war planners on both sides were hurriedly preparing for the next round of warfare.

Admiral Chester Nimitz, Commander in Chief in the Pacific, knew he could not long delay pursuing his advance against the enemy, otherwise he risked losing momentum and allowing the Japanese time for additional defensive preparations. The powerful enemy fortress of Rabaul, originally Admiral King's primary target, was now in range of both carrier and land-based bombers and fighters, but Nimitz no longer deemed it worth the cost of invasion. Both the Admiral and General Douglas MacArthur agreed that American air power was in good position to keep the fortress' offensive capabilities neutralized, and that bypassing the island in favor of enemy territories with lesser fortifications would better suit their offensive needs. Yet, beyond this, the two key leaders could not come to a clear consensus on which direction the offensive should continue.

MacArthur preferred moving his forces westward by way of New Guinea, Biak, Morotai, Mindanao and on through the Philippines (fulfilling his promise of "I shall return.") in pushing toward Japan proper. Nimitz, on the other hand, determined his desired route to Japan to be through the conquest of several key island groups in the Central Pacific (effectively ripping through the interlocking web of Japanese defenses), which included the Gilberts, Marshalls, Marianas, and Philippines, in that order. Both plans were presented to the Joint Chiefs of Staff, and, after careful consideration, both were approved for implementation.

The Joint Chiefs had determined that a single line of advance, by either route, to be far too vulnerable to the full power of Japanese capability, and especially so if the Japanese were to consolidate their strength against the advance as their defensive web was designed to do. Therefore, by executing two offensive lines, each could effectively protect the other's flank while forcing the Japanese defenses into a less supportive structure. In other words, Nimitz's advance should cause the Japanese to shift forces away from MacArthur's advance, and visa versa, a real dilemma for the Japanese defensive web. And if these advances were pursued with speed, refusing to be slowed by areas of Japanese strength that (considering the Imperial Japanese Navy's increasingly weakened state) could otherwise be isolated and bypassed (as Rabaul), there would be little time for the Japanese to regroup.

Now that the directions were clear, the next pressing problem for either offensive operation was that of obtaining the necessary equipment for their completion. Since it had long been established that the defeat of Germany was to be given precedence, the greater abundance of new equipment was being held in reserve in preparation for the Allied invasion of Europe. Therefore, the amounts of new equipment to reach the Pacific were never of the desired levels, and commanders often found themselves scrambling just to meet the minimum requirements for their operations.

For Nimitz, whose operation against the Gilberts (code named "Galvanic") had received the Joint Chiefs' approval on 1 September, the shortages were especially troubling. Targeted for assault were two island groups, Tarawa and Makin. For these operations he had approximately 200 ships, including five new carriers and six new battleships, available for escorting and transporting troops and supplies to the destinations, which were sufficient. Yet for the beach assaults he initially had only 100 (an additional 25 would be located by invasion day) of the crucial new LVTs or amphibious tractors (each having a 20 man capacity) available for landing nearly 28,000 assault troops on reef guarded beaches in two separate landing operations, leaving much of the landing responsibility to lesser capable LCVPs or "Higgins boats." And, of an anticipated 66 destroyers (as many as 20 being of the new 2,100 ton *Fletcher* class) initially promised to be available for the operation, Nimitz came up short nearly a third that number, creating for him a last minute scramble at acquiring additional destroyers from wherever they could be found.

In addition to his supply problems, Nimitz also had a concern with training. Along with all his new ships came an abundance of unseasoned, untested personnel. His new air crews, though well trained, had yet to prove themselves against the veteran Japanese pilots they were likely to encounter. And despite a mixture of veterans of the

Solomons campaign being spread throughout the group, many questions remained as to how the inexperience might play on the operation's outcome.

Lang's return to the Pacific was therefore very timely, as being a destroyer with a veteran crew she fit both of Nimitz's needs. It therefore came as no surprise when she was ordered from Hawaii to sail for a rendezvous with the Admiral's assembling fleet. And by 14 November Captain Payson was again directing his destroyer and crew back to sea, and to the war.

Despite Nimitz's urgency, *Lang* would not join the Gilberts operation immediately; the destroyer's first duty was to give escort to the destroyer tender *Cascade* (AD-16), which was bound for Funafuti, Ellice Islands. Though the seven day journey greatly impeded *Lang*'s ability at advancing quickly, the task was duly completed with both ships arriving at the destination safely.

At Funafuti *Lang* had her fuel tanks topped off and after only a few hours in port was again sailing in open waters. Under a full head of steam the destroyer raced across the ocean's surface in the effort to catch up with and join the Fast Carrier Task Force that Nimitz had assembled for support of the invasion of the Gilberts. By this time, however, the operation was already underway, and nearing completion. For several days the carriers had been giving near continuous support to the effort, aiding in the quick capture of Makin. But Tarawa had proven itself a hard nut to crack, its mass strongly held by a determined group of defenders, and so the fighting continued.

Initially, *Lang* joined in the screen of the Relief Carrier Group (TG 50.4), which included the older fleet carrier *Saratoga*, the new light carrier *Princeton* (CVL-23), heavy cruiser *New Orleans* (CA-32), light cruisers *San Diego* (CL-53), *San Juan* (CL-54), and *Mobile* (CL-63), and several other destroyers. This group was very impressive indeed. And, despite her age, *Saratoga* was the standout of the crowd, her veteran crew expertly sending their flights of fighters and bombers into the air on their missions and later recovering others to be rearmed and refueled in a cycle which seemed never to end.

Screening for "Sara," however, was for *Lang* only to last a few days. On the 27th Captain Payson received orders to depart TG 50.4 and to rendezvous with and rejoin Destroyer Division 15, which was then screening for fleet carrier *Bunker Hill* (CV-17), light carrier *Monterrey* (CVL-26), and the fast battleships *North Carolina*, *South Dakota* (BB-57), *Indiana* (BB-58), *Massachusetts* (BB-59), *Alabama* (BB-60), and *Washington*. The battle for Tarawa had by this time finally ended (at a cost of 980 Marine and 29 sailor's lives and an additional 2,101 men wounded), and the Gilberts were finally under American control; yet enemy air and submarine activity remained a serious and constant threat, requiring all carrier task groups and their protective support to remain in the area.

For as long as the enemy threats continued so too did the need for all ship crews to remain alert, and for *Lang*'s crew each new day began with a ritual as practiced by all throughout the operation. Routinely, each morning there erupted the bonging of alarms and the blaring of P. A. systems, sending sailors rushing topside to their battle stations. Once on the open decks, a cool breeze of fresh sea air slapped each man in the face, awakening him to the moment's reality. Along their line of sight low, broken clouds drifted in the dim of the morning light — light that on the horizon often shown the sky a deep red and the clouds gold trimmed — while wind whipped whitecaps danced on the darkened sea. Obviously, the beauty of the new day brightened the crew's spirit, yet the fear of what the morning might bring often overshadowed its blessing, forcing men to an alertness which overwhelmed their preference for rest. And such "dawn alerts" seemed never ending and would become no easier; despite their growing weariness, sailors would find the war continually demanding more of their energy.

What was to prove only a preview to the way the future was to play, on the 28th the usually short dawn alerts became quite lengthy, as enemy planes made frequent early morning challenges. And throughout the day several marauding enemy bombers appeared off and on to harass the ships — one winged menace dropping its deadly cargo to splash the water some distance astern of *Lang*. Yet, despite such efforts, all intruders on this day were driven away and no ship received any damage.

The following day brought more of the same as yet more enemy bombers tried scoring against the powerful group. But the few planes that were able to pass through the covering air patrol (CAP) were met by a murderous fusillade of anti-aircraft fire; never before had *Lang*'s crew witnessed such awesome firepower, the battleships' erupting with such concentrations as to make their entire length appear ablaze. And again the ships received no damage.

Periodic air attacks continued throughout the next several days, culminating in a large night action on 4 December that scored a torpedo hit on the new carrier *Lexington* (CV-16). The carrier survived her damage but the threat of further attacks were of serious concern. Admiral R. A. Spruance, Fifth Fleet commander, had had enough. Determining the enemy bombers to be nesting on the island of Nauru, which had a large airfield, the admiral sent *Bunker Hill*'s group to put an end to the island's mischief.

By 8 December the task group had arrived at its destination, and almost immediately the two carriers began sending their planes airborne to strike at Nauru's installations. In the meantime, the battleships and half the destroyers (which included *Lang*) moved forward for a massive bombardment effort.

The bombardment group moved within 1,500 yards of the island before presenting itself broadside to the enemy ashore. On *Lang*, gunners directed the destroyer's five-inch batteries to point toward the island's interior. From their vantage point it was clear the enemy airfield had already received heavy damage from the preceding air strikes, yet the destruction was not enough, and they stood ready to add to the enemy's woes.

As their preparations continued, the ships stood quietly, their guns bristling in wait of the signal to open fire. The pause was of little comfort to Nauru's defenders, numbering over 1,000 men. They could do nothing but wait for the murderous bombardment to begin.

Then, the order was given, and with thunderous response the big 16-inch guns of the battleships erupted in violent unity, sending their monstrous one ton shells to rock the island with devastation. With the sound of a roaring freight train, the huge shells passed over *Lang* to strike the island a shocking blow, instantly obliterating large segments of Nauru's interior.

With a simultaneous effort the five-inch batteries from both the battleships and destroyers also joined the fray, sending their smaller but lethal fifty-four pound projectiles to rake the island with death. While ashore, geysers of sand and debris shot high into the air with each explosion, the resulting noise melting into one deafening roar.

For thirty minutes the devastating bombardment shook the island to its very foundation, pounding its surface with a total of 810 sixteen-inch and 3,400 five-inch high-explosive shells. Then it abruptly ended, replaced with the eerie ringing of silence. The powerful display of mass destruction had been awesome, and quite respectfully many sailors acknowledged their sincere appreciation for not having been on the receiving end as had the hapless Japanese. Obviously, enemy bombing sorties from this island was ended.

Their mission now complete, Nimitz ordered the battleships and their screening destroyers away from the Gilberts in preparation for a series of future operations. Departing with the battleship group, *Lang* set her heading for Espiritu Santo, arriving there four days later and remaining only long enough to bring on needed provisions. From there the ships went on to Efate, entering Havannah Harbor on 14 December. And it was here *Lang* was to experience the craziest event of her entire career.

Upon arriving at Efate, *Lang* went alongside the repair ship *Medusa* (AR-1) for some minor repair work. Obviously, during her most recent operations the crew had had little time for housekeeping, and the ship did show areas of rust and crud, though it did not seem excessive. Yet, one morning while ashore, someone made the remark to Captain Payson of what a "ratty, sorry looking ship" was the *Lang*. Striking a nerve with the normally calm Payson, he returned to his ship in an unusually foul mood. Hardly did his feet hit the destroyer's deck than he ordered "all hands" to turn out to "paint ship." And immediately buckets of paint, brushes and rags were issued and the work began.

Certainly the crew had little appreciation for the extra work, especially considering the searing tropical climate. Yet things went pretty well for a while, at least till sometime in the early afternoon.

It was in the afternoon that someone broke out a 200 proof concoction made from torpedo fuel, which sailors appropriately labeled "torpedo juice." Torpedo fuel was nothing less than pure grain alcohol with an inert additive to prevent its consumption. Sailors had long learned, however, that by slicing off the two ends of a loaf of bread and then straining the fuel through the bread removed the additive, returning it to its pure state.

As the afternoon heat reached its pinnacle, *Lang*'s cooks brought out a batch of the potent brew mixed with grape juice and passed it out throughout the ranks. And soon all sense of control was completely lost.

Once the alcohol took effect the painting began to accelerate. Buckets of paint were sloshed out across the decks as brooms were brought out to help in spreading the enormous puddles. Sailors soon went from painting the ship to painting one another, many times just painting over those unfortunate men who had passed out on deck.

The chaos continued throughout the rest of the afternoon, finally peaking with many of the jolly painters purposely jumping overboard into the water, which they had already littered with floating paint cans, brooms, and brushes discarded during the performance. By dusk the ship — and nearly every man aboard — had received a thorough coating. It was a mess, but the purpose had been accomplished; Captain Payson was satisfied and the crew had been able to vent a little steam.

For the next several days *Lang* remained at Efate, periodically participating in combat rehearsals with the battleships. Then on Christmas day she departed in company of *North Carolina* and *Washington*, destined for a patrolling station some 50 miles east of Bougainville and 700 miles southeast of the Japanese fortress of Truk. There they were to intercept and destroy any enemy ships which might try escaping from Kavieng, New Ireland, following upcoming bombing raids against the island's naval and air installations.

What followed was a period of more than one week in which three separate air attacks were carried out against the enemy base, yet not a single ship was chased the way of the battle group. And by 7 January 1944 the ships were all returned to Havannah Harbor.

New Year's Day had come and gone with little celebration. *Lang*'s crew had enjoyed a fine meal, complete with pie, ice cream, cigars, and candy, but had otherwise passed the day with normal routines. This was the beginning of the third year of war in the Pacific and, despite the enormous successes in pushing the Japanese back, there seemed little hope for a quick end to the ongoing conflict. Perhaps Admiral

Halsey's New Year message to his South Pacific command summed up the best that could be hoped for: "To all the Nips I wish a 1944 packed full of devastating destruction. I am confident my South Pacific crew will continue to blast them and thus ensure the happy and prosperous new year you all so justly deserve." The implication that the war would not conclude this year was obvious.

Certainly the first major new operation of the year was not long in coming, and *Lang* was soon on the move again. Departing Efate on the 18th, the destroyer led a line of ships out of the harbor which included battleships *North Carolina*, *Washington*, *South Dakota*, *Indiana*, and *Massachusetts*; destroyers *Conner* (DD-582), *Charrette* (DD-581), and *Wilson*; and a couple subchasers. It began as just another routine departure — but for *Lang* it turned into an unexpected tragedy.

This day the weather was nice but the sea was unusually rough. High crested swells evenly spaced between deep troughs gave the water an appearance of blue corduroy. Just outside the Havannah Harbor entrance *Lang* entered the rough sea, and over the loudspeaker came the urgent order: "Now hear this. All hands, do not come topside — do not come topside!" Unfortunately the order came too late for Gunner's Mate Ted S. Pytynia. He had just come out on the main deck on the port side at midship, making his way forward with a piece of heavy equipment cradled in his arms, when one of the huge swells suddenly crashed over the ship, sending tons of water across the decks. The gunner's mate had no time to react; in an instant he was lifted off his feet and carried over the torpedo tubes, across the fantail, and into the sea astern.

The "man overboard" alarm was quickly sounded but Captain Payson found himself helpless to respond. Under the conditions of the moment he could not turn his ship around to search for the missing gunner's mate. The very best he could do was to have the other ships of the column contacted to be on the lookout for him, and pray for his recovery. But it was not to be. *Lang*'s signalman on duty, G. A. Shannon, had within seconds of the incident alertly signaled the ship directly astern of the destroyer, but it reported no sign of the missing sailor. Soon the other ships of the column followed suit with the same disheartening news. Gunner's Mate Ted S. Pytynia was gone.

To *Lang*'s crew, the loss of the man they best knew as "Petunia" was the saddest event they had so far experienced. It was much like losing a member of their own family. He had been very well liked and was a friend of most everyone aboard, making the shock of his sudden loss very profound.

Captain Payson was also painfully saddened over the young sailor's loss. He too thought well of Pytynia. Many times he questioned himself as to if there was anything else he could have done to have prevented the loss (it was a question he never fully resolved to his own satisfaction), but obviously there was not.

The dubious distinction of being the first *Lang* commander to lose a member of the ship's crew seemed of only minor consequence to Payson. What tore hardest at his gut was how this event reminded him of just how very limited he was in providing security for his ship and crew. So much remained outside of his control. He, his ship and his crew were all mere pawns in a contest of ongoing duels to the death, both natural and man-made. Even if he provided perfect leadership, there were no guarantees of survival. Truly fate held the upper hand. But such knowledge did little to ease his pain of responsibility, especially when faced with the sad task of penning words of condolence to a lost sailor's family. Such limitations and sad tasks were part of the job, however, and so he accepted them and pressed onward.

This initial blow to morale was no way to begin a new mission but, as expected, *Lang*'s crew followed their captain's lead and persevered with their duties. By the following day, while yet remaining in the company of the battleship task group, they had joined the two carriers *Bunker Hill* and *Monterrey* and their screen of six additional destroyers. And, by the 20th this enlarged force had safely made their way to the anchorage at Funafuti.

Certainly the carrier/battleship group with which *Lang* served was in itself a powerful force to behold, but it was nothing compared to what greeted them at Funafuti. Within the anchorage stood the greatest assembly of warships so far witnessed by the veteran *Lang* crew. Ships of every size and description dotted the water nearly as far as the eye could see. And, with each passing hour more and more ships arrived to add even further to the awesome display of naval power — and the scuttlebutt it generated.

On the third day the two new battleships *Iowa* (BB-61) and *New Jersey* (BB-62) made their appearance. *Lang*'s crew had never before seen such big battleships. Long and sleek and covered with armaments, their powerful physiques were alone capable of sending a cold shiver up the spine of any man — whether he be friend or foe. Obviously, therefore, it was a comfort for *Lang*'s crew to know that these great ships were on their side.

Eventually the growing number of ships was to comprise a force of well over 300 vessels. The fast carrier groups that had formed alone had the potential of putting over 700 fighters and bombers into the air (escort carriers could provide another 200). And troop ships carried a landing force that numbered 54,000 men, effectively doubling the number of troops used in the Gilberts assault.

Admiral Nimitz had learned a hard lesson at Tarawa, and it was one he did not plan on repeating in this next operation. The Japanese defenders of Betio Island had proven that presumed ample preliminary bombardments combined with presumed ample numbers of invaders not to be adequate against well manned, well established, layered island defenses like those found on Tarawa Atoll. The miscalculation of the enemy's ability to survive had cost the assault force right at 50 percent casualties, and this was not acceptable by any terms. To prevent such from happening again the Admiral adopted a new stratagem which would in effect completely overwhelm the defenders of his next target.

The invasion of the Marshall Islands had long been a primary goal for Nimitz, but to get there he first had to take the Gilberts. Now that that task had been accomplished, preparations for conquering the Marshall defenders were nearly complete.

Yet Nimitz was not entirely secure with the original plans to simultaneously invade Kwajalein, the most centrally located atoll of the Marshalls, and Maloelap and Wotje, the two easternmost atolls. And after considerable debate — with numerous objections from his junior commanders — he decided to bypass both Maloelap and Wotje in favor of consolidating the power of his entire force against Kwajalein.

Obviously, such a decision was risky. Nimitz placed most of his confidence in the abilities of both his land based air forces (now stationed on new bases at Tarawa) and his new fast carrier task forces at annihilating the regional enemy air power throughout the Marshalls. Even so, he had little intelligence on Kwajalein. He could not be a hundred percent certain the island would be suitable for the planned building of a forward bomber base, key to future operations (he did not know that the Japanese had a 70 percent complete bomber strip already on Kwajalein proper). Nor was he certain of the strength of the islands' defenses or the number and quality of their defenders (both were below what could be considered adequate). Therefore, his bold decision not only shocked his junior commanders but was to totally surprise his Japanese counterparts.

Nimitz's decision set the stage for an unprecedented move deep into enemy territory, and on 23 January his awesome assemblage of warships, now divided into four mighty task forces, departed Funafuti for Kwajalein. *Lang* was part of the screen attached to Task Force 58, the fast carrier force of Rear Admiral Marc Mitscher.

The power and security this massive force projected was indeed overwhelming. Any enemy force which dared confrontation would first have to get past the powerful deployment of fighter planes, bombers, outlying submarines, and screening destroyers before it could ever reach any capital ships. And, should the enemy somehow breakthrough the screen, the amount of firepower prepared to greet their challenge would no doubt send them into oblivion.

Yet the enemy remained capable, still retaining several operational airfields within reach of the ships. Such potential kept ships' crews on alert and carriers increasingly active while steadily closing their objective. Fighters and bombers regularly made their slow runs across the carriers' flight decks, dipping off into the wind to climb high into the sky and then form into groups that soon disappeared from sight. Later, as the flights returned and circle above, each pilot patiently waited to bring his plane back to a rest on the floating platform of steel from whence he had come. And such cycles were non-stop.

As the air operations increased, so too did the hazards. On the second day of the journey northward *Lang*'s crew once again had opportunity at displaying their plane guarding skills. Two Avenger torpedo-bombers had crashed while attempting to land, one being off *Bunker Hill* and the other off *Monterrey*. And *Lang* immediately dispatched to the crash sites, her bow knifing through the water at great speed in the effort to retrieve the valuable pilots and crews.

Lang arrived at the first crash site just moments after the plane disappeared below the sea's wrinkled surface, sadly taking its radioman with it; but the other two crew members had escaped the craft and were soon brought to safety aboard the destroyer. Afterward, Captain Payson quickly directed his ship to the second crash site, where all three crew members were successfully located and retrieved.

Such experiences were always to be gratifying to *Lang*'s crew. Not only were lives saved but the knowledge that these crews would soon be returned to their respective carriers to again fly, keeping their Japanese counterparts occupied and away from the shipping, increased their own personal security.

Thanks in part to the fine abilities of the carrier pilots the task forces met no opposition in their trek to Kwajalein, and by the 29th were each safely setting off their designated targets. The Southern Attack Force of Rear Admiral Richmond Turner stood ready off Kwajalein proper, while likewise the Northern Attack Force of Rear Admiral Richard Conolly stood off the causeway connected islands of Roi and Namur. And a third (reserve) attack force, under the command of Rear Admiral Harry Hill, stood off Majuro Atoll, which had been added to the list of objectives late in the planning.

Mitscher's carriers were also in position and immediately continued preinvasion air sorties, targeting all enemy strong points but especially the airfield on Roi, which had already been under non-stop air attack for five straight days. And these aerial bombardments were to continue for at least two more days.

Meanwhile, that evening *Lang* joined the destroyer *Sterett* and the battleship *North Carolina* for a bombardment mission on Roi-Namur. Under the cover of darkness the three ships departed the rest of the carrier force and cautiously proceeded toward their target.

The ships' approach began very quietly, but as they neared the islands' shores lookouts on *North Carolina* spotted an unidentified enemy vessel in the atoll's lagoon. Then, in what seemed an almost unexcitable, routine-like manner, the battleship's big guns slowly pivoted toward the unsuspecting target and exploded with a deafening blast. A fraction of a second later there pronounced a second large explosion, echoed by smaller ones, as the doomed ship (later to be identified as the 3,535 ton armed cargo ship *Eiko Maru*) was seen to erupt into a flaming mass. Certainly, if the islands' defenders had been previously unaware of the American ships, they were now very much awakened to their presence.

Nevertheless, despite the very real threat from enemy shore batteries, the three ships continued to move closer to the islands' edge. Such a move was not so unusual for destroyers, which were often used in heckling missions to cause enemy gunners to fire and give up their positions. But never before had *Lang*'s crew witnessed a battleship move so close to an enemy held shoreline.

At point blank range *North Carolina* drew herself broadside to the two enemy held islands. Her big 16-inch guns slowly rotated into firing position, as did five of her twin 5-inch batteries. In the meantime, *Lang* and *Sterett* drew themselves broadside of the islands with each of their own four 5-inch guns readied for firing. And then there was silence.

In the distance the targeted islands were just barely visible through the surrounding darkness. Only the burning cargo ship gave evidence to the enemy's presence. Somewhere within Roi and Namur over 3,000 defenders had initially taken shelter, having hoped to outlast the bombardments so they could later reappear in an effort to ward away the invading forces sure to follow. But the previous poundings had taken a heavy toll of both their numbers and will to fight. And it was far from over.

Adding further to the misery of the islands' defenders, the three ships suddenly shattered the previous calm with the momentous volume of a unified blast of their firing batteries. With slow, deliberate rhythm they sent round after round of high-explosives into the islands' interiors in a pace uninterrupted throughout the night, the darkness clearly revealing the many explosions and fires created by the constant shelling. And not till dawn did it end.

By 7:00 A.M. the three ships had ceased the bombardment and made their return to the carriers. But Roi and Namur had not seen the last of this trio just yet; after spending only a very short time with the carriers, they were joined by the battleship *South Dakota* and the cruiser *Indianapolis* (CA-35) and were again heading back to the islands for a second bombardment round.

In the daylight *Lang*'s crew had a much better view of the destruction that had been wrought upon the two causeway connected islands. Their nearly flat surfaces were nearly void of all vegetation, with not a single tree remaining undamaged — few even standing. And, with the eruption of a second round of the naval bombardment, additional plumes of smoke and clouds of dust marked even greater landscape changes in the enemy territory.

By 4:00 P.M. the second bombardment had come to its conclusion and the ships were again returned to the carriers. And again planes flew forward to unleash still more destruction to the already pulverized islands of Roi and Namur.

It seemed impossible that anything living could have survived such a punishing bombardment as had been delivered to the two islands. But, on the morning of 1 February, as Marines made their way ashore, it soon became evident that several enemy soldiers had indeed survived. Resistance, however, was for the most part light and unorganized, and in just a little over 24 hours both islands were securely in American hands.

Of the defenders of Roi and Namur, Marines estimated half their numbers had been annihilated by the preliminary bombardments. Those that remained were quickly and systematically picked off by the Marines themselves. Only 51 Japanese and 40 Korean laborers were taken captive. For their part, the Marines had taken their objective with only 737 casualties, of which only 190 were killed. Clearly the operation was a complete success, and certainly Nimitz had reason to cheer his victory — and sigh a bit of relief for his good fortune.

By 4 February all the islands of Kwajalein Atoll were declared secure and under American control. That same day *Lang* sailed into one of the prizes of the recent victory, beautiful Majuro Lagoon.

Majuro Atoll had fallen to the Americans on 31 January, being the first pre-war Japanese territory to be captured. The Japanese had abandoned the islands in late 1942, and therefore they had escaped the destruction imposed on Kwajalein. What *Lang*'s crew found there was rare for the South and Central Pacific these days, unscarred beauty, rich with color and life. But the islands' pristine landscape was soon to change; the atoll's huge lagoon would now become an important staging area and the islands a vast supply depot area for future operations planned against the Japanese.

For the next month *Lang* remained a part of Destroyer Division 15 and continued as part of the screen for the *Bunker Hill* carrier group. On 12 February this group departed Majuro for a mission to strike at the "impregnable" Japanese fortress at Truk Atoll in the Caroline Islands. Again the Japanese were caught off guard, and by the 18th the carrier planes had successfully sunk two light cruisers, four destroyers, three auxiliary cruisers, two submarine tenders, two submarine chasers, an armed trawler, a plane ferry, and twenty-four merchant ships of the Imperial Japanese Navy, not to mention their destruction of approximately another two hundred fifty planes of the Japanese air force.

The success of the Truk attack prompted the carriers to move even farther west and make strikes against the Marianas Islands of Saipan, Guam and Tinian. And again they delivered a gut wrenching punch to the Japanese, the carrier planes destroying another 168 enemy aircraft and sinking two more large freighters.

Lang's part in the preceding carrier operations had been mostly routine, with just minimal enemy air activity to disrupt normal screening. *Lang*'s crew had, however, successfully rescued another three downed airmen. But by the 26th the air operations were ended and the destroyer was returned to the safety of Majuro Lagoon.

For the next several days *Lang* remained at the Majuro anchorage, allowing the ship some needed repairs and the crew opportunities for shore time and simple relaxation. But the vacation was not to be long.

On 10 March *Lang* again departed the anchorage, this time as screen for four fleet oilers bound for Espiritu Santo, where they arrived five days later. The return to the South Pacific soon saw the destroyer involved in some of the ongoing Bismarcks operations, primarily screening small escort carriers during the invasion and capture of Emirau Island, which lay just northwest of the large Japanese base of Kavieng on New Ireland.

These rather unremarkable duties around the Bismarcks lasted the rest of the month, but by 1 April *Lang* had departed the area for a return to Efate. As she proceeded eastward, on the 4th the destroyer stopped by her old stomping grounds at Tulagi Harbor to refuel. Obviously, the visit served to stir many old memories among *Lang*'s veterans, kindling several stories of the destroyer's glorious Vella Gulf days. Good fortune had served with them back then, and it had so far not deserted their side.

By the 6th *Lang* had finally reached Havannah Harbor. There the ship received several bags of long overdue mail, some of the crew receiving as many as 30 letters. Mail in the Pacific would never be regular, and crews would sometimes go for weeks on end without receiving a single letter. Therefore, this event was truly welcomed. And the hearing from loved ones and the catching up on news from back home was an immediate lift to morale.

The good news, however, did not end with the mail delivery. Of much greater significance was the official word that *Lang* was going back to the States. The crew could have only been happier if the journey which lay ahead was already behind.

On the following day the destroyer departed Efate in company of battleships *Tennessee* (BB-43) and *Mississippi* (BB-41) and the cruiser *Columbia* (CL-56) bound for Pearl Harbor, arriving there on the 16th. Three days later *Lang* continued on to San Francisco.

After many anxious hours of sailing on 26 April the long awaited arrival at their destination was at hand. It had been six long months since the crew had last seen it — many had wondered if they would ever see it again — but there it stood, that grand monument of the Golden Gate. Faces busted open with broad smiles as the word flew throughout the ship that they were again home. Soon they would be united with family and friends. And just maybe the war might even come to an abrupt halt and end during their absence. Oh well, at least they would be home for little while.

Lang as she is being towed from Kearny Shipyard to her commissioning on 30 March 1939. (H. Symons)

Four *Lang* sailors pose in one of the ship's confined and crowded work areas. (T. Sapp)

Lang as seen while carrying President Roosevelt during the second presidential cruise, February 1940. (R. Glass)

Various *Lang* crew enjoy a stroll along the shore-line of Cocos Island. (H. Symons)

The U.S. Pacific Fleet gathered at Lahaina Roads, Maui, April 1940. (H. Symons)

Captain Felix Johnson greets King Neptune and his court during the ship's first crossing of the equator, 24 July 1940. (L. Bisgrove)

Lang in her camouflage colors upon her return to the states from her mission to Malta,
26 May 1942. (U.S. Navy)

Following their victories in the Solomons, a proud and happy *Lang* crew watch as a transfer
is made at sea during their return to the states on 28 August 1943. (U.S. Navy)

7272-43
PLAN VIEW, FORWARD,
MARE ISLAND, CAL.   25 OCTOBER 1943.   (DD399)

A look down *Lang*'s upper decks from midship forward as seen on 25 October 1943.
(U.S. Navy)

399

7314-43   (DD399)
45° OFF CENTERLINE. ALTERATIONS CIRCLED ON M.I
PHOTOS NO. 7272-43 TO 7273-43 INC.
MARE ISLAND, CAL.   26 OCTOBER 1943

With a new paint job and a few minor changes *Lang* prepares to return to the war-torn Pacific, 26 October 1943. (U.S. Navy)

Lovable little George, *Lang*'s mighty mascot from 10 May thru 16 October 1944, with Lt. Joe "Doc" Browning, ship's doctor from May 1943 thru December 1944. (J. Browning)

Aerial view of Saipan as seen during the invasion, June 1944. (U.S. Navy)

Destroyers *Sterett* and *Wilson* as seen from *Lang* during their heckling mission to Rota and Guam, 28 June 1944. (J. Browning)

"Bum boats" welcome
Lang to Leyte Gulf,
October 1944.
(W. Walden/F. Cretors)

The cruiser *St. Louis,* just seconds after having been hit by one kamikaze, fires on a second suicider off Leyte, 27 November 1944. (U.S. Navy)

Undaunted in its mission, the second kamikaze also scores against *St. Louis*. (U.S. Navy)

Captain John Bland enjoys a moment of humor with his Executive Officer, Lt. Dennehy, following his taking command of *Lang*. (W. Walden/F. Cretors)

The huge mushrooming cloud from the exploded *Mount Hood* could be seen for miles and gave testimony to the power of the blast. (U.S. Navy)

Lang receives a precious cargo of mail from the destroyer-escort *Dennis* during their trek to Lingayen Gulf. (W. Walden/ F. Cretors)

A TBM takes off from a carrier while *Lang* is being refueled in the
South China Sea, January 1945. (W. Walden/F. Cretors)

Sterett, Stack, and *Wilson* follow *Lang* as they patrol the Russell Islands before proceeding to Guadalcanal to take part in rehearsals for
the invasion of Okinawa, 27 February 1945. (W. Walden/F. Cretors)

Various types of landing craft make their way to the beaches of
Guadalcanal during rehearsals for Okinawa, March 1945.
(W. Walden/F. Cretors)

Doctor Bernard would have his hands
full at Okinawa though all of his patients
would come from other ships. Here he
relaxes a moment on the tiny island of
Mogmog, Ulithi before *Lang* proceeds on
to the "LOVE Day" invasion. (W. Walden/
F. Cretors)

A 30 knot wake created as *Lang* speeds to the assistance of the crippled destroyer-escort *Wesson* on the morning of 7 April 1945. (W. Walden/F. Cretors)

A dead Japanese pilot found by *Lang* while investigating a sound contact just outside RP#2 at Okinawa on 9 April 1945. (W. Walden/ F. Cretors)

Close-up of dead pilot after being hauled aboard shows his youth.
(W. Walden/F. Cretors)

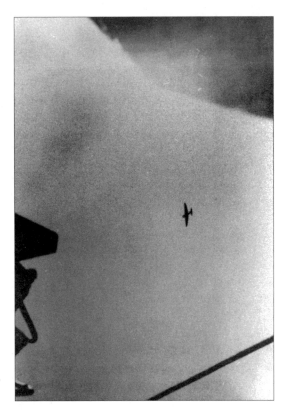

A Japanese Val dives down toward
Lang while at RP#2 on 12 April 1945.
(W. Walden/F. Cretors)

Tiny Ie Shima as seen from *Lang* on 18 April 1945, just a few hours before the death of Ernie Pyle. (W. Walden/F. Cretors)

Lang's buckled bullnose following her being rammed by the oiler *Brazos* at Okinawa on 29 April 1945. (W. Walden/F. Cretors)

Four Okinawans captured by *Lang* of Okinawa on 11 June 1945.
(W. Walden/F. Cretors)

As a cold wind lashes at their half naked bodies, the Okinawan
prisoners partake of a hot meal consisting of hash and hotcakes.
(W. Walden/F. Cretors)

A completely refurbished *Lang* sets at Mare Island on 17 August 1945, but her talents were no longer needed. (U.S. Navy)

Lang proceeds north through one of the locks of the Panama Canal during her trip to her decommissioning, 21 September 1945. (D. Kenzie)

Chapter 8

Saipan and Guam

On 10 May 1944 *Lang* was again slowly steaming beneath the Golden Gate and heading back into the vastness of the blue Pacific. The feelings of the crew toward this most recent of departures from San Francisco Bay were ones of disappointment, sadness and even anger. The war absolutely allowed them — or any other servicemen for that matter — no breaks. They had been in port only 14 days, during which half the time was spent helping dock workers with repairs to the ship, while the other half did afford the crew a ship sponsored dance at the Gold Room of the Palace Hotel and some shore liberties, but at no time did any of the crew receive a single day of leave. Now they found themselves headed right back toward the war's hostilities. And no one, not even the few new men who easily sensed the foreboding of the old timers, was overjoyed at the prospects.

The crew's concern was more than justified. The war in the Pacific was as hot as ever. The Allied forces were gaining offensive momentum and confidence but the Japanese, while seeing their defensive perimeter quickly shrink, remained doggedly determined to hold against any further losses. Obviously, the stakes for both sides were increasing with each new move, but for the Japanese the situation was gravest. And in their desperation Japanese commanders were scrambling to prepare a serious response to the U.S. Navy's next move.

Nimitz's swift victories in the Marshalls had indeed stunned the Japanese high command, who (though having written off the Marshalls prior to their invasion) had hoped to use the islands in an extended defensive effort to buy precious time in preparing their forces for a counterstrike. The Japanese had therefore invested heavily in the Marshalls with their remaining regional air power, but to no avail. Nimitz's immense preliminary bombing campaign combined with his unexpected strike into the heart of the Marshalls at Kwajalein caught the Japanese command by complete surprise and simply overwhelmed all opposition.

The Marshalls' victory also served to bolster Nimitz's stance that his Central Pacific advance be continued, giving the U.S. Joint Chiefs of Staff good reason to review their overall strategy in the pursuance of future offensive operations in the Pacific campaign. And again the direction and the targets of these operations were at the forefront of their debate.

General MacArthur's forces, having on 22 April occupied key positions along the Hollandia coastline, Western New Guinea, at Tanahmerah Bay, Humboldt Bay, and Aitape, were now in position for their next move. In the preceding months MacArthur had fought hard to convince the Joint Chiefs to place Nimitz's Pacific Fleet under his command for one single offensive thrust; with his own forces poised to take Biak and Nimitz's in perfect position to take Truk, the two forces could then converge on the Palaus and from there advance in force to Mindanao. But, despite the general's persistence on the matter, the Joint Chiefs remained resolute on keeping the Pacific offensive a two pronged effort, agreeing with Nimitz's argument that the Marianas were key to winning the Pacific war.

Approximately 3,300 nautical miles west of Hawaii and 1,500 nautical miles due east of Manila, Philippines, the Marianas was made up of 15 islands stretching 425 miles along a north to south arc. Claimed a possession by Spain in 1565, the islands remained under Spanish control until the end of the Spanish-American War when the United States gained possession of the islands along with the Philippines. But only the southernmost island of Guam held American interest, and so the rest of the islands were sold to Germany for 4.5 million dollars. Following Germany's defeat at the end of the First World War, Japan was given mandate by the league of Nations to these islands, whereupon the colonization and development of Saipan, Tinian, and Rota were immediately undertaken by the Japanese Government (secretly and illegally preparing them for military use).

Throughout their Japanese ownership the Marianas remained off limits to foreigners, and American owned Guam (under U.S. Navy control) obviously remained a constant sore spot for the Japanese military. It was therefore of no surprise that Imperial Japanese forces assaulted the American possession only two days after Pearl Harbor, quickly subduing (with the exception of one renegade sailor whom they never caught) the small garrison posted there.

It was not, however, the sudden opportunity to regain this lost American territory which caused the Joint Chiefs to set their sights upon the Marianas. Admiral King, like Nimitz, had long felt the islands to be crucial in the advance to defeat Japan. But General George Marshall (Joint Chief, Army) and General Henry "Hap" Arnold

(Joint Chief, Army Air Force) would not have been so eager to agree had not a new development arrived on the scene. That development was the introduction into service of the new B-29A Superfortress, a long-range heavy bomber with a bomb capacity of 20,000 pounds and a range of 4,100 miles. A combination of this new bomber and the Marianas effectively put Japan proper within reach of a massive bombing operation. And this was an opportunity too important to pass up.

Furthermore, the successful isolation and reduction of Rabaul along with Nimitz's successful bypass of the powerful enemy bases at Wotje and Maloelap through massive bombing campaigns caused the Joint Chiefs to even re-evaluate the importance of taking Truk. The carrier strikes on the enemy facilities there back in February had effectively taken the fortress out of the action and, with the U.S. Navy's new allocations of Kwajalein Lagoon, Majuro Lagoon, and Humbolt Bay, there was no need for another naval staging/supply area in that region. In addition, the Joint Chiefs also determined that planned operations against the powerful enemy naval base of Kavieng, New Ireland, and the enemy submarine base at Wewak, New Guinea, could also be canceled, citing similar reasoning. But MacArthur's planned invasion of Biak would remain, possibly serving to draw Japanese attention south and away from Nimitz's movements toward his next targets in the Marianas.

Aboard *Lang* the crew had no idea of the plans being set for the next Pacific operation of which they were to be involved. But it didn't really matter, for it was obvious to them that they would return to the conflict somewhere and wherever that might be there would be Japanese to fight. The real question came not as to where but how the next battle would be fought. Would it be a surface engagement?... The Imperial Japanese Fleet had retreated from battle following the bloody Solomons campaign and had not been heard from since, but sooner or later they would have to come out of hiding. Would it be another air campaign?... The Japanese Army and Navy Air Forces, as *Lang*'s crew had experienced first hand, were and would continue to be deadly adversaries. Would it be a challenge from an unseen enemy?... Additionally, the Japanese submarine fleet, though tactfully inept compared to the German U-boat fleet, remained a serious threat. Or would it be some combination of any or all the above? Whichever, the closer to the Japanese homeland the U.S. forces got the more aggressive the Japanese forces were sure to be — and the more uncertain the future of *Lang*.

Obviously, few of *Lang*'s crew were feeling at ease with their imminent return to the Pacific conflict. One lone chief, however, had found a friend that was far more nervous about the future than he. Standing alone on the ship's fantail, the chief cradled his arm around his new pal, shared one final view of the near faded shores of the West Coast, and spoke a few words of comfort before accompanying him back to his quarters.

The chief's new found friend was "George," a little brown and white stray dog that had been adopted by the crew during this past visit to San Francisco. He had been aboard ship several days before their departure, but this was his first time at sea and he had yet to gain his "sea legs." The first few days were indeed quite unsettling to him, yet he adjusted rather quickly. Soon he was enjoying his own special bunk up forward in the chiefs' quarters, the chiefs taking charge of his care. Some of the crew even took time to fashion a special "Mae West" life preserver for his little foot high frame; in time he even learned to dash to the preserver at the sound of "general quarters." And there never failed to be someone around to give him attention, which quickly created a strong bond between the new mascot and crew.

Perhaps it was George's inspiring liveliness which finally lifted the crew's spirit, or maybe it was just the normal magic of beautiful starlit nights combined with constant flows of warm, salty air. At any rate, the nine days at sea passed pleasantly and quickly, and at their end the destroyer was again reentering the confines of Pearl Harbor, Hawaii.

Pearl, as always, was a busy place but even more so during this latest of visits. The number of ships, especially the number of transports and cargo ships, and the amount of supplies being loaded did not go unnoticed by the crew. Scuttlebutt ran amuck throughout the gathering fleet, but only days later would the crews be informed of their part in operation "Forager," the planned invasion of the Marianas (likewise, in England, operation "Overlord," the planned invasion of Normandy, was also proceeding on its own tightly secretive schedule). In the meantime, the intensity of the preparations and special training left little doubt that another major offensive was just days away.

During *Lang*'s stay several ships routinely left the harbor to take part in landing rehearsals at Maalaea Bay, Maui, while those that remained were busily being loaded with the materials of war. The anticipation and suspense created by all this operational activity was indeed profound, and the destroyer's crew were certainly not immune to its energy. Yet, they had no idea of the bit of excitement which next they would witness.

Lang's third day in port began as routinely as ever. Sailors set about their normal details, the harbor about them teaming with activity, with all consumed in their immediate tasks. Then, without a hint of warning, an immense blast, so powerful as to be felt for miles in every direction, suddenly rocked the harbor. The explosion was centered among a group of LSTs and LCTs that were anchored in the harbor's West Lock, an ammunition depot area very near where *Lang* was at dock.

At the very moment of the horrifying blast every bit of work within the harbor suddenly came to a paralyzing halt, as nearly every sailor became momentarily affixed by the shock of the sudden detonation. But, as more explosions closely followed the first, throwing additional fire and debris high into the air, men quickly snapped to and joined in an effort at controlling the flames and in the towing away of endangered vessels.

The base fire departments responded quickly, racing to the scene, their sirens adding to the massive confusion while joining the effort at confining the threatening fires. Munitions were stacked throughout the loading areas and the spreading of the flames threatened to add to the disaster. Yet bravery and expertise prevailed and the fire was finally subdued.

Just what had caused the explosion was not immediately known (later it would be determined that faulty fuses on some 4.2-inch mortar shells were likely responsible), but the results were very costly. Six LSTs and two LCTs were destroyed, vessels that would be very difficult to replace for the coming operation. But, even more tragic, 163 irreplaceable lives were lost while another 396 were injured. Not since the Japanese attack had their been a greater tragedy at Pearl.

Several of *Lang*'s crew had been away from the ship enjoying shore liberties and therefore missed most of the excitement. One of those, however, who was still aboard at the time of the explosion was Seaman First Class Randell Knight (the author's father). Eighteen years of age and just fresh aboard the destroyer for his first duty at sea, Knight had yet to even be adjusted to his new home let alone be prepared for such exhibition of carnage. He had been sitting on the after deck house, just forward of five-inch gun #3, consumed with the task of pealing potatoes for the ship's cooks, when suddenly the concussion from the explosion knock him cleanly off the box he had been using as a seat. Surprised and awestruck, he watched as flames leapt in quick succession from one LST to the next. Never before had he witnessed such a violent spectacle. He did not then know that this would pale in comparison to what he was to witness in the months which lay ahead. But one thing was for certain, this day's explosive demonstration awakened him to the grisly reality for which war was so notorious.

The blast itself was immediately brought under suspicion of sabotage (after investigation it would later be determined that poor handling of the munitions had resulted in the accident). Therefore, security on the base quickly tightened while security patrols became more alert to any unusual activity. But no more incidents were to interrupt the rest of destroyer's stay.

Finally, on 24 May *Lang*, now flagship for Destroyer Division 4, Captain J. L. Melgaard commanding, departed Pearl as screen for the battleships *North Carolina* and *Washington* and cruisers *Vincennes* (CL-64), *Houston* (CL-81), and *Miami* (CL-89). Ordered to rendezvous with Admiral Mitscher's Fast Carrier Task Force 58, the ships set sail for Majuro, where they safely arrived six days later.

It was during this trip, however, that *Lang* acquired a problem with her engines, and at Majuro she immediately went alongside the destroyer tender *Prairie* for repairs.

On 3 June the repairs were said to be complete, so Captain Payson took his ship to sea for a trial speed run. The results of the run were not to the captain's satisfaction, the engines only able to make 27 knots, and he returned his ship back to port for more work.

The next day the ship was once again ready for tests, and this time results were much better, the engines running much more smoothly and capable of a speed of 30 knots. It was not ideal but acceptable. And, following one more return to port to take on ammunition and fuel, *Lang* was again ready for action.

Assigned to Rear Admiral W. K. Harrill's Task Group 58.4, *Lang* was to become part of the screen for the carriers *Essex* (CV-9), *Cowpens* (CVL-25), and *Langley* (CVL-27). On the morning of 6 June these ships departed the confines of Majuro Lagoon and headed west, and their crews were finally informed of their destination.

Later that same day a wild cheer was pronounced throughout the fleet at the announcement that Allied forces had made successful landings on the coast of France. It was indeed good news, and morale was given a tremendous boost. Certainly the crews were hopeful they would be sending home a similar success story from their newest effort in the Pacific.

The Japanese, however, had far different plans in mind for the Americans. Admiral Mineichi Koga, successor to the late Admiral Yamamoto's position as Commander in Chief of the Imperial Fleet, had long expected the U.S. Navy to at some point finally reach the edge of the Philippine Sea. In the meantime, he had been waiting, patiently rebuilding his carrier fleet and preparing for the opportune time to engage Nimitz's carriers in a fight to the finish.

Unfortunately for Koga, Nimitz's unexpected quick victory in the Marshalls was to play havoc with his training timetable, leaving his young pilots and air crews short the valuable experience in the air he had previously hoped to provide them. And to add even further to the Imperial Navy's woes, at the end of March Admiral Koga himself became a statistic when a plane carrying he and members of his staff was caught in a storm and lost at sea.

Koga's successor, Admiral Soemu Toyoda, would, however, quickly adopt and press on with his predecessor's plans. Entitling his revised version of Koga's original plans "A-GO," Toyoda hoped to catch Nimitz's fleet at its most vulnerable moment, while being tied down protecting assault ships during an invasion. But knowing just where the next landings were to take place so far eluded his intelligence. He correctly suspected the target to be either the Marianas or Palaus, and to be safe he had both regions reinforced with additional fighters and bombers. But, as was hoped by the Joint Chiefs, MacArthur's operation against Biak, which began on 27 May, momentarily diverted Toyoda's attention south in anticipation that the Palaus would be Nimitz's next target. He soon learned his mistake, however, and responded by committing his fleet to a showdown in the Philippine Sea — where Mitscher and Task Force 58 would be ready and waiting.

As for the trip westward to Saipan, *Lang*'s crew found the sailing to be pretty much routine. Few ships had more experience than their destroyer at working the screen for the carriers, and there were no real surprises with their present duties. As expected, drills were frequent. Sonar and surface and air radar searches were constant. Vigilant watches were set, constantly keeping an eye out for anything possibly overlooked by the electronics, and ready to scream out a warning to the bridge. And communications, with radios silent, were conducted mostly by semaphore, keeping signalmen alert for any incoming messages.

Obviously, the closer the ships got to the shores of Saipan the greater the potential for trouble. Yet their journey westward remained eerily quiet, the only intruders initially encountered being a few friendly goonie birds and porpoises who trailed the ships in search for food. It was not till early morning of the 11th that the first enemy contact was made, and that being a couple reconnaissance planes which were quickly eliminated by the fleet's CAP. And by this time the carriers had already reached a point 200 miles east of Guam.

In fact, Mitscher was already preparing to launch his first air strike. Originally, he had not planned to launch this strike till dawn of the 12th, but hoping to catch the island unprepared — and now uncertain as to whether one of the two reconnaissance planes may have gotten off a warning — led him to revise his plan, moving up the launch time to early afternoon of the 11th. And by 12:59 P.M. the first of 208 fighters (most being new F6F Hellcats) and 8 torpedo-bombers was in the air.

The gathering fighter formations were quickly established, and the concentrated drone of their radial engines was soon fading off into the distance. The contest for Saipan was begun, and all the ships' crews could do now was poise themselves for the long, agonizing wait which customarily accompanied such strikes. And, of course, prepare for the possibility of their own defense.

During this time there was a dramatic increase in tension among the sailors. Nervous eyes searched the sky, straining to see some tiny group of specks in the distance, hoping they would be friendly but expecting the opposite. Yet when evening arrived it was indeed only the "friendlies" who were seen. And such a sight was early evidence of welcomed success, though the total extent of that success had yet to be fully determined.

Later that night the enemy responded as a few of their bombers did make a short appearance, trying desperately to locate the ships with flares but having no luck. And by morning the untouched carriers were again sending their fighters and bombers airborne for a second strike against the enemy held islands.

Finally, just shortly after the planes' early morning departure, news of the previous day's accomplishments was received aboard *Lang*. As Mitscher had hoped, the Japanese had been caught by surprise, with the preliminary estimate of damage reading very well for the American crews: "By this group yesterday fourteen Zekes (Mitsubishi A6M Zero fighters), twelve Tojos (Nakajima Ki-44 fighters), two Emilys (Kawanishi H8K flying-boats), one Mavis (Kawanishi H6K flying-boat), one Rufe (Nakajima 6M2-N seaplane fighter), and four Jakes (Aichi E13A reconnaissance seaplanes) destroyed on the ground or water. Nine Emilys and one Cherry (Yokosuka H5Y flying-boat) probable. And one small cargo ship probable."

That evening additional reports were received of the day's continuing raids. "Estimate (of) today's damage: Many bomb hits (were made) on Marpi air strip and AA (anti-aircraft) battery. (A) small cargo ship (was) straffed (and) left dead in (the) water. (An) ammo dump (was) exploded (and) three or four hangers and 50 percent (of all) barracks destroyed on Pagan. Seven of (a) twelve ship convoy left burning, two abandoned, two destroyer escorts sunk, (and) three left damaged. Three sampans sunk, (and) six left dead in (the) water off Pagan Island." (Actually, all twelve enemy cargo ships were sunk, in addition to the torpedo boat *Otori* and three submarine chasers.)

Despite such success, casualties among the American planes were beginning to add up. One such instance had come that early afternoon when a returning bomber, severely crippled and trailing smoke, flew in low to crash into the water just ahead of *Lang*'s position. Sailors watched as the plane skipped across the choppy sea like a stone across a pond, its travel halted only after its nose dove sharply into the sea's surface, resulting in a spray of water so dense as to momentarily hide it from all view.

Observers on *Lang* had, however, followed the bomber's approach carefully, and the water had barely settled before Captain Payson had the destroyer speeding to the rescue. Only a very few minutes elapse in reaching the crash site, and soon after two designated swimmers from the destroyer were in the water assisting the sinking plane's crew to safety. The two airmen, Ensign John S. Foote and Radioman N. W. Schmidt, both uninjured, were greatly appreciative of *Lang*'s quick response, and equally so for the crew's hospitality and offering of dry clothes.

For the time being the two airmen would be forced to remain aboard *Lang* till arrangements could be made to transfer them back to their own ship, *Essex*. In the meantime, however, both men seemed content and received considerable enjoyment at sharing stories of their airborne exploits with *Lang*'s crew — and in turn hearing a few tales from the proud destroyermen as well.

The airmen's extended stay aboard the destroyer was to last only two days, at which time *Lang* and *Essex* both drew close aboard the fleet oiler *Kaskaskia* (AO-27) for refueling. Obviously, this presented the perfect opportunity for the two airmen their transfer back to their own ship. And, after a hearty salute of sincere appreciation, the two men departed the destroyer's decks for those of their own beloved *Essex*, where a new plane and a new mission eagerly awaited their arrival.

As it were, the ships of two of the carrier task groups (TG 58.1 and TG 58.4) had been proceeding on a north northwest heading for more than 24 hours. Their destination was the two enemy held islands of Iwo and Chichi of the Bonin Group. Air bases on these two islands were loaded with planes which had the capability of interfering with the landings on Saipan, and preemptive airstrikes from the carriers had been ordered to eliminate the threats they posed.

Under the overall command of Rear Admiral Joseph "Jocko" Clark, the two carrier task groups were by 2:30 P.M. of the following afternoon within fighter range of the islands and their planes were preparing for the attack. The sea was rough and the sky was cloud covered. Intermittent rain squalls made the takeoffs from the carriers somewhat hazardous, but Clark's pilots and crews were undaunted in their effort. And their effort was to be nicely rewarded.

Indeed, this first flight caught the Japanese completely unexpectant and found little effective resistance to their attack. As a result, on Iwo alone close to 20 enemy fighters were destroyed, while on Chichi another 21 seaplanes were made into useless junk. Japanese defenses, on the other hand, would account for only three American planes and their pilots.

Meanwhile, *Lang* continued her work in the screen of the carriers of TG 58.4, successfully navigating the choppy seas while awaiting the outcome of this first strike. This newest mission had, however, created a noticeable nervousness among her crew. Being so deep in the heart of enemy territory (only 592 miles southeast of Tokyo) and with a skipper yet untested in combat was of certain discomfort to men who knew well the destructive power of the enemy's air machine. They truly expected a fight, but it was not to happen this day. The reassuring return of the American planes brought with it the news of yet another successful operation. And so their anxiety was temporarily set aside.

Early the next morning the carrier crews were again hurriedly preparing to send another large flight of attackers to Iwo Island. The weather was again foul but not enough so to deter Clark from his mission. Fifty-four planes were soon airborne, defying the tough conditions, and again catching the Japanese unsuspecting. In fact, the weather conditions had so convinced the Japanese of the impossibility of air attack on this day that they had not even disperse their planes as a precaution, leaving neat rows of valuable fighters and bombers to be chewed to pieces by the American pilots. As a result, the Americans again returned victorious, claiming 64 enemy planes destroyed on the ground (a number obviously refuted by the Japanese, but which was probably much closer to actuality than the zero losses the Japanese claimed). Whereby Clark was quick to send a "well done to all hands."

In the meantime, while Clark's carriers had been engaged with the task of neutralizing the Bonin's air offensive capabilities, Turner's Amphibious forces had been busy landing some 20,000 Marines on the shores of Saipan. And, likewise, in quick response to the American move, Admiral Toyoda's "A-GO" operation was quickly put into action, with his carriers departing Tawi Tawi Island, Philippines, for their ultimate confrontation with the American fleet.

Toyoda had given tactical command of his massive fleet over to Vice Admiral Jisaburo Ozawa, the extremely capable Commander in Chief of the Imperial Navy's First Mobile Fleet. He had at his disposal nearly every capital ship left in the Japanese Navy, including five fleet carriers, four light carriers, five battleships, eleven heavy cruisers, two light cruisers and twenty-eight destroyers. Among the number was the 29,000 ton *Taiho*, the then second largest carrier in world (only the 33,000 ton USS *Saratoga* was larger) which alone was capable of hauling 53 aircraft. And also included were the two giant 64,000 ton battleships *Yamato* and *Musashi*, the undisputed Goliaths of the seas. Without question his was a formidable force.

By 17 June Admiral Mitscher was given conformation of Ozawa's advance. And soon, all his commanders were receiving word of the enemy approach: "The enemy who appears to be determined to interfere with our landings on Saipan can be within range today in force. That is where we want him. All units, all personnel alert to this opportunity."

The message was obviously intended to be optimistic, but most of the men aboard *Lang* weren't so sure they wanted a powerful Japanese carrier fleet within range of them. As far as they knew, there were still several enemy fighter/bomber land bases operating in the area, and if those planes successfully combined their attacks with those of the enemy carriers it was sure to get very nasty very quick.

Reluctant or not, *Lang*'s crew was destined to meet the enemy challenge, continuing their screening duties for the carriers of Task Group 58.4, which was itself racing to rejoin the rest of Task Force 58 for the ensuing battle. *Lang* had since been teamed up with the destroyer *Ellett* as one of three torpedo attack units for Destroyer Squadron 12, in the unlikely event any enemy ships should actually get so close. But it was the enemy's fighters and bombers which continued to be of the greatest concern aboard the destroyer. For few doubted that such a massive contest between carriers (15 carriers on the American side with total launching capacities of 891 planes, and 9 carriers on the Japanese side with total launching capacities of 430 planes) would be fought without the enemy managing to break through with at least a portion of their air arm.

Throughout the rest of afternoon and evening of the 18th, however, the skies remained quiet. The only planes airborne were only those searching for the enemy's location and those on routine CAP duty. Yet such serenity was assured to be short-lived.

Indeed, the first report of the enemy's presence came at 10:15 A.M. on the following morning. This first report claimed "enemy aircraft bearing 250 degrees true, range 116 miles and closing." And only seconds later planes were scrambling from the decks of the American carriers.

Lang, as with the rest of the carrier escorts, moved quickly to take up her anti-air-craft position. But Captain Payson would wait a few more minutes before sounding general quarters. Obviously, this short delay caused some uneasiness among others on the bridge, yet the captain seemed very confident in his procedure. In fact, in future situations he was often to wait till planes were within sight before sending his crew to their battle stations. Indeed, while under his command, the crew would quickly learn that the general quarters alarm meant that battle was imminent. And such procedure was to keep the crew sharply tuned, which was to prove invaluable to their own survival in the coming months.

At 10:30 A.M. the TBS reported, "Enemy aircraft bearing 254 degrees true, range 70 miles." By this time *Lang*'s guns were fully manned and ready to engage in battle. With the enemy planes under ten minutes away, the sailors nervously searched the sky. Five minutes later came the welcomed report, "Large group of enemy aircraft bearing 250 degrees true, at 55 miles, intercepted by our fighters." And for a moment their fears were eased.

Hardly was this the time to relax, however, and the crew remained expectant of much more enemy activity. Twelve minutes later their expectations proved true as "enemy torpedo planes" were reported "bearing 260 degrees true, at a range of 20 miles and closing." And again nerves wrenched with anticipation.

Suddenly, everyone jumped as a volley of gunfire diverted the crew's attention from the sky to the direction of cruiser *Vincennes* and destroyer *Sterett*. Both ships had fired several five-inch rounds toward what they initially reported as an enemy submarine. But further investigation proved their target a stray sampan instead.

This bit of excitement ended, attention was again focused upward into the sky. Almost immediately, a Japanese torpedo bomber was sighted quickly closing the force from a distance of only five miles. And *Lang*'s five-inch guns were quick to respond.

Traversing toward the fast approaching enemy, the destroyer's main batteries began tracking their target's approach. *Lang*'s fire-control directed the guns to the bomber and Captain Payson gave the order to fire. Then, in what seemed a near unified volley, the destroyer's batteries erupted right along with another three or four ships, each giving their best effort at stopping the onrush of the intruder.

121

Lang's entire structure jarred from the recoil of the gunfire, effectively informing everyone aboard that she was now entered into battle. Yet the plane continued its approach, initially defying the concentrations of exploding rounds thrown its way. But the volleys continued and, as more and more ships joined the effort, the wall of flak became so thick the pilot finally determined his attempt useless and pulled away to escape certain death.

Throughout this short action the many vessels of the task force had commenced emergency evasive maneuvers, trying desperately to avoid giving the enemy pilot any easy targets. *Lang*, too, began an evasive turn just as the plane was spotted, but almost immediately the helmsman lost steering control on the bridge. Captain Payson quickly ordered the after steering station to take temporary control till the bridge could correct the problem. Three uneasy minutes later the bridge was again in control of steering, but by then the threat from the enemy plane had long ceased. Thankfully, the incident had not placed the ship in any direct danger — this time.

The threats from the air continued, however. At 11:27 A.M., just five minutes after having regained steering control to the bridge, yet another report of a "large group of enemy aircraft" was received, this group "bearing 250 degrees true, at a range of 100 miles and closing." Eighteen minutes later the report was updated stating the group contained "20 to 30 Japanese torpedo and dive bombers" and was continuing to close, their range now reduced to "43 miles." It appeared this group might well break through when just moments before their suspected arrival friendly fighters appeared and tore into the enemy formation. No Japanese planes got by and again the ships were spared.

For the next hour the area around Task Group 58.4 remained quiet. Radar displayed only the silhouettes of friendly planes in the surrounding sky. Yet the welcomed serenity was not to last.

Again, at 2:18 P.M., warnings of "unidentified planes" sent *Lang*'s crew to their battle stations. These planes were reported 62 miles distant, but hardly had the report been received when an undetected enemy dive bomber suddenly came screaming out of the sky on the attack. With *Essex* as its target, the plane made its pass with hardly a single defensive shot to block its path. Certainly an experienced pilot would not have failed such an easy opportunity. Fortunately for *Essex*, however, this poorly trained aviator's aim was tremendously lacking, and he sent his deadly cargo of bombs to splash harmlessly into the sea.

To the enemy pilot's credit, however, he did make good his escape. By pulling his plane out of its dive low over the water and in the middle of the group of ships, he made naval gunnery against him impossible without the ships endangering each other. Therefore, only after the bomber cleared the formation were the naval gunners free to open fire. And by then the plane's speed and angle made it an impossible target.

Twenty minutes later another report warned of still more enemy planes approaching, this group closing from 60 miles. This time crews were far more alert to surprises and trigger fingers were anxious to blast some luckless enemy from the sky. But just moments before the planes appeared came an urgent message to the ships for their gunners to hold their fire — these planes were "friendlies." The first report had been in error and nearly got some American boys shot at or worse.

By 2:55 P.M. radars were completely clear of all enemy air activity, and on *Lang* general quarters was relaxed, allowing the crew some valuable rest. Carrier planes continued to perform their periodic air searches, and lookouts continued their watches, but all remained quiet. And it appeared this action was finished.

For the next several hours the serenity continued. Then, at 7:00 P.M., *Lang*'s lookouts suddenly spotted a large splash dead ahead of the ship. The splash was initially thought to have been caused by a plane crash, and a rescue party was immediately called to stations. But closer examination revealed no evidence of a downed plane. This left but one obvious alternative as to the cause of the splash — a bomb.

Captain Payson quickly sounded "general quarters." The alarm sent the crew rushing to their battle stations, and a determined search was immediately begun for the suspected enemy intruder. In the meantime, a warning was sent out to the rest of the task group that a possible undetected enemy bomber was in the area, and the entire force went on alert. Then, after some further investigation, one of the carriers clarified the mistake. What *Lang*'s lookouts had seen was not a bomb splash but rather the splash from a depth-charge that had been jettisoned by a friendly plane prior to its landing on the carrier. Despite the mistake, Captain Payson had responded correctly to the occurrence. Clearly, his original assessment was justified, and had it proved correct his action could have saved lives.

For Task Group 58.4 the first battle of the Philippine Sea was indeed ended, for at the end of the day these ships were ordered back to Saipan for refueling. For the most part the actual battle had been fought in the air, far out of the sight of the ships. Most crews had yet to even be informed of all that had transpired during the action of the day, though it had been dramatic. Nor were they aware of the extent of the continuing effort to keep the enemy engaged. And, once detailed word was received, even then the full effect of the victory was to temporarily elude its participants, including the most senior officers.

In truth, the first day's victory was profound. American fighters joined ship's gunnery for accounting the downing of 330 of Ozawa's own carrier based fighters and bombers, nearly 77 percent of his total air strength. And, though not immediately known to Mitscher and his crew, the two fleet submarines *Albacore* (SS-218) and *Cavalla* (SS-244) had each respectfully dispatched the two enemy fleet carriers *Taiho* (Ozawa's flagship) and *Shokaku* to the deep.

123

The rest of Task Force 58 continued to pursue Ozawa's fleet into the next day, again forcing costly air battles for the Japanese. Another 65 enemy planes were downed. And Ozawa also lost the fleet carrier *Hiyo* to an aerial torpedo attack.

In all, the Imperial Japanese Navy's Mobile Fleet lost in two days of air combat a total of 395 combat planes and nearly all their irreplaceable pilots and crews. In addition, they also lost three irreplaceable fleet carriers and most of their crews. As a result, the Imperial Fleet's air arm would be impotent for the rest of the war's duration.

Mitscher's own air losses for the two days amounted to a total of 130 combat planes and 76 pilots and crew. His ships had at most suffered only the slightest injury, mainly from near misses, and a very few casualties among their crews. Still, these were losses that were deeply felt, especially among the carriers. And the initial understanding that Ozawa's fleet had been able to escape (the fates of *Taiho*, *Shokaku*, and *Hiyo* yet unlearned) led the fleet's most senior officers to be most mournful of what seemed only a partial victory for the cost. Later they would more fully learn the true extent the blow they had handed the Japanese.

Back in the waters around Saipan *Lang* continued her screening for the carriers of Task Group 58.4 as air operations against Saipan and neighboring islands of Rota and Guam shifted into high gear. Airstrikes on Saipan were mostly to aid the ongoing ground assault while on Guam the daily poundings were to soften the island's defenses in preparation for its upcoming planned invasion.

By the evening of 22 June the rest of Task Force 58 had returned to Saipan, their search for Ozawa's fleet ended and their attention again focused on the securing of the Marianas. The invasion of Guam was to have taken place on the 18th, but the tough resistance on Saipan and the approach of Ozawa's carrier fleet made certain its postponement. Now that the naval action was ended and the fleet's air support was back at the ready, Guam was again targeted.

The actual invasion of Guam had been pushed back to 21 July, but there would be little reprieve for its defenders. In the meantime Admiral Spruance had prepared plans to keep the island under near constant bombardment from both sea and air. And *Lang* was to help initiate some of the first shoreline strikes.

It was on the morning of 28 June that *Lang* along with *Sterett* and *Wilson* departed the screen of Task Group 58.4 to proceed to the islands of Rota and Guam in what was described as a "heckling mission" against the islands' defenses. In column, spaced at 2,000 yard intervals, the three destroyers began their trek at 7:35 A.M., and at a speed of 25 knots made for their first objective.

The ships moved swiftly across the sea and by 9:36 A.M. were within sight of Rota, the island bearing 110 degrees true and at a distance of 32 miles. Moving closer still, the group was by 11:38 A.M. within eight miles and eventually, by 11:55 A.M., only six miles from the island's shore. At this point general quarters was established and lookouts scoured the coast for enemy activity. When none was found the group continued on for Guam.

Remaining clear of any enemy interference, the three destroyers arrived eight miles off Guam at 2:54 P.M. Twenty-one minutes later they had their first enemy contact, when a small boat was spotted moving along the beach near Orote Point. General quarters was again set and the group moved closer to investigate. During the approach smoke could be seen on the beach just east of Orote Airfield, apparently the work of a previously made airstrike. Then, at 3:35 P.M., *Wilson* spotted a small barge on the beach and began firing on the craft. Within the next two hours several more small boats or barges were sighted and fired upon by both *Sterett* and *Wilson*.

After dark the group moved back out to sea. Throughout the night there were occasional radar contacts of enemy planes, though none came close to the ships' position. On one of these occasions, however, one enemy plane, which was approximately 30 miles distant, was seen by lookouts to explode into a huge ball of flames, apparently the victim of a roving American night fighter (the newly introduced radar equipped P-61 Black Widow).

The next morning the destroyers once again headed back toward the island of Rota. Approaching in column on a zigzag course, they were back within eyesight of the island by early afternoon. Continuing their approach, in the area of Sosanjaya Bay lookouts from the destroyers sighted four small craft near the shore. This time *Lang* responded as Captain Payson gave the order to fire on the targeted boats, and the destroyer's main batteries boomed in response, delivering a deadly concentration of explosives and steel to the island's shore.

Most interesting was, just prior to this bombardment, within the bay itself was a lone fisherman in an outrigger canoe. Obviously a native of the island, the day for him had begun routinely. But *Lang*'s opening volley quickly shattered his tranquility and sent him desperately paddling toward shore. At what appeared a record speed the canoe hit the beach hard and the fisherman, with no pause to his forward motion, continued at high speed out of the canoe and across the sand to safety. Though certainly not so for the native, to those observing the scene from the *Lang* the episode was especially humorous.

Ironically, at the same time and nearby, another native of the island was seen working on the roof of his house. Yet his reaction to *Lang*'s opening bombardment was much different to that of the fisherman's. His work did seem to accelerate some but otherwise he continued his effort, defying the danger tossed his way. Explosion after explosion erupted in his area but he refused to budge. The firing continued, the dust and smoke finally obscuring him from view, and his outcome could only be guessed.

Lang continued to throw one shell after another toward shore, pausing only a few minutes as a flight of carrier planes arrived to strike at Rota Airfield. Following this airstrike, firing from *Lang* recommenced, sinking two or three sampans in the process. A TBF (Avenger torpedo bomber) that remained in the area following the earlier airstrike began circling over the beach to locate additional targets for *Lang*'s gunners. With more boats spotted by the plane, the destroyer continued its fire, destroying yet another two or three boats and an old sugar mill before ceasing its fire at 4:30 P.M.

Following this bombardment of Rota the ships again headed in the direction of Guam. By 9:00 P.M. they were again off the larger island's shore, positioned just off the northwest coast, and preparing to take known enemy positions under fire.

Ten minutes later *Sterett* began the bombardment by firing a star-shell over Agana Airfield. Searchlights immediately pierced the sky and anti-aircraft guns fired blindly into the air, the enemy obviously convinced they were under air attack. *Sterett* fired again. This time a searchlight snapped on to send its bright beam across the water, sweeping low over the ships but apparently missing their silhouettes, and just as quickly switched off. Then, just a few minutes later, the light again snapped on. The beam again swept out across the water, this time followed by some random, unaimed shore gunnery. But again the results were negative.

By 10:00 P.M. *Sterett* had completed her firing mission without being located by the enemy or receiving any damage from the random enemy gunfire. Afterwards, *Wilson* moved into position to continue the bombardment. Once again wildly inaccurate gunfire came from the beach. But 50 minutes later *Wilson* had safely completed her run, and the ships then moved farther south to a position just off Orote Point.

Unhampered in their effort, the three destroyers reached their next target area at midnight. This time *Lang* would be first in turn in the bombardment mission, and Captain Payson immediately directed his ship forward.

Though having proceeded slowly, it did not take long for *Lang* to reach her bombardment position. Once in range, the destroyer turned broadside the shoreline to expose all its main batteries to the targets ashore, primarily consisting of known gun positions and Orote Airfield. A quiet pause followed. Then, in a unified volley, her four 5-inch guns suddenly shattered the silence with a deafening blast. And for the next hour and a half the destroyer continued a slow, deliberate fire, doggedly pounding its targets over and over again.

Sterett next took over, relieving *Lang* temporarily, and independently continued the bombardment for another hour. Then *Lang* again moved forward and both ships united in yet another 30 minutes of shelling. Finally, at 3:00 A.M., the firing ended and the three destroyers departed, destined to return to the task force at Saipan.

As the trio retired through the darkness, behind them they left a blanket of destruction at Agana and Orote Airfields. The crews could see the evidence of their effort by

126

the glowing light of numerous fires which heavily dotted the shoreline. Many continued their observance for several minutes, the fires dimming as the distance grew greater till finally all was darkness. And again the night reverted to the peaceful sounds awarded by a calm Pacific sea.

This mission was ended, and with success. Such should have been a positive influence on *Lang*'s crew. But in truth morale on the ship was dwindling rapidly. The month had been long and tiring, spent almost entirely at sea. Faces that were once young and innocent were now seasoned to a hardness by the salt of the sea and a war that appeared many years from ending. Space upon the destroyer seemed to grow smaller with each passing day. Tempers grew shorter, and the days became hotter. Such frustrations were to take a heavy toll on the men's spirits. Even Captain Payson, who often used a skipping rope to overcome his own confinement and frustration, was not immune. And, indeed, neither their fight nor their frustration was soon to end.

Chapter 9

New Guinea to Morotai

June 1944 had ended in great success for the Allied war effort, and especially so for the Americans. At the beginning of the month many planners and leaders throughout the Allied high command had certainly had much to be concerned about. Indeed, there was a lot riding on the successes of the two major campaigns planned for the month, whereby any failures at either Normandy or Saipan could have proven devastating, even to the point of prolonging the conflict by many additional years. Fortunately, the previous months of tedious preparations had paid off substantially, even having produced several welcomed bonuses. And, finally, the Allies had reason to be assured that total victory was within their reach.

Yet, despite the weight placed upon these two new campaigns, the first real taste of success for the month had come from the ongoing old campaign in Italy. Having begun nearly a year earlier with the invasion and conquest of Sicily, the initial momentum of this massive Allied effort quickly stalled. Following a series of secret negotiations, a newly restructured Italian leadership had signed a formal surrender just one day prior to the 9 September 1943 invasion at Selerno. Certainly this surrender was greatly welcomed, but a strong German army still occupied the Italian landscape and was fully prepared to stop any Allied advances. As a result, the battles which followed were lengthy and costly for both sides, but the months of slow progress proved especially embarrassing for the Allies. Every effort to punch through the German defensive line failed. Finally, near desperation and hoping to force a reconfiguration of German forces (thus to weaken their defensive grip), on 22 January 1944 the Allies circumvented the strong German line by making a new coastal landing at Anzio. This move caught the German high command completely by surprise;

but an Allied failure to quickly seize the advantage more than gave the Germans enough time to regroup, and with near catastrophic consequences for the Allied invaders. A tremendous fight ensued, but on 4 June the Allies victoriously entered into the city of Rome and the German army was finally forced to begin a stubborn withdrawal northward.

Just two days later, on 6 June, following months of highly secretive preparations, the Allies successfully made their long-awaited return to the northern European continent, amassing powerful landings on the beaches of Normandy, in northern France. Though these landings were met with fierce German resistance, the beachheads were quickly consolidated and, while costly, with much fewer casualties than initially expected. By the end of the month American forces had successfully captured the strategic deep water port of Cherbourg, which was to allow the Allies quick access at bringing ashore the massive amounts of heavy equipment and supplies needed for the following month's planned breakout. As a result, the second front for which Stalin had been pleading for so long was now reality. And the nightmare that Hitler had so hoped to avoid was now to bedevil him through to his pitiful end.

In the Pacific, General MacArthur's forces had been meting success in their systematic push to drive the Japanese from their occupations along northern New Guinea, retaking the key areas of Aitape, Hollandia, Wakde and, by June, Biak. And this effectively placed his forces within 800 miles of the Philippines, helping to set the stage for the general's long-awaited promised return.

The successful landings on Saipan on 15 June only added to the growing list of reasons for the Allied high command to be self-congratulating. Prophetically, that same day B-29's flying from bases in China delivered their first bombing raid on Japan proper, striking steel mills on the home island of Kyushu, as only a taste of what was about to come. Soon massive groups of B-29's would be making routine trips from new bases in the Marianas to deliver a destruction never before experienced by the Japanese populous. Add to this the great American naval victory in the Philippine Sea, which effectively destroyed the Japanese carrier fleet as a fighting force and left the U.S. Fleet in near uncontested control of the Pacific sea lanes, and certainly there was every reason for the Allies to display cautious celebration. Indeed, Japan was now doomed to total defeat — only the cost remained in question.

Aboard *Lang* the crew were well abreast of all this current news; a wireless and ship's newspaper kept the men up-to-date on not only the war effort but also of the happenings back home. The influx of the month's positive reports was certainly well received by the crew, but it did little to ease their personal fears and expectations of the future. For them the war was certain to become more intense and riskier with each new move, and they had no reason to expect any immediate relief or pause in the action.

In fact, the continuing land battle on Saipan and its aftermath was to testify greatly to the legitimacy of every serviceman's caution. The defiant Japanese behavior experienced on Saipan was horrific, and probably to have as much to do with the future decision to drop the atomic bombs on Japan as any other factor considered. And, ironically, those bombs were to begin their flights from the new American air bases to be established on these very islands.

Truly, Saipan was unlike any previously captured Japanese territory. During their tenure the Japanese had invested a lot in Saipan's development, not only for its military importance but also for its economic value, being a primary supplier of sugar to the homeland. Its many acres of low lying flatlands were rich with fertile soil, growing abundant amounts of sugarcane and corn. The island's own mills processed these crops, and small gauge railways delivered them to shipping docks for transport to Japan proper. To oversee these operations Saipan had gained a hearty population of Japanese nationals (a number estimated to have been near 30,000 at the time of the invasion), and with them had come Japanese culture and architecture, making the island nearly as Japanese as any of the home islands.

As for its military function, Saipan had also had a healthy population of both Army and Navy personnel (by 1944 totaling over 31,000; effectively double the number expected by U.S. military planners). Yet the island's military purpose had never exceeded being anything more than a centralized supply redistribution area, especially for the Japanese air services. In fact, it was its large air facilities on its southern end which had made it such an attractive prize to U.S. planners. Still, though they had suspected the island to be a future target for invasion, the Japanese had did little in preparing for its defense; as it turned out, they never expected it to be threatened so soon. But, despite its weakness in manmade defenses, the island's commanding high ground and naturally cavernous structuring was to aid its defenders greatly, proving it a prize not easily to be won.

The bitter contest that followed was to last nearly a month, but by 7 July the fighting on Saipan was drawing to a close (on 9 July the island would be pronounced secure); even though, many stubborn defenders continued to fight to their own end. Throughout the entirety of this time *Lang* and her crew had been at sea, and the battles ashore had been out of sight and impersonal. On this day, however, the need for fuel and supplies had determined their entry into newly won Saipan Harbor. Obviously, the visit was to allow the crew no vacation from duty, but it did award their first opportunity at a closer look at the former enemy held territory and reminded them of the life and death struggle that even then was continuing ashore.

From the destroyer's outer decks the crew could see the results of some of the hard fighting that had taken place. The island's once natural beauty had now been replaced by a shell scarred and scorched landscape, where at various points dense columns of black smoke still rose high into the sky. Of the few structures visible to the sailors, none had escaped the wrath of the violent warfare of the previous battles. And there were the occasional wisps of death's stench borne from somewhere inland on the back of a lazy breeze reaching out into the bay.

Such sights and smells many of *Lang*'s veterans had experienced before; at Guadalcanal, New Georgia, Nauru and/or Roi-Namur. And, obviously, the warfare going on ashore seemed no different — but it most definitely was.

That evening, as *Lang* departed the harbor to return to sea and rejoin the carriers, news of that morning's massive suicide attack by Japanese soldiers on the island's north end had finally reached the ship. Certainly such acts from the Japanese soldier had come to be expected. But at Marpi Point the acts of suicide far surpassed anything before witnessed by the American servicemen. In this single attack over 3,000 Japanese, including several civilians, had raged forward to overrun many American positions before finally being stopped, the attackers wiped out to nearly the last man. Thereafter, suicidal Japanese could not die fast enough. Of those soldiers that remained, most committed suicide rather than face capture (at least 30,000 Japanese soldiers of Saipan's total garrison perished in combat or by their own hands); while thousands of civilians (an estimated 22,000), misled and confused by their own propaganda, began a systematic and ritualistic killing of themselves. So mothers were seen to toss their small children from high cliffs into the sea below, to then follow; and, likewise, fathers were witnessed to gather their entire families around them to then exploded a grenade in their midst. And, though the Americans tried in every way to prevent the unnecessary deaths, such wasteful carnage continued for days.

Thankfully, *Lang*'s patrol did not take the crew close enough to witness any of the actual seaside suicides. But even at their distance from shore there was still an occasional body floating by their ship to remind them of the ongoing slaughter. Certainly each sighting was very disturbing, not solely due to the great amount of unnecessary death, but more for the fact that these were mostly all civilians, and from an island that so fully exacted the Japanese home culture. For *Lang*'s crew, as much as any other witnessing serviceman, the implications of the event were clear — if all Japanese civilians could be expected to react in the same fanatical way, the future cost at defeating Japan, in both lives and material, had just increased dramatically.

Still, the Pacific war continued unabated. obviously, *Lang* and crew had no choice but to continue the course that was destiny's choosing. And by the end of July the destroyer's duty around the bloody island of Saipan had come to its conclusion, relieved of her patrols and directed back to the Marshalls for a much needed rest for her crew and repairs for herself.

By 2 August *Lang* was sitting in Eniwetok's harbor and tied next to the destroyer tender *Piedmont* (AD-17). During the past two months there had been little time for any major repairs or upkeep, and Captain Payson's ship was again looking pretty rough. Soon, though, the necessary gear was aboard the tender for repairs, rigging was being mended, and the entire ship was receiving a fresh coat of paint.

Rest for the crew, however, did not immediately materialize. At Eniwetok such an opportunity just was not in the offering. The ship demanded most of their attention during the stay, keeping each man rather busy mending, cleaning, scraping, and/or painting. Still, the visit did produce some special rewards; bags of long-overdue mail finally caught up with the ship to bring word from home, and a fresh replenishment of provisions awarded the crew some tastier meals. These rewards were indeed most welcome, as morale was given a tremendous boost. And certainly Captain Payson was most appreciative of the renewed spirit returned to his vessel.

Yet the stay at Eniwetok was short. After only two days *Lang* was again at sea, departing as escort for the "Liberty Ship" SS *Henry Meiggs* to Makin Island in the Gilberts. Granted, the ship was in a much improved condition, with new paint glistening in the sunlight and a crew momentarily relieved to be out of the action, but it fell far short her every need. Rest, for both ship and crew, was needed in a much greater supply before they returned to the war — and they had no doubts that they would return soon.

At Makin the crew did finally have a greater opportunity to escape both duty and the confinement of their restrictive home. Yet Makin, like most Pacific isles, had little to offer in the way of distractions. Swimming was the primary recreation, and, though healthy exercise, was not very excitable. Still, Makin's environment was peaceful and the water was crystal clear and warm, providing a most leisurely atmosphere. And the crew did take advantage of its offering.

This stay was also quite short, however. And by 11 August the destroyer was again back at sea, this time headed south for the Solomons.

Lang arrived at Tulagi on the 16th, refueled and then proceeded on into Purvis Bay. This ended a journey that very much retraced in reverse the ship's Pacific war past, from the Marianas to the Marshalls to the Gilberts and finally to the Solomons. In the process they had again crossed the equator, and again new Shellbacks were added to the rolls. And, while several of the former Polywogs recuperated from their sore bottoms and wounded dignity, they were treated to one story after another — some true, some not — of *Lang*'s wonderful Solomons battle history.

Indeed, the stop at Purvis brought back a lot of memories to the "old hands" aboard *Lang*. Certainly the stories they shared gave the junior members of the crew considerable prospective of their ship's wonderful heritage, bolstering everyone's confidence that their little sea riding warrior could yet see them safely through this war. And, no doubt, such inspiration would be greatly needed when they returned to the fight.

For five days *Lang* remained in the confines of Purvis Bay, finally allowing the crew the real rest they so desperately needed. Again, swimming proved to be the greatest source of exercise, but this time there were alternatives. On the second day of their visit the officers and crew engaged in a "friendly" game of softball. The final score for this truly American contest: enlisted men — 10; officers — 2.

The hands of time did not slow, however. All too soon *Lang* and crew were back at sea and, as had been expected, heading westward back toward the war which continued its rage. But, instead of returning to Nimitz's Central Pacific push, this time Captain Payson's command was being directed to join General MacArthur's South Pacific forces at New Guinea. Just what duty would be expected of *Lang* to perform remained a mystery, but it was certain that her past duty of screening for Nimitz's fleet carriers had ended, for a while at least.

Lang made her first stop at New Guinea, arriving at Langemak Bay, near Finsch-hafen, on 23 August. There the ship became an official part of Admiral Thomas C. Kinkaid's Seventh Fleet. But the stay here was brief, and *Lang* departed the following day for Humboldt Bay, arriving there just two days later.

Entering this important coastal anchorage, Captain Payson gave the order, "All ahead one-third," and his destroyer slowed. Before his ship stood a group of green hills peaking above a cloud of steam which, in turn, rose from above a dense jungle interior. Typical of New Guinea, Humboldt was a most primitive and brutally hot territory, high in humidity and thick with insects. Each minute that the sun rose higher the metal on the ship grew hotter, even blistering to the touch. The destroyer's confines soon sweltered with unbearable heat. And the crew quickly withered at even the most conservative exertions.

That night many of the men moved to the ship's outer decks to sleep. Even with the sun gone the destroyer's interior refused to cool, whereby the humid outside air — though somewhat putrid with the smell of rotting jungle — gave a share of relief.

On the following day, in allowing his men some escape from the ship's heated confines, Captain Payson sent various boatloads of sailors ashore. There men disembarked to travel along the island's edge, keeping within the shade of the neighboring jungle's heavy foliage while walking the hard-packed mud paths. The trails led them past the tent cities of the occupying soldiers, who lived among the insects and lizards, and who secured their precious supply of warm drinking water in lister bags from nearby trees. Such sights quickly gave notice that no luxuries were to be found here.

Continuing their explorations, a few men disregarded safety and took dangerous treks into the thick jungle, braving hidden dangers in search of souvenirs. Others visited the black sandy beaches along the coast, drinking a warm beer under some shading tree or wading into the ocean's edge for a refreshing swim. Still, others opted to search for one of Humboldt's more elusive sights, that of women. The news of a nearby Army hospital being occupied by several American Army nurses had indeed peaked the interest of several of *Lang*'s company.

Meanwhile, as the crew spent their time acquainting themselves with the sites ashore, Captain Payson remained aboard ship busily studying his newest orders. *Lang*'s next mission involved the destroyer becoming a screen and bombardment unit for a minelaying task group headed some 200 miles east/south east along the New Guinea coast. Their intended target was to be the previously bypassed enemy held base at Wewak, there to reinforce a defensive minefield at the harbor's entrance in denying the cutoff outpost any possible support from the sea (American intelligence had previously intercepted Japanese communications mentioning the possible efforts at re-supplying Wewak by using submarines).

By 10:30 P.M. on the night of the 29th *Lang* was again out to sea. In the company of two other American destroyers and the British minelayer *Ariadne*, *Lang* quietly edged along the New Guinea shoreline en route to the target.

Early the next morning the little task group arrived at Aitape and remained there throughout the daylight hours, awaiting dusk before proceeding on. That night the usual precautions for security were taken, but all remained quiet. And by daylight of the following day they were successfully within striking distance of Wewak, pausing beyond sight of shore in wait of darkness before closing their objective.

Once darkness fell, the four ships slowly and cautiously moved toward the harbor entrance. Lookouts kept alert for any threat from the enemy. By this time, however, the Japanese offensive capabilities in the region were close to nil; very few Japanese planes were operational in the area, and the Imperial Fleet's long-range submarines had been dwindled down to only a couple dozen operational boats. But the possibilities remained, and so every precaution was taken.

The task group finally arrived just outside Wewak Harbor at just slightly past midnight. Various ones of *Lang*'s crew could see the dim glow of lights off in the distance, acknowledging their undetected arrival. In truth, the moment seemed almost surreal; the ships being so close to the enemy, practically within his camp, yet all remaining so eerily quiet. Shortly, the order to execute would be given, and a thunderous challenge was to follow. What after that, no one knew for certain.

Following this short pause, the minelayer suddenly moved to initiate the action, quietly slipping up to the harbor entrance and systematically placing her mines across its opening. The destroyers, meanwhile, held their positions offshore, readied for the bombardment that was soon to follow. And still, the night's peace remained undisturbed.

Lang's readiness was set at condition "III," meaning that those men on watch, not necessarily the regular gun crews, would be manning the guns. A few more seconds of stillness remained. Then the order was given, and the quiet Pacific night suddenly erupted with the violent thunder of the three destroyers as they combined their five-inch firepower.

Slowly and deliberately, round after round was launched toward the enemy base ashore. The initial surprise quickly ended, and almost immediately the previously seen lights were extinguished. Replacing them, however, were a flash of explosions and the eruption of fires as the five-inch shells displayed their accuracy. For a short moment a searchlight from shore switched on to seek out the bombarding ships, warning of retaliation from shore batteries; but the enemy guns refused to fire and the light switched off.

The operation had to this point went totally as planned. The minelayer finished its task and rejoined the destroyers, but its captain then decided to join the bombardment effort. Suddenly, there was a simultaneous boom and bright flash, and a brilliant flame lit up the entire area, illuminating all three destroyers. The darkness returned only to be chased away again by a second boom and bright flash. Each volley from the minelayer drew several well chosen curses from the American sailors before finally its gunners were ordered to cease their firing. But the damage to the operation was done, and the bombardment abruptly ended.

The idiocy of the moment was profound; the minelayer had not used flashless powder as had the other ships. Therefore, the bright flashes this created had given up the ships' positions to the enemy gunners on shore, not to mention making the ships easy targets for any lurking submarines. Fortunately, the enemy gunners continued their refusal at giving up their own positions, and obviously no submarines were momentarily present. And, with a sigh of relief, the four ships quickly vacated the area and rushed back for Humboldt, arriving there safely later that day.

For the next several days *Lang* was destined to remain in port. And this allowed the crew even more opportunities at rest and recreation, while *Lang* too benefited with time for additional repairs and upkeep.

On the third day of this stay all work was given pause, as different groups of the ship's company were given a turn at going ashore to share in a ship sponsored beer party. Near the sandy beach several makeshift tables had been constructed, sheltered somewhat by the shade of some tall tropical trees for the convenience of those who gathered. Soon, wild stories and laughter were erupting all around the area, as many of the men displayed their talents at catching the spewing warm beer upon the opening of each can — some of the less talented efforts being rewarded with near empty cans and some less than sympathetic laughter from their mates.

That evening the entire crew gathered in preparation to view a movie on the ship's forecastle deck. As a warm evening breeze flowed pleasantly across the decks, an echo of jolly conversation could be heard resonating from the crowd as they waited. And then there was a sudden hush.

A group of the ship's officers had just arrived, and with them some very special guests. Drawing immediate attention, the six nurses slowly made their way forward the group. In response, nearly 200 sets of eyes followed their every move, while every nose breathed in deeply the sweet smell of their alluring perfume. It had been a very long time since any of the crew had seen any women, and especially American women. And the resulting boost in morale was clear, with one small exception, that is.

The exception came when one of the chiefs appeared through the forward deck hatchway with little George resting in his arms. Immediately upon seeing the ship mascot, one of the nurses jumped from her seat and exclaimed, "Oh! Look at the cute little puppy." Quickly moving over to the chief she gathered little George into her own arms. Suddenly, in a manner never before exhibited, George began to snarl, growl, and wiggle about in a desperate attempt to escape the grip of the nurse. With a burst of laughter from the crew, he finally freed himself, hit the deck in a run, and reentered the forward hatchway to never be seen the rest of the night. It was later deduced by the crew that George had never before been near a woman, and evidently the smell of perfume was so foreign to him that it caused him to go wild and run away. Most of the crew could understand going wild over a good-looking woman but, admittedly, had to question having a mascot that would run away from one; it just was not sailor-like.

The restful visit at Humboldt finally concluded on 10 September, when at 10:30 P.M. Captain Payson again directed his command back to sea. His crew was well rested now, and his ship was back in good working order. And together they headed back for the war.

A brief stop was made at Aitape on the following morning. There *Lang* joined in the escort of 25 LCIs en route to the enemy held island of Morotai. This left little doubt in the minds of the crew that they were once again headed back into some serious action.

Indeed, *Lang*'s role was to be an important one, as she had taken aboard an Army Air Force officer, First Lieutenant Paul A. Richardson, just prior to leaving Humboldt. And from the destroyer this lieutenant would direct a patrol of fighter planes against the enemy wherever it was needed.

Five days later, just one day after the initial invasion, *Lang* arrived at her destination. There, while the LCIs she had accompanied delivered their reinforcements and supplies ashore, the destroyer quickly deployed to take up her new fighter-director duties.

On Morotai itself the enemy offered little resistance to the invasion, yet several enemy planes did make appearances while flying sorties from airfields on the neighboring large Japanese held island of Halmahera. This is when *Lang*'s fighter-director came into play. And it was during one of these episodes that several of *Lang*'s crew had front row seats to a wild dogfight which orchestrated high above them.

The moment had begun most unsuspectedly. In fact, by the time the crew first noticed the action, the Japanese plane was already on the attack. Diving headlong at the two American fighters, the engine of the dark painted Zeke (Mitsubishi A6M Reisen/famed Zero fighter) screamed as its guns spit out hot steel. Caught completely by surprise, the first American plane quickly dropped from the sky, its fuselage ablaze and trailing black smoke, just as its pilot escaped its cockpit to parachute to safety.

As the first pilot descended to the water's surface, high above him the second American plane twisted through the sky in a desperate but vain attempt to escape the gun sights of the enemy fighter. The skill of this enemy pilot proved him a veteran, as he duplicated every move of his American counterpart, and soon this plane too was making its final plunge to the sea.

Again, the American pilot made his escape from his doomed fighter. With the opening of his chute it appeared the battle over when yet a third American plane suddenly arrived on the scene. And again the hotshot Japanese flyer was given challenge.

This time, however, the contest was more of a match. Through a totally undefiled blue background the two planes twisted and turned, desperately trying to gain an advantage over the other. Looking much more like a game than the deadly contest it was, the two continued to loop and spiral as they covered the sky. Suddenly, the Zeke puffed out a bit of smoke and a burst of flame erupted from its side. Its nose arched downward, pointing the way of its final dive. Farther and farther it fell, its pilot never appearing to make his escape. And when the flaming enemy struck the ocean's surface, sending a spouting geyser high into the air, the men of *Lang* gave out a cheer to the demise of one more "good Jap."

That night the crew received little rest, as still more enemy planes made periodic appearances, and calls to general quarters frequently interrupted any possible efforts at sleep. Yet at least two more enemy planes were seen to drop from the darkened sky, their flaming forms arching to a silent death.

The next night was more of the same, as still more enemy planes made their appearances. Two such planes, evidently searching for targets on the sea's darkened surface, flew directly over *Lang*. One flew so low over the ship that "you could have swatted him out of the sky with a flyswatter." Indeed, his exhaust's blue flame was plainly visible as he passed by so very near. But Captain Payson wisely had his gunners hold their fire, refusing to give away his ship's position. And soon the threat vanished.

The third night at Morotai continued as the others, the crew's rest again interrupted by the appearances of still more enemy planes. This night, however, soon erupted into a blaze of anti-aircraft fire, as all the ships in the area took on the nighttime challenge of the high-flying enemy bombers. Thousands of tracer rounds and booming high explosives turned the night sky into what appeared a 4th of July celebration. Lively lines created by the tracers shot up from the ships to often cross paths and then spread off into some wild direction, while bright explosions erupted in their midst. The sky flashed with brilliance, ever so often being highlighted by the blazing streak of a stricken enemy plane, its form plunging to its grave among the deep. Then the planes disappeared, and for a short while the night sky was again quiet, allowing the crew some moments to rest before morning's light would introduce another day of challenges.

Lang remained on duty at Morotai till the morning of 19 September, then she departed for a return to Humboldt. Other than a false submarine contact near Biak on the trip's third day, this voyage encountered no interference. And by the 23rd the destroyer was again anchored in Humboldt's bay.

At Humboldt *Lang* took on supplies, fuel and, much more importantly to the crew, mail. But otherwise this stop was nothing more than routine. And two days later the destroyer was again at sea, this time in escort of five LSTs and four Liberty ships that were destined back to Morotai.

Following five additional days of uninterrupted sailing, *Lang* was again off Morotai and immediately pursuant of a patrol off the island's shore. This patrolling lasted two days, then ended on the night of 2 October as *Lang* departed in company of destroyer *Stevens* (DD-479) for a return to Humboldt. But this trip was soon to be interrupted, as in the early morning hours of the third both ships received an urgent call to assist a nearby destroyer-escort that had been torpedoed.

Shelton (DE-407) had been serving as a part of the screen for the two escort carriers *Midway* (CVE-63), and *Fanshaw Bay* (CVE-70) some 38 miles east of the northern tip of Morotai, which had taken her near a submarine safety lane set up for U.S. submarines. Unfortunately, on this morning the submarine nearest the DE was not American but was instead the Japanese boat RO-41, and at 8:07 A.M. she launched a spread of torpedoes headed directly for the U.S. warship.

From aboard *Shelton* lookouts saw the torpedoes' wakes, but it was too late. Before any evasive action could be taken, one of the deadly underwater missiles struck the targeted vessel solidly astern, killing two officers and eleven enlisted men and wounding twenty-two others while destroying her propulsion and filling several of her aft compartments with water.

Racing to her immediate aid was the destroyer-escort *Richard L. Rowell* (DE-403), which searched the area, dropped a few depth-charges, and then proceeded to take aboard *Shelton*'s crew. In the meantime, a patrolling plane from *Midway* had located a sub nearby and had dropped two depth charges and marked the area with dye. And upon hearing this report — despite this sighting being 18 miles from where *Shelton* was first torpedoed — *Rowell*'s captain quickly ordered his ship to speed to the site of the suspected enemy.

Upon its arrival, *Rowell* almost immediately picked up the fleeing sub on sonar. An attack was made using hedgehogs, a scattering of underwater bomblets that exploded upon contact. This first attack failed. But afterwards, a faint signal was heard to come from the sub. This obvious effort at communication, however, was quickly dismissed by *Rowell*'s captain as an enemy effort at jamming his sonar, and a second attack was commenced. This time the attack met with success, with the ocean jarring from several deep underwater explosions. And the crews of both DEs cheered as the submarine was most assuredly destroyed.

Indeed, a submarine had been sunk, but instead of RO-41 the determined DE had accidentally killed America's ace submarine *Seawolf* (SS-197). *Seawolf*, with 18 accredited sinkings, totaling nearly 72,000 tons of Japanese merchant shipping, had just a few days earlier departed Manus en route to deliver some Army specialists and supplies to guerrillas on Samar, in the Philippines. She was already a day behind schedule due to bad weather, but her captain had relayed this information to the Seventh Fleet command. Unfortunately, this information had not been properly passed on and so, despite the safety lane in which she traveled, led to the mistaken identity which would be her sad demise. (The real villain, RO-41, escaped, and would survive till 4 April 1945, when at that time she would be sunk by the destroyer *Hudson* (DD-475) off Okinawa.)

In the meantime, *Lang* and *Stevens* had quickly knifed their way across the sea, stubbornly surging across spirited waves to arrive near *Shelton* at around 1:15 P.M. Though yet distant, a signalman immediately flashed her a signal using the signal lamp. There was no reply. As the two ships drew closer there could be seen no visible signs of life aboard the crippled DE. Through binoculars the ship could be seen to be at a slight list, her stern missing, and the remaining deck rear of the after five-inch gun bent upward at about a thirty degree angle. But it was a group of signal flags displayed at the vessel's yardarm that initially peaked the interest of *Lang*'s observers.

The signalman aboard *Lang* began to call out the flags: "Able, Love, Oboe, How and fourth repeater." With a puzzled look the small group of men around him questioned, "What is it?" "I don't know!" he replied. They looked in the signal book, but it wasn't there. Finally, someone suggested writing it down, and then it dawned on them. It wasn't in code. It was just a simple spelling out of "Aloha." Evidently *Shelton*'s own signalman had thought it fitting that the ship tell her abandoning crew "goodbye."

Having now determined *Shelton* to be vacant, Captain Payson next began a thorough search of the area for any additional enemy threats. This completed, by 2:30 P.M.

it was determined safe to close within a few yards of the DE and prepare to begin salvage operations. And by 3:15 P.M. a boarding party from *Lang* had made their way over to the stricken vessel for the initial assessment of its damage.

What the boarding party found was somewhat disappointing. Apparently *Shelton*'s crew had tried to control their ship's intake of water, but their efforts had seemed to have ended somewhat prematurely. By this time the after engine room had seven feet of water, and the after fire room had two feet; but all spaces forward were dry. In addition, the boilers had been drained, making power for the ship impossible. Regardless, once the inspection was complete, it was decided to try to tow the wounded ship back to port. It was obvious that *Shelton*'s situation was very critical. But there was a chance that she could still be saved.

Hoping to increase the DE's chance, the boarding party quickly began tossing off all the loose gear to lighten her load. *Shelton*'s own crew had already destroyed her sensitive materials, but they had also thrown away several important tools, wedges and pumps which could have aided the boarding party's salvage efforts greatly. These had to be brought over from *Lang*, which further delayed their efforts. Despite such hamperings, a six-inch manila line was finally brought over from *Lang* to be attached to the DE's bow. And at 4:15 P.M. *Shelton* was taken under tow.

Stevens screened nearby and patrol planes guarded from above. Still, the pace of the towing was painfully slow, usually no faster than four knots. Understandably, this made *Lang*'s crew very nervous. As far as they knew, the very enemy sub that had torpedoed *Shelton* most likely remained somewhere nearby. And at this slow speed they knew they were easy prey.

In addition, the situation aboard *Shelton* continued to worsen. Rough seas increased the ship's water intake, and nothing (even the use of bucket brigades) helped to reduce the flooding. A strong wind also caused a serious increase in the ship's list, and this too only worsened. Soon, it was evident that the crippled DE was not going to make it.

The salvage efforts continued for while longer but, unable to do anything more, the boarding party was finally ordered to return to *Lang*. Soon after, at 9:45 P.M., *Shelton* rolled over on her starboard side and capsized.

With the DE's fate now sealed, Captain J. L. Melgaard, Commander of Destroyer Division 4 aboard *Lang*, ordered the tow line cast off and the five-inch guns to sink her remains. In response, *Lang*'s five-inch battery fired into the hulk. A hit in the forward magazine started an intense fire, and by 10:22 P.M. *Shelton* was gone.

Captain Payson would later write in his report, "It is believed that salvage of the *Shelton* would have been possible if *Lang* had been able to arrive a few hours earlier." Obviously, even at the time of *Lang*'s late arrival, it still appeared the destroyer escort could have been saved. Yet, despite all their valiant efforts, *Lang*'s crew could not overcome all the obstacles required at keeping the doomed DE afloat. Indeed, from the very beginning, "Aloha," that haunting Hawaiian farewell left behind by her abandoning crew, seemed to stubbornly ensure her fate. And so *Shelton* retired to the deep, and her demise added one more sad page in naval history.

Witnessing the death of a ship is always an emotional ordeal for a sailor, especially when such an effort was given at keeping the vessel alive. Now that *Shelton* was gone, *Lang* and *Stevens* both turned back to their original courses destined for Humboldt, giving both their crews considerable time to study over their latest experience. For *Lang*'s crew, however, the episode had once more reminded them of just how fortunate their ship really was. *Shelton* had been in service only six months. *Lang*'s service, on the other hand, was deep into its fifth year. Such reality was quick to awaken the crew to just how charmed their destroyer truly was. Such might explain why from this point on the crew more often than not referred to their warrior as the "Lucky *Lang*." Surely, if "Aloha" could help ensure doom for one ship, "Lucky" could help ensure safety for another. Certainly there would be plenty more war to test the theory. And test it it would, even more severely than they could have ever imagined.

Chapter 10

Leyte Gulf

During the same time frame of the Morotai operation there had been two more important acquisitions completed in preparation for the forthcoming invasion of the Philippines. The invasion of Peleliu in the Palaus islands group began on the same day as Morotai. Halsey had suggested this group be bypassed, but Nimitz felt the Japanese air facilities built there had too much potential at harassing the supply routes for the coming invasion of Leyte; whereby its capture would deny the Japanese any such opportunity plus, in turn, provide for the American forces another forward air base for the bombardment phase of the forthcoming operations. Whether or not Nimitz's initial assessment of the Palaus' importance was correct is still debated, nevertheless, the taking of Peleliu proceeded, and after the first week — at a cost of 3,946 Marine casualties — the island's strategic positions were consolidated; though all enemy opposition would not cease till 25 November (on this date the Japanese commander, Colonel Kunio Nakagawa, committed suicide and 45 soldiers — nearly all that remained of an original contingent that numbered over 10,000 — were killed in one final assault). In addition, on 23 September, Ulithi Atoll was occupied for the purpose of its large lagoon providing a forward fleet staging area, which was to indeed prove very important to the support of all naval efforts in the Philippines. Unlike Peleliu, however, this acquisition was acquired without opposition or cost.

As a result, the stage was finally set for one of the Pacific war's most epic battles, the climax to Japan's assured defeat. After months of successfully forcing a two-pronged offensive across the South and Central Pacific (and not discounting the equally successful northern push across the Aleutians), Nimitz and MacArthur were finally poised to join forces. MacArthur had eagerly looked forward to this day, the day he could finally fulfill his past promise to the Filipino people. And American planners looked equally forward to busting this last major obstacle prior to proceeding with their final push to Japan proper.

For the Japanese the Philippines was to indeed be their last real opportunity at stopping the American onslaught. To command their ground troops they sent one of their most experienced and capable leaders, General Tomoyuki Yamashita, the renowned "Tiger of Malaya"; though he would have little time and far too few resources to provide an adequate defense. Additionally, Admiral Toyoda, Commander in Chief of the Imperial Fleet, was prepared to commit his remaining battle fleet at one final effort at destroying the American Fleet; unfortunately, he could not risk making such commitment till being fully certain of just where the American forces were to strike, information deprived him till too late to have the most desired opportunity. And, finally, their was Vice Admiral Takijiro Onishi, new commander of the Philippine based First Air Fleet, whose command would have sole responsibility at unleashing Japan's most effective — and most desperate — offensive weapon of the war's final months.

Back at Humboldt activities in preparation of the war's next set of events were increasing daily. Aboard *Lang* sailors constantly searched the eyes of their mates, sensing each others quiet anxiety over all the new commotions around the bay. As a result, tight-lipped sailors suddenly spoke a good word to another with whom they had just griped at earlier. While still others took opportunity to quickly write one more letter home, hoping to catch the mailbag before their next departure. Indeed, they had seen this all before; the gatherings of ships, the increased stockpiles of supplies, and the high-level meetings. There was no doubt another big operation was approaching quickly.

That the Philippines was to be the next target was of little secret; it had been talked about for months now, and certainly little else stood in the way of proceeding on to Japan. That it would be a long and hard fought campaign also seemed logical to the thinking; after all, Japanese forces were being increasingly squeezed into a smaller area, forcing their consolidations and increasing their desperations. Obviously, the veterans on both sides knew what to expect.

Certainly *Lang*'s veteran crew were aware of all the probabilities. They remembered the most recent campaigns. They remembered the long nights at general quarters, being served hot cups of strong coffee and hard "G. Q." biscuits at the posts they could not leave. They remembered the dehydrated food when the fresh meals had long expired. They remembered the fresh water supplies running low, and the showers being turned off. They remembered, too, the many restless hours at duty, when sleep seemed impossible. But, most of all, they remembered the fear of the unknown, uncertain of what deadly menace might strike next, or when. And yet, even these past experiences were to fall far short the extremes of this next group of campaigns.

Duty did not allow *Lang*'s crew much time to contemplate the possibilities, however. By the morning of 8 October the destroyer was back at sea, patrolling beyond the bay area for any snooping underwater predators which might try to prey on the shipping gathered inside.

This patrol began rather routinely, and continued quietly throughout the rest of the day and evening. The early morning hours of the 9th also began in the same routine manner. Then, at 2:19 A.M., *Lang*'s sound gear suddenly picked up the echo of a definite submarine contact. The contact was at a distance of 2,700 yards, running shallow at a speed of five knots. *Lang*'s speed was fifteen knots, and she was quickly closing the submarine's position, both courses on a five-degree variance and intersecting.

Captain Payson listened to the soundman's contact, agreed with his assessment and quickly flipped on the ship's P. A. "Sub contact!," he shouted into the microphone. "Sub contact — Man your stations!" And within seconds men were manning the depth-charges and preparing to let loose a lethal barrage of the explosive canisters onto the enemy below.

Meanwhile, the soundman continued to listen, keeping Captain Payson informed of the enemy's position. Within the next five minutes the first group of depth-charges were away, the Y-guns firing two 300-pound canisters to the ship's sides (one to port and one to starboard) while an additional 600-pound canister rolled off the rack at the ship's stern.

Within seconds of the canisters' dropping into the sea there came a deep, near simultaneous rumble of three explosions. Behind the ship the sea jarred, boiled and then erupted into three foaming geysers. Three minutes later another 600-pound canister rolled into the sea astern. Again the sea reacted violently at the canister's explosive eruption beneath its surface. Within the next six minutes five more explosive canisters sank below the ocean's surface, each sending a tremendous shock throughout its nearby depths in the attempt to shatter the sub's hull. Then all was quiet.

The soundman again listened to his phones. Nothing. All was quiet. The enemy was in hiding, hoping to evade any more attacks. *Lang* continued its search, remaining in the area for the next hour and a half, trying to force the sub into some movement. But, despite the effort, nothing more was heard of the elusive enemy. And Captain Payson finally abandoned the search and turned his ship back toward Humboldt.

During the destroyer's short absence the increase in the number of ships in port at Humboldt had been dramatic. The bay area was more crowded and busier than ever before witnessed by *Lang*'s crew. Commanders were called ashore for meetings, and orders were given out. Thus Captain Payson soon learned his command was to become a part of Rear Admiral Jesse B. Oldendorf's Task Group 78.4, destined for a preliminary exploratory penetration of Leyte Gulf on the 17th, three days ahead of the rest of the assault force.

For most of the rest of *Lang*'s crew the details of the approaching operation remained very scarce. But on 10 October the destroyer departed with a group of cruisers, destroyers, and fast attack transports (APDs) for landing rehearsals at nearby Tanahmerah Bay. From that point it wasn't too difficult for the crew to figure out that they would soon be involved in a major operation.

On the following day the ships returned to Humboldt, and there *Lang* picked up some additional passengers. Naval Reserve Lieutenant (jg) William S. McPherson and Army Air Force Second Lieutenant Lloyd W. Brooks had already reported aboard the destroyer three days earlier to serve temporary duty as fighter-director crew. On this day three more men were added. Army Colonel Charles R. Lehner and Lieutenant Colonel Arthur C. Bass both reported aboard from the Headquarters of the Sixth Army, and were to be observers for the forthcoming landings. The third fellow, however, was a Navy Lieutenant Commander, and it was he, above all the others, who caught the crew's attention the most.

Lieutenant Commander John T. Bland III was a man of medium height and build, with dark hair, and an appearance that, according to some, reminded one of the tough-guy movie star Edward G. Robinson. He was a serious fellow, all Navy, and very confident in his own abilities. No doubt, too, he was eager to prove his abilities capable of meeting any challenge. And very soon he would have just such an opportunity, as he was destined to be *Lang*'s next skipper.

Obviously, *Lang*'s crew were not at all thrilled with the idea of going into combat with a new, untested leader. Momentarily, however, it was decided by Commodore Melgaard, who still remained aboard the destroyer, that due to Lieutenant Commander Bland being unfamiliar with the new operation's order he should ride along only as a passenger. Once he had familiarized himself, and at the first available opportunity, there would then be a change of command. Until that time Commander Payson would continue as *Lang*'s commanding officer. Certainly this was quite a relief to the crew, and a most welcomed decision on the commodore's part. Even Bland, understanding his arrival's bad timing, was somewhat relieved.

Indeed, there was little time left for late preparations. By early the next morning Task Group 78.4 was at sea and the 1,250 mile trip to Leyte was begun. Aboard *Lang* every available bit of space was stacked with extra supplies, giving strong hint to anticipated length of this campaign. Certainly there was little doubt of the Japanese unwillingness to relinquish any additional territory, and definitely not without first a very serious fight. But just what would be in store for the American's remained a mystery. And this unknown was to keep everyone on edge.

Sailing as a part of Task Group 78.4 were three old survivors of Pearl Harbor: battleships *Pennsylvania* (BB-38), *California* (BB-44), and *Tennessee*. Also included in the group were the three heavy cruisers *Louisville* (CA-28), *Portland* (CA-33), and *Minneapolis* (CA-36); the three light cruisers *Denver* (CL-58), *Honolulu*, and *Columbia*; a screen of fourteen destroyers; and five APDs.

Aboard the APDs were members of Lieutenant Colonel H. A. Mucci's Sixth Ranger Battalion and teams of underwater demolition specialists. The Rangers were destined to occupy and clear off any enemy troops on the islands of Dinagat, Suluan and Homonhon at the gulf entrance, while the UDTs were to proceed to the designated landing areas and locate and destroy any underwater obstacles or mines.

On the 15th, the group was joined by the minesweepers of Commander Wayne R. Loud, which had sailed from Manus five days earlier. To this point everything remained on schedule. But nature was beginning to have her say in the matter. Throughout the day the weather progressively deteriorated, and the smaller ships were having trouble keeping up to speed.

That night the storm struck its full fury. Winds cranked up to 30 knots, causing the sea to rage, sending tons of water crashing across the decks of every ship. Aboard *Lang*'s bridge Captain Payson, Commodore Melgaard and others there on station kept a close watch of their instruments, hoping to keep their ship out of trouble as rain blasted against the portlights to impair all outside visibility.

Below decks men worked at their stations or gathered in groups to swap stories and drink hard to handle coffee, trying to ride out the storm as best they could, while their ship constantly rolled and bucked its way across the fierce sea. Obviously, there would be no sleep for any of the crew this night.

At dawn, just as the morning sky began to lighten, the worst of the storm finally began to subside. Surprisingly, all the ships had survived nature's tremendous pounding; some — especially the sweepers — were lagging behind, but none were lost. Still, the rollers remained large, and mighty rushes of water continued to blast across the ships' decks.

Lang had ridden the storm fairly well. In the ship's mess, where several sailors had gathered during the storm's peak hours, some utensils and cookware were found far out of place and spilt coffee yet ran across the decking. On the forecastle deck a half dozen flying fish were found stranded; these Captain Payson would soon have taken to the galley to be prepared into a fine meal for himself. Otherwise there was little visible evidence of all the ship had been through. But, just when the worst seemed to have passed, then came tragedy.

Throughout the morning hours most of the destroyer's outer hatchways remained dogged down, but a couple were being used. It was unfortunate that little George managed to locate one of open exits and wandered out from the safety of the ship's interior. For just as he reached the outer deck there came a sudden "whoosh," and a huge roller came crashing over the destroyer's bow. Just as suddenly the little pup was gone. *Lang*'s mighty mascot had been carried away into the vastness of the cruel sea, helpless and hopeless any salvation. His little "Mae West" still hung at its usual place, its intended purpose unattainable. No doubt, under the extreme conditions it would have did him little good anyway, serving only to prolong his agony and the inevitable.

Suddenly not only did Captain Payson have a nervous and tired crew, but one also wherewith morale had just been dealt a serious blow. Truly, the loss of the little pet was very disheartening to all aboard, but especially so for the chiefs, who were in many ways the most crucial strength of the ship's company. Certainly this was by no means the way any captain would want to enter an important campaign, and especially one that had the potential of being the most lethal of any yet undertaken. But obviously, at this point Captain Payson had little choice.

Indeed, in the early morning hours of the 17th (A-Day minus three) Task Group 78.4 arrived at Point Fin, the rendezvous area just outside Leyte Gulf. And preparations were immediately undertaken for the coming operations.

Clouds still covered the sky this morning, as the rain still fell, and the water was still rough, but they had finally reached sight of their intended objective. Off in the distance, stretching before them lay the jungle covered, mountainous islands of the Philippines. Off to the north and bordering that portion of the gulf lay the island of Samar, and to the southwest lay the island where General Douglas MacArthur was destined to fulfill his unwavering promise to the Philippine people, Leyte.

From this point the offensive operations were quickly set in motion. At 6:30 A.M. Commander Loud's minesweepers entered the gulf and commenced sweeping the southern entrance for mines. An hour and a half later the cruiser *Denver* closed to 6,500 yards of Suluan and opened the first shots of the campaign, softening up the island for the Rangers; who landed at 8:20 A.M., sending the small Japanese garrison fleeing, and successfully taking back the first bit of Philippine real estate.

In the meantime, just prior to the Ranger landing, at 6:50 A.M. a Japanese lookout on Suluan spotted the sweepers. He immediately notified his commander, who in turn notified Admiral Toyoda. Suspecting this at being preliminary to a major landing on Leyte, but not totally satisfied his suspicions were correct, at 8:09 A.M. Toyoda ordered SHO-1, his Philippine battle plan, to a state of alert.

At about this same time, Admiral Onishi arrived at Air Fleet Headquarters in Manila to assume his new post as head of the First Air Fleet. He soon learned of the SHO-1 alert and quickly began assessing his air strength. What he found was very discouraging; for the defense of the Philippines he had only 100 operational warplanes, of which only 30 were fighters.

Meanwhile, back in Leyte Gulf the preliminary operations were continuing. The next target for the Rangers was the island of Dinagat. But by 11:30 A.M. the weather had again deteriorated, and gale force winds of up to 60 knots were hampering the Rangers' landing efforts. Nevertheless, the Rangers reached the island's shore, found no opposition, and proceeded to set up a marker light to help guide the shipping in through the entrance.

The minesweeping was also made very difficult by the increased weather activity. But Loud's sweepers were relentless in pursuing their task, and stopped only when conditions became totally impossible.

By the early morning hours of the 18th the storm again subsided, and plans were again put in play for the next set of operations. Aboard *Lang* tension was high. At this point there was little doubt the Japanese were aware of the group of ships. But all remained quiet — far too quiet. Because of this lack of response, most of the ships had little to do but wait. Sailors remained at general quarters, waiting for and anticipating a strong enemy response that never appeared. And thus everyone's nerves were set on razor's edge.

Lang was scheduled to give fire support for the next Ranger operation which was to begin at 9:00 A.M. At around dawn, Captain Payson decided a measure was needed to calm his crew before their move forward, and he slipped from his perch on the bridge to disappear into his cabin. When he reappeared, in his hands he held his favorite rod-and-reel. He then proceeded out to the open deck, strolled down to the ship's bullnose, sit down, and dropped the fishing line into the sea as if he had no cares in the world. The move worked; seeing the captain respond in such a carefree and unpredictable manner soon brought forth some laughter, and soon the crew was loosened from their state of anxiety. Captain Payson even caught a few fish in the process.

Finally it was time for *Lang* to enter the gulf. The minesweepers were still working at a steady pace to clear the entrance of all mines, but the area remained a hazard. The Ranger's next target was the island of Homonhon, designated Black Beach #2, and *Lang*, in company of *Herbert* (APD-22), *Bisbee* (PF-46), and *Ross* (DD-563), carefully approached to within 4,000 yards of the island before dropping anchor.

At 9:00 A.M. the Rangers disembarked *Herbert* and headed for shore. At the same time, both *Bisbee* and *Ross* opened a bombardment of the beach area, ceasing only as the Rangers neared the shore. Once ashore, the Rangers established communication with *Lang*, and the destroyer's gunners prepared to provide any needed fire support. But none would be needed; the Rangers found no opposition and soon had a second guide light erected at the island's southern tip. The entrance to Leyte Gulf was now secure.

By this time Admiral Toyoda had finally determined that Leyte was indeed the American target. At 11:10 A.M. he sent the message giving the order to "execute"

SHO-1. And Japan's remaining fleet carriers, battleships, and heavy cruisers, and most of their remaining light cruisers and destroyers headed forward to do battle with the American Fleet.

Later that afternoon, while a few of the larger American ships made their approach to bombard the main landing beaches, *Lang* moved to help guard Loud's busy sweepers. The area between Dinagat and Homonhon proved to be heavily ladened with enemy mines, and their clearing was essential to the operation's continued success. That morning a few individual Japanese planes had finally appeared, and a few attacks had been made on the sweepers. Obviously, more attacks were expected, and *Lang* readied as fighter-director to add her own personal defense should that happen. But no more intruders appeared. Other than taking time out to help land a small group of Rangers on a small island just off the southern tip of Leyte and then later to transfer the two Sixth Army observers, the day passed by without any further interruptions.

On the next day, A-Day minus one, things continued to remain fairly calm. A few more enemy planes were occasionally picked up on radar, but the morning was quiet enough that several Filipinos took the opportunity to sail their outrigger canoes out to meet and welcome *Lang* to their home islands.

Known as "bum boats" to the sailors, they came not only to welcome but also to trade and or beg for whatever they could get from the good-hearted swabbies. As these boats eagerly drew near, the sailors gathered along the railings to trade for a souvenir or, as in many instances, just give away cigarettes, clothes, food, or fresh water.

A short time later the trading ended and the native-filled canoes returned to shore. *Lang*'s crew, in the meantime, returned to their duties. Yet the quiet continued throughout the rest of the day and evening — at least from *Lang*'s vantage — and the crew had a rare opportunity to steal a good rest.

That night the rest of the landing forces finally arrived and made their entrance into the gulf. The sight was awesome. Counting Halsey's Task Force 38, which would operate far outside the gulf, the ships numbered even more than the amount used for the Normandy invasion. And very soon they would unleash their power upon the Philippine occupying forces of Japan.

It was about 1:00 A.M. of the next morning (A-Day, the designated day of the invasion) that *Lang*'s restful quiet suddenly ended. The crew's hearts raced as they jumped at the call to general quarters, the P. A. blaring reports of simultaneous sound, air and surface contacts. Men quickly manned their stations, expecting the worst. Fortunately, the sound contact proved to be false, the surface contact proved to be natives in an outrigger, and the air contact kept its distance and never directly threatened the ship. General quarters ended, and a huge sigh of relief encompassed the destroyer.

A short time later, two men on watch spotted what appeared to be torpedo wakes headed directly for the ship. Again general quarters was sounded. And again there was no action; the torpedoes turned out to be a pair of sharks at the water's surface. And again sleep had been unduly interrupted.

At just before daybreak, and while the main landing forces were moving into position, *Lang* moved to take up a patrol just off the coast of Samar. As was now routine, at dawn's first light there came the usual call to general quarters. Though somewhat grumpy from the previous night's non-action action, sailors were soon at their stations and reporting "manned and ready." Almost immediately enemy planes were being reported at several different locations. It suddenly appeared that real action was just around the corner. But, for *Lang*, the morning hours continued without any direct threats.

That afternoon the destroyer moved to the Southern Transport Area. The landings had begun on schedule at 10:00 A.M., and by this time (approximately 4:00 P.M.) were several hours along and proceeding with only slight resistance from the Japanese. Settling near the cruiser *Honolulu*, *Lang* had just gotten in position when suddenly an enemy plane came swooping in from low over Leyte. Caught totally by surprise, *Lang*'s shipboard communications blared a short warning and startled gunners quickly struggled to direct their guns in the determined enemy's direction.

The plane, a *Francis* (Yokosuka P1Y Ginga) medium bomber, came straight down *Lang*'s starboard side. The destroyer's 5-inch and 40-millimeter batteries began to bang, shooting hot steel toward the intruder. Other ships also joined the fray, but the plane was soon out of range and making its escape back over Leyte, seemingly untouched in its effort. Unfortunately for its target, *Honolulu*, the same could not be said.

The cruiser's crew had fought desperately to avoid the torpedo unleashed by the bomber, but to no avail. Within seconds of its release into the sea, the torpedo slammed solidly into her port side, rocking the ship with its tremendous explosion. *Honolulu* quickly began to list, as water filled her interior and smoke rose from fires started below decks. At first only confusion could be made of the excitement created aboard the stricken ship. Then for the next several minutes, *Lang* had front row seats to an exemplary example at damage control. And the cruiser's crew gallantly rescued their ship to fight yet another day.

That night *Lang* was once again moved, this time to the Northern Transport Area at the western end of San Pedro Bay. Here again the crew spent most of their time at general quarters, as enemy planes steadily increased their harassment of the ships offshore and began bombing the beaches. This continued action, combined with an already insufficient amount of rest, was beginning to show its wear upon the men. And, obviously, the real fight had hardly begun.

Indeed, at dawn came even more excitement. *Lang* still remained at the Northern Transport Area when at 5:30 A.M. the crew was startled by the sudden eruption of anti-aircraft fire. Not far from the destroyer the Australian cruiser *Australia* was battling it out with a couple enemy planes, her guns hammering away desperately. With the additional firepower of other nearby ships, the two planes were soon dispatched in flames to their graves in the sea. Then, as several men topside of *Lang* continued their observance, a third plane suddenly sailed from over a mountain to dive headlong into the *Australia*, slamming directly into the cruiser's bridge.

The strike's resulting explosion was very loud, sending forth a ball of flame and smoke high into the sky, and turning the ship's bridge into a tangled and twisted mass of steel. Twenty men, including the ship's captain, perished while another 54, including the naval commander of all Australian forces present, were wounded. Never before had any of *Lang*'s crew witnessed such a suicidal act, the pilot deliberately destroying himself in order to strike a blow. Unknown to the crew, however, this was just the beginning of a brand new and even deadlier type of warfare.

On the day before, Admiral Onishi had went to Mabalacat Airfield (a part of the former American Clark Field) on Luzon and gathered several of his pilots and flight leaders for a talk. He announced the order to execute the SHO-1 operation, as given by Toyoda, explained their mission, and then paused. Knowing he had more to say, the pilots patiently waited. Then he slowly continued. What he next proposed not only shocked his pilots, but would also equally shock all who witnessed its results. His words "organize suicide attack units" were destined to again change the character of the Pacific war. And a brand new fear was to be placed in the hearts of all Pacific sailors.

The attack on *Australia* was the first of Onishi's new Kamikaze Corp (probably carried out by Lieutenant (jg) Yoshiyasu Kuno, who had taken off at 4:25 P.M. in search of a target at Leyte). Certainly it would not be the last.

Japanese planes continued to make their presence known throughout the rest of the day, though no additional suicide attacks were witnessed. At this same time American fighter planes were airborne and provided their additional protection, while bombers took turns unloading their lethal cargoes on the enemy positions ashore.

That night the crew continued to remain mostly at general quarters, drinking coffee to stay awake or taking turns napping at their stations between calls. They had now moved to a fire support station just 2,500 yards off Red Beach, northeast of Palo Town. At regular intervals throughout the entirety of the night *Lang*'s guns provided starshell illumination for the troops ashore and added some harassing fire at an area still occupied by a few enemy troops.

The next two days and nights brought about no serious changes to the routines. The American ships continued to battle off enemy planes, to which *Lang* joined on a couple additional occasions. And, at night, more support was given to the troops ashore by providing illumination fire and harassing bombardments of enemy positions.

At the breaking of dawn on 24 October everything continued as normal. The routine dawn alert produced no immediate excitement for *Lang*'s crew, and for awhile all was relaxed. Then, at 8:00 A.M., the call to general quarters again rang out. A dozen or so enemy planes came over dropping bombs but made no hits. Fighter-directors aboard the destroyer directed the CAP, and soon enemy planes began dropping from the sky to the cheers of the crew.

Then a group of enemy dive-bombers suddenly came streaking down toward the amphibious force flagship *Blue Ridge* (AGC-2), and *Lang*'s gunners immediately swung into action. Five-inch, 40-millimeter, and 20-millimeter guns all began to report in each their own distinctive tone. Round after round chased after the enemy, and the intensity of fire finally forced their turning away.

Friendly fighters joined the fray, oftentimes risking the intense anti-aircraft fire in their determined effort at downing the enemy intruders. Despite such efforts, the ships were still vulnerable. In one such case, a crippled Dinah (Mitsubishi Ki-46 Reconnaissance Plane) dove headlong into an LCI not far from *Lang*, its impact marked by a shattering explosion as flame shot high into the air and a pillar of smoke followed to ascend nearly a mile into the sky.

Hoping to hide the vulnerable shipping from the enemy above, smoke boats quickly began moving around the transport area to spread their covering blanket. This heavy concentration of smoke combined with the constant noise of gunfire and the impossible visual track of the swarming enemy and friendly planes soon set the crew into a state of confusion. Then, nearly as suddenly as it had begun, the attack ended, and the smoke and confusion dissipated.

This lull was not to last long, however. That early afternoon another, much larger group of enemy planes was reported closing the ships. At 3:00 P.M. the attack came, and heavy anti-aircraft fire again erupted throughout the transport area.

Quickly moving into the range of *Lang*'s guns, a Betty (Mitsubishi G4M1 Attack Bomber) came speeding in low over the water, once again headed for *Blue Ridge*. The destroyer's gunners responded quickly, each battery intently spitting hot steel toward the intruder, trying desperately to knock it from the sky. But no sooner had they begun this concentration of fire when a Zeke suddenly came screaming in from a different direction, immediately requiring some of the guns to be diverted. The gunfire was intense, but neither plane was apparently hit, as both were soon out of range. Yet *Blue Ridge* also escaped any harm.

More enemy planes continued to make attacks throughout the rest of the day and into the night. But there was now a new concern. Just prior to the 3:00 P.M. attack it was learned that a Japanese battle fleet was headed toward Leyte, and a battle of immense proportions was brewing for that night. Obviously, there would again be no rest for the crew of *Lang*, or any other ship, throughout the coming hours of darkness.

That night *Lang* remained at "Condition II Readiness." The sea was calm and the night was clear, with a quarter moon making its way to the horizon. By midnight most all of the combat ships had left the transport areas to stand outside the gulf in wait of the enemy fleet. Only the cruiser *Nashville*, which had aboard General MacArthur, and a handful of destroyers remained. *Lang*, which was one of the destroyers to remain in the gulf, continued her watch nearby *Blue Ridge*.

Shortly after midnight the moon set and clouds covered the sky. The night quickly became an eerie pitch black. From this point time passed by very slowly. *Lang*'s crew waited, impatiently wondering what would be the night's outcome. Certainly they were all very much aware that should the Japanese Fleet make it through to enter into the gulf, they, along with all the vulnerable transports, would be "setting ducks" with little to no chance at escaping the enemy gunnery.

Then came the reports that contact had been made with an enemy force just outside the gulf. A few minutes shy of 4:00 A.M. the men at *Lang*'s topside observed a bright flash to the south. Following this initial flash, more flashes began to lighten the southern sky. The crew immediately recognized these flashes as those from the big guns of the battleships, and they knew the battle was on.

Indeed, at Surigao Strait, the southern entrance to Leyte Gulf which lies between Leyte and Dinagat Islands, Rear Admiral Oldendorf had established a formidable line of defense. There he had strategically placed six battleships, four heavy cruisers, four light cruisers, two destroyer divisions and thirty-nine torpedo boats. Moving against this line was Admiral Shoji Nishimura's Force C, consisting of the two battleships *Fuso* and *Yamashiro*; the heavy cruiser *Mogami*; and the destroyers *Asagumo*, *Yamagumo*, *Mishishio*, and *Shigure*. And there the battle raged.

Back aboard *Lang*, sailors nervously awaited the outcome, hoping the Japanese ships were being sent to their glorious end at the bottom of the sea. The flashes continued for a short while longer, then they ended and all was quiet. The silence became so very painful as they awaited some news. Then the news came, and it was good; the enemy had been stopped. With a cheer, the tension was released and all began to relax.

The battle of Surigao Strait had ended in victory for the Allied warships, and had handed the Imperial Japanese Fleet another terrible defeat. All that remained of Nishimura's force of ships were the cruiser *Mogami* (she would be sunk the following day by carrier planes) and the destroyer *Shigure* (as in the battle of Vella Gulf she was once again the sole survivor). On the American side only 39 men were killed and an additional 114 wounded, and most of these were from the destroyer *Albert W. Grant*, which had accidentally took more hits from the American ships than from the Japanese. Yet despite this great victory, relaxation on the part of any of the American crews was premature.

At dawn there came the usual call to general quarters. The weather this morning was excellent, with a few fluffy clouds lazily drifting across a beautiful sky, and a steady but gentle breeze making its way across a wonderfully calm sea. Momentarily, all was quiet. Soon though, enemy planes were once again being reported at various locations, and again the anti-aircraft guns around the transport areas began to pop.

These air attacks increased with intensity throughout the early morning hours, and then it was suddenly learned that yet another enemy battle group was threatening the gulf. The small escort carriers on station just outside the northern entrance to the gulf were already engaged in a desperate battle for their lives, and pleading for help.

For the men in San Pedro Bay, their fear was now divided between the threat of the enemy planes and the possibility of being trapped within their bottled-up positions by these enemy ships. The latter threat looked even more likely as news was received that the escort carriers were being overtaken by a much superior enemy battle force.

The gulf's northern entrance defense had been left to the care of three Taffy units under the command of Rear Admiral Thomas L. Sprague, each consisting of six small escort-carriers, three destroyers and five destroyer-escorts (Taffy 3 with four destroyer-escorts). Just as Toyoda had hoped, Halsey's powerful task force was far off to the north chasing a decoy carrier fleet. Oldendorf's ships still remained far to the south, continuing to guard the southern entrance. Therefore, the Taffys were on their own. Facing them was Rear Admiral Takeo Kurita's Main Attack Group, consisting of four battleships (including the super battleship *Yamato*) six heavy cruisers, two light cruisers and eleven destroyers. And the likelihood of a serious breach in the American defenses appeared inevitable.

In lieu of this new threat, *Lang* and a destroyer-escort were ordered to depart the transport area and proceed to a patrol out in the gulf. It was quite obvious to all aboard *Lang*, however, that if the Japanese ships made it through, there would be very little they could do to stop them. But just when all looked its darkest, a stroke of luck befell the American ships, and the Japanese turned their ships away in confusion.

Though the weather had indeed been good this morning, visibility was somewhat limited. Since Kurita was expecting a much larger force, it was difficult for him to believe that he was in such a superior position. With the ferocity of the attacks of the planes from the carriers combined with the bravery of the screening destroyers and destroyer-escorts, Kurita's lookouts were soon reporting the escort carriers as fleet carriers, the destroyers as cruisers, and the destroyer-escorts as destroyers. Thus the ill-informed admiral soon determined his opposition as that of Halsey's Task Force 38. Had he truly understood what was his opposition, and had he known that Halsey was miles away chasing the decoy strike force as planned, he could have entered Leyte Gulf with devastating effect. Instead, in the ensuing confusion of battle, he decided to retreat. What had looked to be certain defeat for the Americans, suddenly turned into victory. Not only had the attacking Japanese been turned away but the Taffy planes had managed to sink three of their heavy cruisers and heavily damage two others. But it was a costly victory just the same; two escort-carriers, two destroyers and a destroyer-escort were lost while several other of the Taffys' ships sustained heavy damage.

Throughout the rest of the day *Lang* continued to patrol in the gulf. Enemy air attacks were still being reported all around, but the immediate area of the destroyer's patrol remained quiet.

That night the air attacks ended, and the situation finally began to relax. Several of *Lang*'s crew took advantage of this opportunity to catch up on some much needed rest. There was little doubt that such an opportunity would not be long lasting.

In the meantime, watches remained at their stations, strong coffee in hand, while lookouts searched out across the darkness. Occasionally gunfire erupted from another ship off in the distance, either firing at enemy "snoopers" or sometimes at American planes by mistake, yet for *Lang* the night continued to remain calm.

On the next morning the destroyer was ordered to join up with Sprague's escort carriers. Along the way she passed through the area of the previous battle, and debris and flotsam covered the water around her. The sight was a stark reminder to the crew to the recent deaths of ships and men.

Then, someone suddenly screamed out a warning of "mines, close aboard!" To everyone's surprise two floating mines went sliding past the side of the ship, one barely five feet away. Distracted by the battle debris, lookouts had allowed their job to escape their attention, and these mines nearly achieved what no enemy planc or ship had so far been able to do, sink or damage "Lucky *Lang*." Everyone held their breath, but fortunately the mines failed their mission. Tragedy had again been avoided. And once the mines had passed a safe distance from the ship, gunners blasted them out of the water.

From this point *Lang* would only remain in the area of Leyte for a period of two additional days. There would be no more sea battles. Air attacks, on the other hand, continued throughout this time, but to no harm to the destroyer. On 29 October, in company of the battleships *Maryland* and *West Virginia* (BB-48), *Lang* set a course for Manus, Admiralities, where she safely arrived on 3 November. And there the ship and crew would begin a new adventure — and with a new leader.

Chapter 11

Kamikaze

W ith the great naval battles around Leyte Gulf ended, the campaign to seize Leyte proper reverted primarily to a ground operation, which was destined to continue for several additional weeks. The air campaign also continued throughout this time, with the Japanese greatly utilizing both conventional (torpedo/bombing) and non-conventional (kamikaze) methods with increasing amounts of success. As for the large numbers of Allied warships, their roles quickly decreased to secondary support status. With the remaining Japanese Fleet terribly battered and unable — or at the very least unwilling — to try another surface engagement, Allied warships diverted most of their attention to patrolling against Japanese efforts to reinforce by sea the island's defenders and providing anti-aircraft defense for all the support vessels used in the constant effort at keeping the Allied ground troops well supplied. Yet this role reduction did little to ease the minds of the Navy's many war weary sailors. Indeed, the Japanese air arm, though weak in many ways, was quickly proving itself an increased hazard to all naval shipping, making life aboard ship more and more difficult, even to the point of being horrific.

With *Lang*'s arrival at Manus Island, however, her duties around Leyte were temporarily ended. It was a most welcomed and timely departure, as the many long hours spent at general quarters had exacted a price of the crew. For by this time the destroyer's group of sailors were very tired, and disgruntled. Their many days at sea had caused their vessel to seem more and more cramped, and the ongoing confinement was taking serious toll on morale. Tempers grew short, as the men increasingly took out their frustrations upon one another. Certainly they were in desperate need of some R&R, and Manus would provide the crew with just such an opportunity.

Manus, at 49 miles in length and 16 miles in width, was largest of the Admiralty islands. It was volcanic, and the island's surface was rough and thickly covered in jungle, initially offering no amenities. But, primarily due to its fine harbor, 15 miles long and 4 miles wide, being able to support an entire task force of shipping, the Allies were to find it ideally suited for an advanced naval base.

In fact, the Japanese had occupied the island in early 1942 for this same purpose. There, in 1943, they had built two airfields (one on Manus and another on neighboring Los Negros). But, due to the existence of the nearby powerful Truk, Kavieng, and Rabaul bases, the Japanese saw no reason to develop it further or provide it with any meaningful defense, either in manpower or equipment. Therefore, it was easy prey when in February and March 1944 American forces arrived to wrench it from the enemy's hands. And soon after, Manus' Seeadler Harbor was under American supervision and teaming with Allied shipping in preparation of the invasion of the Philippines.

When on 3 November *Lang* first arrived at Manus, Seeadler was indeed full of ships of nearly every size and description. Most of these ships were veterans of the recent operations around Leyte, and were there in need of provisions, fuel, and or repairs. But much more importantly to the crew of *Lang*, Manus was also a place in which to escape the hot confines of their tiny vessel. At this rear area naval support base they could safely relax either aboard ship or ashore, write a letter to loved ones at home, watch a movie, go to a beer party, or just enjoy a quiet moment alone. It was indeed a refreshing change of pace from the hostile waters around the Philippines. And for a little while the cruel Pacific war could be set aside.

But it was also at Manus that *Lang*'s crew finally caught up with the day they had so been dreading. For it was here that they would say farewell to their grand skipper, Captain Payson.

It was on the morning of 5 November that the destroyer had moved alongside the repair ship *Cebu* (ARG-6), as *Lang* also needed some special attention. Almost immediately following this mooring all duties were paused and the crew was gathered on deck for the short ceremony of the change of command. And, shortly afterward, Captain Payson officially turned command of the "Lucky *Lang*" over to Lieutenant Commander Bland.

It was indeed a most sullen moment for *Lang*'s crew. Certainly Commander Payson was extremely well liked by all aboard. He was a sailor's captain, strict but always thinking of his men, and insisting that his officers do the same. He trusted his crew, many times overlooking their crazy antics, aware of the special spirit of unity which had always brought them through the tough times. And it was in this spirit that the crew had went together to present their now former captain a special farewell gift; displaying their appreciation and stating their farewells with a matched set of Kaywoodie smoking pipes, the case commemorating his service to the ship with embossed gold lettering which read:

Crew, USS *Lang*
Harold Payson, Jr.
18 October 1943 – 5 November 1944

As for Captain Bland, his trial was just beginning. His new crew was very suspicious of him. They didn't enjoy the thought of going back — and they were sure to go back — into the torrent of combat with this untested C. O., or putting up with his much stricter attitude. But, despite such distrust, Captain Bland was the new leader. And, fortunately, he would have a quick opportunity to display an example of the type of devotion to ship and crew he was to bring to *Lang*.

It just so happened that shortly after the change of command ceremony ended that the destroyer *Albert W. Grant* came into Seeadler in tow. During the battle of Surigau Strait *Grant* had just made a torpedo attack on the Japanese cruiser *Mogami* when she suddenly got caught between the gun-dueling Japanese and American ships. As a result, she received hits from at least seven Japanese 4.7-inch projectiles and eleven American 6-inch. Though badly damaged and left without power, her gallant crew succeeded in keeping her afloat.

For Captain Bland the arrival of *Grant* had another even greater significance, for this was the ship on which he had served before making his move to *Lang*. He quickly contacted his old ship and only then learned that there were still several wounded men aboard who had elected to remain till the ship had reached a safe port. With this news, the captain gathered Lieutenant A. J. Bernard, *Lang*'s Medical Officer, and took a launch over to the badly battered destroyer. There the two officers assisted in removing shrapnel from at least a half dozen men before returning to *Lang*. No doubt, it seemed only a small favor for an old friend. But it was destined to gain him his first accolades of respect from his new crew; after all, he had given up his own special moment of celebration, his first coveted moments at his own first command, to give aid to someone in need.

Remaining at Manus another five days, *Lang* departed on the morning of 10 November, in company of the battleship *Maryland*, cruiser *Columbia* and four other destroyers headed for Palau. At 8:55 A.M. the group had just slipped outside the harbor when a tremendous explosion suddenly rocked the area behind them. Looking aft, *Lang*'s crew could see a huge cloud of smoke and debris covering the harbor area. Soon after, it was learned that the ammunition ship *Mount Hood* (AE-1), loaded with an esti-mated 3,800 tons of ammunition, had just exploded (cause undetermined).

The huge mushrooming cloud from *Mount Hood*'s explosion rose an estimated 7,000 feet and engulfed an area 500 yards radius. The crater on the ocean floor beneath the spot where the ship had stood measured 300 feet long, 50 feet wide, and 30 to 40 feet deep. Little remained of the former 13,910 ton ammunition ship, with the largest fragment of metal left measuring no bigger than 16 by 10 feet. Only 18 of *Mount Hood*'s crew survived, and all of these were ashore at the time of the explosion.

Several other vessels were also damaged from the explosion, with casualties mounting to 45 known dead, 327 missing and 371 injured. Of the other ships dam-aged, most noted by *Lang*'s officers and crew was the CEBU, the repair ship *Lang* had been tied next to before her departure. She had been showered with numerous steel fragments, killing five of her crew and wounding another six. Had *Lang* been delayed in her departure by even a few minutes she, too, would have most likely received some type of damage and casualties. Certainly for Captain Bland it appeared that *Lang*'s good fortune was to continue, and for years to come he would refer to this moment as being "luck #1" of his command.

As *Lang* continued to move farther and farther away, the ominous cloud which continued to hang above Seeadler began to fade in the distance. Different ones of the crew could not help but think how quickly circumstances change; earlier the harbor had provided shelter and safety, now it yielded death and confusion. But, again, they had managed to escape tragedy and so on they sailed toward their next adventure.

No longer a part of an invasion force, *Lang*'s duty as a fighter-director ship was complete, and Lieutenants McPherson, Richardson, and Brooks had departed the ship on their first day at Manus. Now *Lang* was back at serving her old destroyer duty as a part of the screen for the larger ships. Once again her radar searched the ocean's sur-face and the sky above while her soundman listened for the enemy below, serving as a first line of defense for the battleships and cruisers. But, with the slight exception of her gunners taking in some target practice, she made the trip to Palau without inci-dent, arriving there on 13 November.

Palau was the advanced base area, which included the costly Peleliu, that Nimitz had so determined imperative to the security of the Philippine operation. Indeed, it was finding some use as a service area for ships in transit to and from Leyte, but it offered little else.

Lang's stay at the anchorage lasted less than 24 hours before she was again at sea. Continuing as part of the screen for the battleship task group, with the addition of cruiser *St. Louis*, the destroyer headed on to Leyte, and back to the deadly contest of defeating the Japanese.

The two day trip from Palau to Leyte proceeded quietly, but no sooner had the group arrived back in the gulf when they were greeted by an enemy welcoming committee. General quarters sounded and the crews scrambled to their respective stations, each reporting "manned and ready" upon the successful filling of each position. Immediately after, high flying enemy bombers made their appearance and anti-aircraft fire erupted in pronounced unison. The sky quickly began to fill with the black puffs of exploding projectiles, as gunners all around the area answered the challenge of the enemy. Certainly Leyte had not changed one bit since *Lang*'s last visit. It was almost as though she had never left; as though time here had stood still in wait of her return.

Later in the day things became much quieter, and many of *Lang*'s sailors manned the rails in wait of a very important cargo making its way to the ship. News from loved ones was always looked forward to, and this was the first mail they had received in over a month. Obviously the bundles of letters and packages were eagerly accepted. Then quietly the group dispersed, and each man began to delve into the treasures sent them from home.

Thoughts of home and family so often filled the minds of the men. Thousands of miles separated these sailors from their loved ones, and the war which caused that separation was far from ending soon. And though mail was often an initial morale lifter, its end results often produced just the opposite effect.

Like the swells that often rose and fell around them, so too did the spirits of the men. How much longer could this war last? How long would it be before their hopes and dreams of a peaceful future would be turned to reality? And for whom? Who would survive and who would forever remain separated from home by the deep waters of the Pacific? These were the questions most often brought to mind during these quiet times. Yet time in the Pacific was seldom to be quiet, and the closer their ship sailed to the shores of Japan, the busier the days became.

On the 17th, the battleship task group began a defensive patrol just outside the gulf. Throughout this day and the next the situation around the area changed little, each day filled with calls to general quarters as enemy planes continued to make challenges. And, even more disgusting was of how the enemy seemed to have gotten "down pat" the ship's chow schedules, time after time forcing sailors to leave behind freshly served hot meals in answer to the call to general quarters.

Then, on 19 November, the sky suddenly became much quieter. There remained a few enemy planes nosing around here and there, but it was nothing like the previous days. In fact, it was quiet enough that the natives again took opportunity to make their way out to the ships for another round of trading with the sailors. Soon several "bum boats" were again gathered at *Lang*'s stern, and bargaining was quickly put in play.

Obviously, in most cases the natives had little to offer, with handmade items and bananas being their most common products. But on this day some of the men were able to trade a couple of blankets for a dog, naming their newly acquired pet "Gum-drop." Yet, though lovable and loved, the new pup was never to fill the void left by lit-tle George. And sometime later Gumdrop was lost and left behind on one of the islands the crew was to visit.

The task group's defensive patrol was destined to continue throughout the rest of the month. Throughout this time air attacks also continued, but whereas previously Onishi's kamikazes had had only limited success, they were now on the verge of per-fecting their new deadly art. And this was to produce three quick occasions where *Lang* was again put in harm's way.

The first occasion came on 23 November, when once again the task group came under heavy air attack. All of the ships were firing. Suddenly, most of the gunners began focusing most of their attention on an incoming Judy (Yokosuka D4Y Navy carrier bomber). *Lang*'s gunners were also hammering away at the fast diving bomber, noting its descent was quickly bringing the plane their direction. Their fire intensified, desperate but without noticeable effect, yet the bomber diverted to fly at low altitude past the entire length of the ship. Meanwhile, the gunners aboard the cruiser *Columbia* had continued to trail the bomber's path unchecked. As a result their gunfire became more of hazard to *Lang* than did the bomber's threat. Five-inch shells began bursting over the destroyer's mast, sending shrapnel zinging down toward the decks below. Tiny bits of steel pinged off the helmets of several of *Lang*'s sailors, but luckily no one was hurt. Even the enemy plane made it through the storm of steel to make its escape. Later that day Third Class Radioman Francis Lihosit, whose G. Q. station was gunner at the forward port 20-millimeter machine gun, wrote in his diary of *Columbia*'s mis-guided marksmanship stating: "A close hit boiled the water 20 feet from my gun. That was too damn close."

Having survived this first near disastrous episode, *Lang*'s next frightful experi-ence came on the 27th. On the morning of this day the task group had rendezvoused with a Navy tanker and was paused to take on fuel. The scene was right out of the "Old West"; like the old wagon trains of the past, the ships had formed a defensive circle around the tanker. Each ship than took a turn at being refueled, depending on the others for protection during the vulnerable operation.

The sky was heavily overcast this morning, and initially there was no air activity — even the CAP had been kept grounded. The likelihood of an enemy air attack seemed remote, but just shortly after 11:00 A.M. the group was startled by a sudden loud pop. Then, from out of the dense clouds overhead came a portion of a plane flopping down toward the sea. Having quickly determined the incident that of a mid-air collision between two enemy planes, the group commander immediately sent out a warning of pending air attack across the tactical circuit. And all the ships responded with calls to general quarters.

Captain Bland responded in kind, and again *Lang*'s crew hurried to their stations. High above, the sky suddenly erupted with angry flights of enemy bombers. At least 12 enemy planes were counted as they seemed to approach from every conceivable direction. *Lang*'s gunners directed their weapons toward the many targets, pounding desperately, but it was near impossible to keep up with all their movements. And though the sky became thickened by a wall of flak, the enemy was not detoured.

Having joined the task group at Leyte on the 20th, the battleship *Colorado* (BB-45) was steaming at about 400 yards directly astern of *Lang*. High above the two ships a Val suddenly veered into a steep downward dive. An obvious kamikaze, both ships began to concentrate heavy fire in a desperate effort at stopping his attack. Round after round raced upward toward the enemy plane, but its determined pilot did not waver in his vicious descent. The bomber screamed as it continued downward, then it leveled off and slammed into the battleship's rear-end, sliding up its port side. Every gun mount along the plane's fiery path was wiped out, till finally only the plane's engine remained to bounce off the forecastle and over into the water. "The carnage was something terrible," wrote Lihosit.

The wounded battleship, now ablaze and sending forth a telltale trail of smoke, was unwillingly signaling its vulnerability. Seconds later a second kamikaze also came screaming headlong on the attack. This time, however, and thanks to some sharp shooting from the destroyer *Mustin* (DD-413), the effort was quickly stopped.

Meanwhile, the group commander had sent an urgent plea for CAP cover. But throughout this first attack no friendly planes arrived in aid of the battling warships, and the Japanese pilots had complete rule of the sky.

By 11:30 A.M. the first attack had ended, but a second attack by an additional ten enemy bombers immediately followed. High above *Lang* another Val broke over into a steep dive. So straight above the ship was the bomber's descent that many of the destroyer's guns could not elevate to the angle needed to fire. It appeared the enemy pilot had picked *Lang* for his target and it would mostly be up to the other nearby ships to prevent his success.

Off to *Lang*'s port was the cruiser *St. Louis*, and her gunners were putting up a horrendous fusillade against the attacking Val. Suddenly the enemy pilot diverted his aim and veered sharply toward the cruiser. With the plane's track angle changed, *Lang*'s gunners quickly joined the heated barrage. But no amount of firepower could stop the determined pilot's effort, and he slammed his craft into *St. Louis'* port quarter with a ripping explosion.

The hit pronounced with a loud bang, staggering the cruiser from the blow. Afterwards, smoke billowed upward, again notifying other attackers of the cruiser's vulnerability. Within the next 12 minutes three more enemy planes tried crashing *St. Louis*. The first two missed, but the last one struck the cruiser's port side very near where the first had hit.

Again the cruiser staggered from the blow, and again smoke billowed upward. The two strikes had caused considerable damage to the fantail, catapults, planes, and hanger space, and several men had been killed or wounded. A handful of the cruiser's sailors had been knocked overboard, and they were to ride out the rest of the action in a life raft. Yet *St. Louis* continued under power and was able to avoid all enemy efforts of a third attack, this time from Kate (Nakajima B5M, Navy Type 97 Carrier Attack Bomber) torpedo planes using conventional methods.

Maryland, too, had a serious encounter with one of the Kates, the torpedo-bomber gliding in low toward her to release a torpedo into the sea. The big battleship's anti-aircraft batteries pounded, and black puffs of exploding projectiles surrounded the enemy plane during its approach. Initially, however, the defensive fire had no effect. But just as the craft released its deadly cargo it was seen to stagger, having encountered a lethal dose of hot steel.

The Kate began to smoke heavily, and its altitude decreased quickly. The pilot struggled with the damaged plane, trying desperately to fly it on to crash into the battleship, but his effort fell well short its objective. Water spouted high into the air when the bomber struck the sea, and loud cheers went up from the observing crews. And, to further enhance the pilot's vain death, the torpedo he had launched also missed the mark, just going past *Maryland*'s bow.

Meanwhile, the cruiser *Montpelier* (CL-57) had also been very busy. Warding off three consecutive attacks, the cruiser's sharpshooting gunners managed to splash all three enemy attackers; one plane's momentum did carry it in for a close hit but caused no serious damage.

Two additional kamikazes targeted the vulnerable tanker, endeavoring to break through the thick wall of anti-aircraft fire thrown upward by the surrounding ships. Both pilots failed, and both splashed into the sea far short of success.

During one 15 minute period of the action at least 15 enemy planes were observed to fall from the sky. The action had been so intense it was near impossible to accurately account for the total number of enemy planes downed, but nearly all were downed by the ships. Indeed, friendly fighter cover did not finally arrive till very near the end of the action, when a handful of Army P-38 Lightnings dove into the fight to account for a couple of the last enemy planes to be flamed. And even the P-38s found the ships' flak a bit overwhelming, with one unlucky pilot mistakenly shot down by the battleship *New Mexico* (BB-40).

By noon the attacks were ended and suddenly all had returned to an eerie state of quiet. In the meantime, both *Colorado*'s and *St. Louis*' crews had successfully put out their respective fires and were managing to make emergency repairs. Despite the intensity and viciousness of the enemy's recent effort, no ship was to be lost this day.

For as long as the defensive patrols were destined to continue, however, the threat of further suicide attacks remained. So it was only a matter of time before the ships would again meet another challenge of the enemy.

Just two days later, on 29 November, the enemy did indeed decide to revisit the embattled task group. This time the cruisers and destroyers were circled about the battleship *Maryland* while on their patrol. It was near sundown and the sky was covered with low overhanging clouds. And, again the group was totally unaware of any air activity.

Suddenly, an enemy plane came bursting through the clouds in a near vertical dive, headed straight toward *Maryland*. There was obviously some initial surprise at the enemy's appearance. This time, however, the response time was almost immediate, as well over a hundred guns from the task group quickly began to hammer. Lihosit would later write, "I bet there was enough AA fired at him to buy two planes." Certainly every effort was made to knock the threatening enemy from the sky, as literally hundreds of rounds of high-explosives filled the air around him, but to no avail. Undaunted in his mission, the determined pilot guided his craft through the firestorm to strike the big battleship squarely on the port bow, just between gun mounts #1 and #2.

Lang's observing crew watched as fire and smoke engulfed the forward section of the battleship's outer deck. It initially looked to be very bad, but *Maryland*'s crew was determined not to allow the dead kamikaze pilot any additional victory. And soon the fires were out and the big dreadnought was continuing its patrol at speed.

In the meantime, a second suicider had suddenly appeared to streak toward the cruiser *Portland*. Again gunners responded quickly. This time aim was a little sharper, and a fortunate round found its target just in time, sending the enemy craft crashing into the sea a short distance aft of the cruiser's fantail. And again crews had reason to cheer the demise of "one more good Jap."

Throughout the rest of that day and night the sky returned to a peaceful state. The following morning began with the usual dawn alerts, but the enemy still made no appearances. Taking advantage of this lull, *Lang* spent most of the day going from ship to ship, attaching lines and making mail deliveries. While the crews of the other ships appreciated the gifts *Lang* brought their way, her own crew was somewhat edgy about the duty, fearing being caught off guard again by some deadly kamikaze. By day's end, however, the deliveries had all been made without incident. But for all of *Lang*'s effort, her own crew found not a single letter for themselves. Such was certainly a very disgusting end to the month of November.

December opened with the enemy again presenting a threat to the task group. But this time the threats came from below rather than above. Sudden submarine contacts were nearly simultaneously made by four different screening destroyers. In response, the rest of the ships immediately began evasive actions, making emergency turns to avoid any possible torpedo attacks. Meanwhile reports continued; one notifying a periscope sighting, and others warning of torpedo wakes being seen passing through the formation.

Aboard *Lang*, the crew clearly felt each concussion of the attacking destroyers' exploding depth-charges. For several minutes the episode continued, again causing considerable anxiety among the men. Then, it abruptly ended. If they had really existed, no submarines were sunk. Neither had any of the American ships received any damage.

Later that day *Lang* drew alongside the battleship *Maryland*. The destroyer's crew was finally to get a close-up look at the big ship's previously received kamikaze damage. Obviously, they expected to see considerable destruction, but its immensity was to the point of being shocking. The plane had completely penetrated through three decks, leaving nothing but a jagged and scorched hollow at its point of impact. The resulting explosion had twisted the ship's heavy steel into masses of confusion, triggered a blistering fire, and killed 31 of the ship's company. One could only imagine the death and destruction such a hit could cause aboard a ship the size of *Lang*. And certainly *Lang*'s crew had no desire for the experience.

Without a doubt the past week had been one of the most horrifying so far experienced by the destroyer and her crew. Onishi's kamikazes were affecting even those ships and crews they had yet to directly strike. Just the fear of the sneaky suiciders was alone taking a serious toll on morale. If Onishi had only known the true degree to which his kamikazes were having success, he would surely have increased his efforts. But, obviously kamikazes did not return to their bases (at least not with honor) and, though sent strictly for the purpose of detailing the successes of the operations, most observation planes failed to return as well, leaving the "Divine Wind" originator far short an accurate assessment of his campaign. Certainly the American Naval command understood clearly the severity of the threats, and by the morning 2 December had ordered all the battleships to depart the area. Lihosit wrote, "I guess things are too rough, and the boys don't want to lose a battleship." Yet the cruisers and destroyers were to continue the risky defensive patrols.

Indeed, no sooner had the battleships gone than attacks by the suiciders recommenced. General quarters sounded and the men again rushed to their stations prepared to face what they knew was to be a determined adversary. *Lang*'s gunners had barely reached their weapons when the enemy was sighted. Approaching low from out of the rising sun, a Kate torpedo bomber was heading straight for the destroyer. And, with near immediate response, the ship's batteries erupted in full fury, trying desperately to knock the intruder from the sky.

Black puffs from the exploding projectiles appeared to engulf the incoming plane but, almost unbelievably, it continued to move ever nearer through the storm of steel. It looked to *Lang*'s crew as though maybe their luck was about to run out. Many of the men felt the strong urge to run. But where was they to go? With a ship the size of their destroyer, no place could be considered safe. After all, they had seen what destruction a similar suicider had caused to a battleship. So they remained, unwilling characters in a performance to its end.

Meanwhile, the plane continued unabated with its run. The ship's guns continued to pound, but results remained negative. It appeared all hope for the ship was lost. But, surprisingly, the plane just kept on going, passing low overhead with its bright red "meatball" markings looking larger than life and its pilot clearly seen through his canopy.

Fortunately for *Lang*, the pilot had chosen for his target a cruiser on the destroyer's other side. For a brief moment a great sense of relief befell the crew, but their performance continued without pause. The guns of both ships continued to pursue the determined Kate. Despite such efforts, just as the plane cleared the destroyer it released its deadly cargo, and the torpedo splashed into the water to race straight for the larger ship.

Lang's observing crew expected the torpedo to rip into the cruiser at any moment, but nothing happened. Fortunately, the destroyer's position had caused the enemy pilot to wait till he was too close to his target before releasing his "fish." Therefore, it didn't have enough room to return to the correct depth needed to ensure a hit, and the torpedo merely passed beneath the lucky cruiser.

In the meantime, the enemy plane had been much less fortunate. Round after round of anti-aircraft fire chased after the plane, and finally one found its target. Black smoke belched from underneath the craft, and seconds later it arched into the sea with a great white splash of salty spray.

The following day was much quieter with respect to enemy air activity. Still, it was strangely different, and in many ways unsettling to the crew. The water around the destroyer had come to life, teaming with poisonous sea snakes and hungry sharks. Everywhere the crew looked there could be seen these creatures of death. The yard long green sea snakes lurked lazily upon the water's surface, while the sharks circled as in wait. It appeared the creatures were expecting a meal and, obviously, the crew could not help but wonder if maybe these snakes and sharks knew something that they themselves did not.

Despite such suspicious omens, nothing occurred which directly threatened the ship and crew. But the constant movement of the patrol and the anxiety it created had brought the crew nearly to a point of exhaustion. They desperately needed a rest, as did their ship. Indeed, *Lang* was also in need of making port, troubled with a damaged screw which had become inoperative. Finally, on the afternoon of 4 December, they would have their chance, as the destroyer was relieved of her patrol duty and released to return to Hollandia.

Joining the screen for several transports and landing ships, *Lang* made her way cautiously southeastward back toward New Guinea. Many threats persisted, yet the ship's transit proceeded without interruption. At Leyte, however, the dreaded suiciders were again striking their deadly vengeance. This time it was the screening destroyers they chose to target the brunt of their beating, as on the afternoon of the 5th *Drayton* (DD-366) and *Mugford* (DD-389) each sustained considerable damage and received several casualties from crashing kamikazes. *Lang*, it appeared, had once again just barely escaped serious trouble.

Truly the members of the crew were happy to be sailing away from the embattled Philippines. Despite several sound contacts along the route, the trip to Hollandia passed without any enemy interference, which was refreshing. And on the morning of the 9th, the entire group of ships safely made their entrance into Homboldt Bay.

Lang immediately tied up next to the destroyer tender *Dobbin* (AD-3) for her needed repairs. And for the next 16 days the ship and crew remained in port, given a substantial break from the ongoing Pacific conflict.

Throughout this time, however, many rumors were passed around pertaining to the ship's future role. Obviously, the crew hoped to hear something on the order of "home" or "States" included in their next set of orders. Yet, with the 22 December arrival of U.S. Army Sergeant Irving M. Wagen, boarding for temporary duty as Army Signal Corp Photographer from the office of Task Force 78, the likelihood of any travel farther east quickly disappeared. And, indeed, on Christmas morning *Lang* departed Humboldt Bay as escort for three LSDs and headed back toward Leyte.

On the following day this group made a brief stop at Biak before proceeding on for Sansapor. Then, having arrived at Sansapor on the 27th, *Lang* left two of the LSDs behind and continued as escort for the third on course for Morotai. Certainly it first appeared these stops were mere convenience duty along a route back to the volatile waters of the Philippines; but not so. Despite the crew's expectations, after arriving at Morotai that next morning, where the last LSD was safely delivered, *Lang* was ordered back to Sansapor.

Arriving back at the roadstead off Sansapor on the 29th, *Lang* anchored amidst considerable activity. Large numbers of transports and LSTs were now concentrated in the area, fully loaded with troops and preparing for departure. In the meantime, U.S. Naval Reserve Lieutenant (jg) Jack Tillotson, U.S. Naval Reserve Ensign Thad J. DeHart, and Australian Army 2nd Lieutenant Edward Segal each reported aboard the destroyer for temporary duty as fighter-director crew from COMAIRSUPCONTUNIT 7th Fleet. It was now certain; another big operation was about to happen and, as usual, *Lang* was to be right in the middle of it.

As had been their past experience, the crew expected the future to bear many restless hours. So, on this final night before again departing for hostile territory, they bedded down in the hopes of receiving some uninterrupted sleep. Such was not to be, however. Just shortly after midnight general quarters suddenly sent the men bounding from the comfort of the bunks and to their stations for battle. An enemy plane had been picked up on radar closing the ship, and sleepy eyed sailors strained to pick out the nighttime intruder as it quickly approached through the darkness.

The enemy bomber was first sighted while yet some distance away, but its speed closed the gap quickly. *Lang*'s forties were first to find the range, and their staccato rhythm began beating the air steadily. Lively lines of tracers arched out toward the darkened enemy, searching his path before losing velocity and wildly tumbling off in various directions. Still the plane continued its approach. The determined gunners also continued their blistering fire. The glowing tracers greatly aided their effort and, suddenly, they found their mark.

Off in the distance a burst of flame momentarily lit a portion of the darkness. A dull thud pronounced through the night air. Then, with a quick arch downward, the flame disappeared, squelched by a darkened sea. The gunnery ended. General quarters were secured. And *Lang*'s crew quietly returned to their bunks, all much too tired to celebrate their latest victory.

Response to general quarters no longer required thought, it was purely reactionary. With routine precision the crew manned their stations, bitterly and fearfully awaiting the enemy's arrival, hating him and his presence, and wanting to kill him in the hopes it would hasten the war to an end. Certainly the increased intensity of the Pacific war had hardened the crew to a new temperament. They cursed the conflict, and they cursed the enemy who prolonged it. The extreme suicidal tactics now utilized by the Japanese disclosed their own awareness that the war for them was lost, yet they stubbornly continued to drag out the whole affair. How could an enemy with such little consideration for life ever be defeated? Curse the Japanese! How many more lives would it take? Curse the Japanese again! And so *Lang* and crew fought on.

Later that morning the destroyer departed the roadstead and, guarding the transports and LSTs, once again headed back toward the volatile Philippines. Quartermaster Eldon Coward would write in his diary, "Looks like this is it!"; seeming somewhat doubtful and ominous. Indeed, how many more major operations could *Lang* bring them through safely? How much longer could her luck possibly hold? And thus 1944 came to an end.

Chapter 12

Lingayen Gulf

Overall, 1944 had been a good year for the Allies, but its ending was somewhat a mixed bag. Since the 6 June landings at Normandy the Allied armies had progressed fairly steadily, but on 16 December the Germans struck back, mounting a massive counter-offensive along an area some 25 miles at either side of the Belgium/Luxemburg border. This winter assault caught the Allies by complete surprise and sent their front lines reeling, creating a huge bulge that threatened to break but somehow held together. Allied losses were high and fighting continued into the new year, but the German advance was halted. On the Eastern Front the Russians were continuing a steady step by step capture of Germany's eastern satellite states, with Finland first and then Estonia, Latvia, Yugoslavia, Bulgaria, and Hungary in that order, though with heavy cost. In Italy, following their successful capture of Rome, the British and American armies were again stalled, blocked by a stout German line of defense which showed little signs of breaking at year's end. In the Pacific the progress against Japanese forces had been measurably good to great. American forces had steadily pushed their way across the Central and South Pacific, success-fully completing their return to the Philippines. By year's end MacArthur's forces had retaken Leyte, destroyed a greater part of what remained of the Imperial Japanese Navy, and retaken Mindoro (this island captured without loss of a single man). Also, on 24 November, American B-29s flying from their bases in the Marianas had deliv-ered their first daylight bombing of Tokyo, the first of its kind since Jimmy Doolit-tle's raid back in April of 1942. But the Japanese had in turn introduced Onishi's new Kamikaze Corp, and with deadly effect, somewhat deflating these earlier American victories. And in China, it was Japanese forces who still garnished the greater suc-cesses, forcing the American 14th Air Force to abandon several of its forward bases.

171

Indeed, the closing days of 1944 proved only to confirm that much more fighting lay ahead. This was destined to be especially true in the Pacific, where the intensity of the fight increased with each new step toward the shores of Japan. New Year's Day, 1945, gave little initial promise that the conflict might end soon. In fact, the Pacific Fleet was already sailing toward its next target, Lingayen Gulf and the invasion of Luzon, which was destined to be another lengthy, hard fought campaign.

This new target, Luzon, MacArthur had steadfastly argued was the next best step toward the eventual invasion of Japan proper. Northernmost and most important of the Philippine islands, the general was emphatic in his determination to retake this former American real estate and to avenge his initial loss of this property to the Japanese. The island held the Philippine capital, Manila, where he had been forced to abandon his headquarters and home, leaving behind many personal effects. There were the former American Naval base at Manila and nearby Clark air base which he had been forced to leave to the Japanese. There were also Bataan Peninsula and offshore Corregidor Island, where after MacArthur's secret escape his stranded garrison, left to the command of Lieutenant General Jonathan Wainwright, had made their final stands before surrender. Then had come the humiliating and brutal "Death March" that the Japanese captors forced upon the thousands of American and Filipino prisoners, whereupon a high percentage were murdered. And, finally, there were the many abuses the Japanese had brought upon the Philippine populous, the people who throughout it all determined to remain loyal to the United States and to MacArthur.

Certainly the general's passion for the campaign was without question. His case was indeed strong, both for the purposes of revenge and honor. But was its necessity strategically wise? At first the Joint Chiefs had their doubts about Luzon, initially preferring its bypass in favor of Formosa. But after further deliberation it was determined that Nimitz, who would be entrusted with the Formosa operation, did not have the troop strength readily available, as the required numbers simply did not exist. MacArthur's plan, on the other hand, allowed for easy transfer of troops already committed to the Philippines operation on Leyte. Therefore, the Joint Chiefs decided MacArthur would get his revenge, as his own troops were to be solely responsible for the Luzon conquest. In turn, this was to allow Nimitz the freedom to use his available manpower in the short term for the invasions of Iwo Jima in the Bonins and Okinawa in the Ryukyus. Thus the Pacific campaign, by not targeting Formosa, would be allowed to proceed without having to await the end of the European campaign for additional troop strength.

Meanwhile, on Luzon, General Yamashita's forces, numbering right at a quarter million men, had been busy in their own right making hasty preparations for defense. Manila, the general decided, was to be abandoned, and stronger more tenable positions would be prepared in the mountainous regions farther inland. Unfortunately for

172

Yamashita, time and equipment were both in short supply. And despite the general's best efforts, by 1 January the Japanese on Luzon had been able to transfer only a fraction of the equipment and supplies originally hoped for — by which time MacArthur's landing forces were already at sea.

Indeed, three task force sized attack groups were headed for Luzon. Task Force 77, under the command of Vice Admiral Thomas C. Kinkaid, made up the bombardment, fire support, demolitions, and carrier air support element. Task Force 78, under the command of Vice Admiral D. E. Barbey, made up the amphibious group responsible for landing two infantry divisions on the beachhead at San Fabian. And Task Force 79, under the command of Vice Admiral T. S. Wilkinson, made up the amphibious group responsible for landing another two infantry divisions on the beachhead at Lingayen.

Lang's departure from Sansapor was with Rear Admiral W. M. Fechteler's Task Group 78.5, which was half of the San Fabian Attack Group under the command of Vice Admiral Barbey, and marked one of the earliest departures for the coming 9 January invasion. Fechteler's main group consisted of transports, laden with the men of the 6th U.S. Infantry Division. These transports were steaming in four long columns, followed closely by six additional columns of LSTs, LSMs and LCIs, and screened by a group of destroyers and destroyer-escorts. All in all, some 60 ships made up the convoy.

For this group the first day of 1945 passed rather quietly. At dawn there were the usual alerts, long established as precaution to avoid any possible early morning air attacks. But no enemy planes appeared. Therefore, gunners were given opportunity to check out their guns and ammunition with live fire, knowing that, though this day may have begun peacefully, such peace was certain to soon end. Indeed, an estimated 400 enemy planes remained on Luzon, and several of these were set aside for use by Onishi's dreaded Kamikaze Corp. And it was only a matter of time before the enemy was to unleash this airborne menace upon the Lingayen invaders.

Still, for Fechteler's ships, the second day of the new year continued to produce no excitement. There were a couple of sound contacts made by the screen, but these proved to be non-submarine. Gunners were also given additional opportunity at target practice. Otherwise, the voyage remained unremarkable.

Early on the morning of the third day Fechteler's group arrived near the Palaus, and there joined the other half of Barbey's task force, this group carrying the 43rd U.S. Infantry Division. Also joining in the company of ships were two escort carriers of the Carrier Task Group 77.4, which provided a most welcomed umbrella of fighter protection, and the fleet oiler *Tallulah* (AO-50), which was to begin refueling operations for the screening destroyers.

Obviously, fueling operations at sea were always a hazard. But, as *Lang*'s crew had so directly learned during their recent encounters at Leyte, these dangers were greatly increased since the introduction of the kamikaze. Understandably, sailors were fearful of being caught during the most vulnerable moments of such an operation, unable to use their ship's speed and mobility as a part of their defense. And immobility in a combat situation usually led to death and disaster for a ship, especially when confronting a determined suicide pilot.

As feared, no sooner had this fueling operation begun than enemy planes were indeed reported on the approach. As quickly as possible the screening ships maneuvered into their anti-aircraft positions, and their gunners prepared to fight. Minutes passed by and sailors nervously awaited the enemy attack. It did not happen, however. The escort carriers' pilots had met the attackers, and none were allowed through to threaten Barbey's shipping. And the rest of the day proceeded without further incident.

On the morning of the 4th the task force arrived at Leyte Gulf on schedule, changed course, and headed south to pass through Surigao Strait. In a strangeness quite unbefitting the waters around Leyte, Barbey's ships proceeded unmolested. Obviously, this non action, though welcomed, provoked much uneasiness among the sailors and their guest soldiers, as they could not help but question the enemy's motives.

That night the passage continued, still unmolested, and at 7:14 A.M. Barbey's ships proceeded past Bohol Island. Throughout the morning and early afternoon nothing interfered with their progress. But at 4:24 P.M. a torpedo wake was reported being sighted coming from the starboard side of the formation. And ten minutes later *Lang* picked up a sound contact on her sonar.

Excitement quickly generated throughout the destroyer as Captain Bland ordered general quarters and directed his ship in preparation to fire a full pattern of depth-charges. Meanwhile, Second Class Soundman Bill Walden exclaimed to the captain, "It's a good one," feeling confident the contact was an enemy sub. Seconds later the Y-guns sent the first set of deadly canisters arching through the air and into the water nearby. Afterwards, from deep below the water's surface came the familiar dull thuds and intense vibrations of the canisters' successful detonations. Seven more followed. Then, all was quiet.

Walden again listened to his phones, carefully focusing his attention on any sound coming from below. There was none. He had felt so positive about the initial contact, but was now unsure. There was no doubt that something had been there, but it was obvious now it had not been an enemy submarine. As all too often had happened to other soundmen, Walden's sonar had been fooled, this time by a large school of fish.

At 12:25 A.M., 6 January, the task force proceeded to change course and head north toward the South China Sea. Throughout the morning hours several reports were received of enemy planes being in the area but, other than witnessing some anti-aircraft fire off in the distance, none came near *Lang*'s position.

Onishi's kamikazes, however, were on the prowl. Though Barbey's transport group had so far been spared, the same had not been so for Kinkaid's bombardment group. On the 4th, escort carrier *Ommaney Bay* (CVE-79) had been sunk with heavy casualties. On the 5th, nine additional ships were hit with varying degrees of damage. And on the afternoon of the 6th, sixteen more ships were hit, including destroyer minesweeper *Long* (DMS-12), which sank.

Despite these deadly attacks, on the morning of the 7th Barbey's group continued unmolested. His screening destroyers were again successfully refueled. And, though a few enemy planes were airborne and reported nearby, his gunners were given no reason to break the morning's silence.

That evening, at 7:17 P.M., Captain Bland received orders redirecting *Lang* to a picket station just outside nearby Manila Bay. Joining her was the destroyer *Mustin*, and both ships arrived at the patrol area at around 9:45.

By this date nearly all Japanese naval vessels had been evacuated from the bay in anticipation of the American arrival. Yet a few stragglers remained. And one such vessel, the light Matsu Class destroyer *Hinoki*, chose this night to make her escape.

As it so happened, shortly after *Lang* and *Mustin* began their joint patrol, a surface contact was picked up bearing 33 degrees true and at a distance of 17 miles. Then it was momentarily lost. Continuing to search, however, at 10:13 the contact was regained, this time displaying "two clear pips" on the radar scope, bearing 30 degrees true, at a distance of fifteen miles and closing at a speed of 19 knots.

Captain Bland immediately sent a report of the contact to Fechteler. In the meantime, Commander W. T. McGarry, Commander of DesDiv 4 aboard *Lang*, ordered both destroyers to assume an attack formation, *Mustin* to form up 2,000 yards astern of *Lang*.

At 10:25 Captain Bland ordered his crew to general quarters in preparation of a surface engagement. The bells rang out and *Lang*'s sailors responded with their usual quickness, manning their weapons and emergency stations with expectations of immediate combat. Somewhere in the distant darkness, and closing fast, were two enemy surface warships — or so they thought. And it initially appeared that *Lang* and *Mustin* were to face the threat alone.

Unknown to most of the crew, four additional destroyers, *Charles Ausburne* (DD-570), *Shaw* (DD-373), *Russell* (DD-414), and *Braine* (DD-630), dispatched from their screening stations with Task Group 78.1, were quickly approaching from the north. *Lang*'s gunners were expecting an even match-up, but were soon to be given a welcomed surprise. Still, several anxious moments were to pass beforehand.

As *Lang*'s radar continued to track the enemy target(s), its approach quickly closed to within 21,000 yards. Gun crews expected the order to fire at any moment. Then, at

10:30, there was a sudden distant blast and the night sky immediately erupted with light. The other four destroyers had arrived, having picked up the target(s), and had fired an initial volley of starshells for illumination of the target area. Two minutes later they began firing for effect.

Certainly *Lang*'s crew were relieved to see the additional help, though they remained very observant to the situation. Meanwhile, the distant blasts of gunfire began closing in on the target(s). In response, the enemy ship(s) began a feeble though highly inaccurate attempt at return fire. All the while, it continued to close *Lang* and *Mustin*; obviously unaware of their presence.

By 10:46 the enemy ship(s) had closed within 15,800 yards of *Lang* and *Mustin*. Shells from the pursuing four destroyers continued their chase. Then, at 10:53, a sudden small fire was observed a distance off *Lang*'s starboard bow, followed closely by a large explosion. One minute later a second explosion was seen to erupt a short distance from the first. And five minutes after that the radar cleared of the enemy shipping.

Initially, the enemy contact had been reported as "two pips." McGarry would later state: "It is believed there were two targets but this may be in error." Though some uncertainty remains, historical records seem to concur that only one vessel, *Hinoki*, was sunk on this date outside Manila. And visually, the enemy ship had at first been identified as a Hatsuharu class destroyer. This too was in error. Though similar in silhouette to the Hatsuharu class, *Hinoki* was a late war production ship, smaller and slower, yet very capable — and very much missing from the Imperial Fleet's roll call after this date.

With this latest bit of excitement suddenly ended, general quarters was secured, and crews slowly returned to their previous duties. Certainly the nighttime action had produced "quite a show" for the sailors aboard *Lang* and *Mustin*. And they applauded the grand performance of their fellow destroyermen, and cheered the end of a career for another of the Imperial Fleet.

Both *Lang* and *Mustin* were to remain at the picket for the duration of the night. No further action interrupted their patrol, however. And on the following morning they rejoined the rest of Fechteler's ships in their continuing journey northward.

By 7:58 A.M. *Lang* had been returned to the task force screen by about a half hour. The morning sky was both clear and quiet. Again there were no warnings of impending air attack. But considering the suddenness with which the kamikaze could strike, Captain Bland had already given Lieutenant (jg) W. H. Conaway, *Lang*'s Gunnery Officer, standing permission to fire at will upon any attacking planes. This being the case, the next thing Bland knew, his ship's five-inch batteries were pounding rapidly, jarring the destroyer with each multiple eruption.

Captain Bland quickly turned his attention to the direction of the firing, and immediately he spotted a plane diving vertically out of the clear blue sky toward the lead group of transports. Black puffs of *Lang*'s exploding projectiles were surrounding the plane's track, yet its plunge continued. Conaway, however, was determined. He directed the fire lower and lower, relentless in his chase of the target, even to the point, as it appeared to Bland, of placing other ships in the convoy at risk. Despite such effort, the maze of steel thrown upward did little to prevent the enemy pilot from hitting his target. And the attack transport *Callaway* (APA-35) was staggered by the plane's violent blow.

The suicider struck the transport hard on the starboard wing of her bridge. Its impact was profound, and immediately followed by the eruption of a violent fire. The resulting explosion killed 29 of the ship's crew, and wounded another 22. Fortunately, however, none of the 1,188 soldiers aboard were even slightly injured. And, despite the enemy pilot's determined effort, all fires aboard the ship were quickly extinguished, allowing *Callaway* to continue in fulfillment of her duty.

Meanwhile, Captain Bland stood nervously upon *Lang*'s bridge, fearing Conaway's dangerously low fire was certain to bring a reprimand from the task group commander, Admiral Fechteler, who was on *Fremont* (APA-44). Sure enough, the tactical circuit was soon cracking with the voice of one very angry commodore. To Captain Bland's surprise, however, the admiral's hostility was directed not at *Lang* but rather at the other destroyers of the screen. With a severe tongue lashing, he complained that of all the ships in the surrounding screen that only one had fired on the enemy — he then, in turn, commended *Lang* for her effort. Obviously, Bland was as relieved as he was proud. And Conaway, who undoubtedly had just barely escaped his own butt chewing, came out appearing every bit the hero.

Off and on throughout the rest of the morning several more enemy planes were reported in the area. Of these, most were either shot down or chased away by the CAP. Still, tension among the crews eased very little. And, due in part to the *Callaway* episode, Fechteler had decided that all ships of the task group should remain at general quarters throughout the rest of the day.

Though air attacks did continue against the invasion forces, Fechteler's group had no further close encounters with kamikazes this day. And by 1:50 A.M., 9 January, designated "S-Day" (invasion day Luzon), his ships finally arrived at "Point Fin" in preparation for entering Lingayen Gulf.

From here the group cautiously began making their way toward the gulf's entrance. Throughout this approach, however, reports quickly circulated of mines being sighted at various locations. Obviously, such news raised considerable concern among the task group commanders. On *Lang*, Captain Bland wisely posted mine watches on the forecastle as a precaution. But no mines were spotted. And, though the threat did somewhat slow the advance, all the ships were successfully entered into Lingayen Gulf by 3:40 A.M. without incident.

At this point *Lang*'s duty as screen ended. She was now to proceed forward as a part of the bombardment group for the San Fabian landings. For this purpose Captain Bland had already briefed his crew, explaining *Lang*'s mission was to fire 500 rounds of five-inch high explosives into a pre-designated 400 square yard area ashore. Afterwards, she was to stand by for further instructions, awaiting any additional needs for fire support.

At 6:30 *Lang* was still proceeding with a slow approach to her pre-assigned station when anti-aircraft fire was suddenly observed to erupt nearby. Captain Bland immediately ordered his crew to general quarters. Some anxious moments followed, but no direct threats came the destroyer's way. And by 7:25 *Lang* had safely arrived within the fire support area.

Meanwhile, the heavy ships had already begun their bombardment of the targets ashore. Their huge shells were roaring over *Lang* as she proceeded to her assigned station, where she finally reached at 8:40. And by 9:00 the destroyer had joined the bombardment effort, her own salvos adding to the already considerable amount of destruction ashore.

Lang's five-inch batteries fired in solid unison, sending salvo after salvo sizzling through the air toward their target ashore. The destroyer shook with each violent recoil of her guns, and her sailors stuffed cotton in their ears to protect their hearing from their deafening blasts.

From his special ship borne vantage Sergeant Wagen had already begun capturing the historical moment on film. He panned his camera from its focus on *Lang*'s firing batteries to the distant explosions ashore and then back out to catch the fast approach of the many amphibs as they roared toward shore. Multitudes of LSTs, LCIs, LCTs, LCMs, LCVPs, and LVTs filled his lense as they carried their valuable cargoes of men and equipment for delivery to the targeted beach, while some leading LCTs fired multiple waves of screaming rockets to add to the intensity of the moment.

Ashore, the beach area shattered from the concussion of hundreds of high explosive shells. Entire groups of trees and foliage were blown away. Buildings within the bombardment area disintegrated. And smoke and bits of debris gathered in the air above.

As the barrage of explosives slowly crept farther inland, landing craft began hitting the beach. Masses of troops began racing ashore as enemy mortar and artillery rounds sporadically fell along the water's edge. Yet, despite this bit of resistance, casualties were to remain light.

Back aboard *Lang* the five-inch batteries continued to pound. Then, at 9:21, with the guns having fired non-stop to this point, gun #1's gas ejection system suddenly failed. Noxious gas quickly filled the powder room and gun shield, and sailors manning these areas were just as quickly found gasping for air. Second Class Gunner's Mate William Roshko struggled to open the gun's outside hatch and fell to the deck unconscious. Other men were quick to Roshko's aid, and soon had the other crew members out in the fresh air, all the while keeping the gun firing toward shore.

Nineteen minutes later the naval gunnery ended, and *Lang*'s batteries fell silent. The shore bombardment had lasted a period of 40 minutes, during which the destroyer's guns had expanded 435 rounds of high explosive ammunition. The episode with gun #1 had caused the ship to fall short its intended numbers, but there was no doubt the crew had put forth their maximum effort.

Afterwards, *Lang* was to remain at her fire support station just offshore. For a short while her guns were rested, their paint blistered barrels cooled by a hosing of salt water spray. But this was a rest destined to be very short lived, as calls for her helpful gunnery were received off and on throughout the rest of the day.

That afternoon *Lang*'s guns fired on several enemy gun emplacements ashore, successfully knocking out four in the process. But one of these got more than expected as confusion created a most unusual moment.

It was at 6:47 P.M. that Bland received orders from the OTC (Officer in Tactical Command) to prepare and await instructions for a fire support mission. An enemy gun had been sighted being rolled in and out of a hillside cave, and *Lang* was given the job to remove it from play.

Within three minutes *Lang*'s gunners had received the coordinates, computed the range, and begun a slow fire under local control. Slowly and surely, round after round pounded the area around the targeted cave. All was routine. Then at 6:57 two enemy planes suddenly appeared to swoop from the hills inland toward the ships standing just off the beach, and all action immediately intensified.

Again Lieutenant Conaway took over, quickly ordering all four main batteries to switch over to automatic and rapid fire. Apparently, however, Second Class Boatswain's Mate W. E. Allen, the gun captain for gun #2, didn't hear the order. Conaway's director easily took control of the other guns, bringing their fire starboard to bear on the attacking planes; but Allen's gun remained turned to port, and continued to target the enemy held cave.

Conaway's rapid fire jarred the ship heavily. Allen, who was still very much unaware of the circumstances, felt the other guns firing rapidly and so he too began firing his gun just as fast as his crew could load its chamber. Conaway's guns trailed after the enemy planes, while Allen's continued to slam round after round into the hillside, both relentless in their efforts.

By 7:00 the planes had escaped the range of Conaways guns, and the gunnery officer immediately gave the order to cease firing. For just a couple of seconds there was silence. Then, the ship's P. A. cracked, and Conaway's voice stabbed the air. "We didn't do too good, Allen. How did you do?" the Lieutenant quipped. Only then did the boatswain realize his error. Obviously, he was somewhat embarrassed. But at least that enemy gun was to menace no one again, and the rest of the crew was awarded a rare bit of wartime humor.

Lang remained off San Fabian throughout the rest of the night, providing harassing fire on enemy positions for most of the darkened hours. Sporadic action continued to take place all around, but it amounted to no serious consequence.

In the meantime, at 4:40 A.M., *Lang* received a report of enemy gunboat attacks on ships of Task Force 79. Captain Bland immediately cautioned his watches to "be alert." Yet no threats came the destroyer's way.

About an hour and a half later another report was received of enemy planes on the approach. This time Bland did not hesitate; being close to shore and without ample room for maneuvering, he ordered his weary crew to general quarters. And once again the destroyer's guns were fully manned and readied for action.

At 6:30, anti-aircraft fire was observed some distance in the west. By this time several ships were already making smoke, hoping the chemically made clouds would hide the vulnerable transports from any enemy planes penetrating the defensive fire. Meanwhile, *Lang*'s crew remained at their stations and waited. And it was this waiting they hated most. If they were to fight, they would just as soon get to it — win or loose. Indeed, when at 7:40 the "all clear" was given and general quarters canceled without a shot being fired, most became angry rather than relieved.

That early afternoon *Lang* maneuvered over to a station just off White Beach #1 (the northernmost landing area at San Fabian), and there prepared to give fire support for the troops ashore. Coordinates were received from the fire control party ashore, and the destroyer's guns responded delivering a slow deliberate fire toward the intended targets. For three hours *Lang* directed her accurate gunnery at enemy gun emplacements and troop concentrations as directed from shore, expanding a total of 106 high explosive five-inch rounds in the process.

That evening *Lang*'s duty in the fire support area ended, and at 6:52 she took up a new assignment. Again, the destroyer returned to screening for the larger ships. This time she was to escort two transports back to Leyte.

As was to be Captain Bland's preferred defensive strategy, *Lang*'s guns were fully manned whenever enemy planes were nearby, regardless of their immediate threat. This strategy, though not particularly wrong, seemed to take away from his crew's mental sharpness. His sailors were tired, and this inactive wait inevitably stole away their adrenaline for action. In the past, when general quarters sounded, they knew enemy planes were there; now it signaled only a wait for their possible appearance.

For this reason it seemed, just 12 minutes after beginning the destroyer's newest assignment, *Lang*'s somewhat complacent gunners were suddenly startled by the unexpected fast approach of two unidentified planes. The first was quickly recognized as a Japanese medium bomber but the second momentarily remained a mystery. And by the time the destroyer's guns were to react, both planes had already passed over her starboard bow.

Fortunately, the enemy bomber was too preoccupied to care about *Lang*'s lack of response. The second plane proved to be an Army P-61 "Black Widow" night-fighter, in a rare daylight appearance (in fact, *Lang*'s gunners, after assuming their role, were so unfamiliar with its silhouette as to mistakenly target the American fighter with several rounds before being corrected). Therefore, the Japanese bomber was much more interested in making an escape, jettisoning its bomb load harmlessly into the sea and speeding away from the area as fast as possible in search of safety. And while *Lang*'s gunners did finally get off a few well directed rounds, none seemed to have affect, and both planes continued their courses to conclude their duel somewhere far out of sight.

Just 14 minutes later, heavy anti-aircraft fire was observed coming from the starboard side of the formation. From *Lang*'s position, observers watched as lively lines of tracer rounds chased one another upward, rising through a darkening sky to meet the challenge of another enemy plane. Yet despite the intensity of the barrage, this pilot was undeterred, and with a rapid descent he slammed his craft into the port side of the attack transport *Dupage* (APA-41).

Black smoke immediately belched upward from the transport's wound, and fires created by the hit were destined to burn throughout the night. Ultimately, 35 men of *Dupage*'s crew died from the deadly blast, while another 136 men received varying degrees of injuries. By daylight, however, the stubborn transport was found to have survived, her remaining crew having successfully extinguished all her fires while managing to keep the ship under power.

Not too surprising, this event proved to be an all too sobering reminder to *Lang*'s crew of just how fortunate their own ship had been. Had the previous bomber decided to attack *Lang* in the same fashion, the destroyer's slow response would've most likely guaranteed a death and destruction of an equal or greater degree to that of *Dupage*. Despite their weariness, it was imperative that the crew exercise much more caution in the future, or else be dead. For it was certain this was not a war with a habit of allowing such lethargy go unpunished.

At 1:30 A.M., 11 January, Captain Bland received orders redirecting his ship to join the destroyer-minesweeper *Southard* in escorting another group of transports. This group, made up of transports *Harry Lee* (APA-l0), *Lamar* (APA-47), and *Alpine* (APA-92), was headed back to Lingayen Gulf. And *Lang* and *Southard* had charge of ensuring their safe and timely arrival, which they did without incident.

By noon, however, *Lang* was again on the move and headed back for Leyte. This time, in company of the destroyer *Charles J. Badger* (DD-657), she was to proceed out into the China Sea to join in escort of the escort-carrier *Kitkun Bay* (CVE-71) (*Kitkun Bay* had three days earlier been severely damaged by a kamikaze and was now headed back to Leyte for emergency repairs).

This trip to Leyte was nearly unremarkable. There were a couple of surface contacts — one initially thought to be three Japanese ships but proved to be "friendlies," and another which turned out to be nothing but a pile of brush. There were also a few air contacts, but none of these closed the ships. Therefore, the voyage proved rather peaceful, and provided a most welcome break in the action for the crew.

By the morning of the 15th all three ships were safely returned to Leyte. There *Lang* gathered supplies and ammunition and refueled in preparation of her next departure. There, too, Lieutenant Tillotson of the fighter-director crew was transferred to shore, as was Sergeant Wagen with his historical film footage of the Lingayen invasion. This done, the destroyer was by the following morning again sailing back to Lingayen Gulf.

As with the previous voyage, nothing interfered with the destroyer's travels. And after five days of uninterrupted sailing, *Lang* safely returned to the gulf entrance where she immediately joined in a routine security patrol.

This patrol's first evening was quiet, but on the following morning, at 8:20, a sound contact again sent the crew to general quarters. Bearing 40 degrees true, at a distance of 1,500 yards, the contact appeared certain a submarine. But just as Captain Bland began maneuvering the destroyer to investigate, the contact was lost. Continuing to search, at 8:30 the contact was regained, this time bearing 145 degrees true, at a distance of 1,000 yards. The target appeared definite, so Bland ordered the firing of a full pattern of depth-charges, and away went the first of nine canisters. When the explosions ended, there was a pause. Again, the soundman checked his instruments. Nothing. The search continued and at 8:55 the contact was once again located, this time bearing 180 degrees true, at a distance of 1,500 yards. Five minutes later it again disappeared. Observers, searching the sea's surface for any debris, soon located a small oil slick and a scattering of surfacing bubbles of air. Yet, after more careful examination, it was determined the contact was not a sub after all but rather a previously sunk ship. Thus the hunt ended.

Lang remained on patrol the rest of the day, and without any additional interruption. That night, however, an unidentified plane was suddenly spotted by the ship's radar as it closed from a distance of just three miles. General quarters was immediately sounded and the men rushed and stumbled about the darkened ship in the effort to reach their stations. In the meantime, Captain Bland had the ship's speed slowed in order to reduce the visible wake. He then ordered his gunners to hold their fire. If the plane, which was determined to be enemy, had no radar, perhaps it would fail to locate the destroyer on the darkened sea.

At their battle stations, the sailors impatiently waited. Their eyes strained, coolly piercing into a pitch black in the effort to locate the plane in its approach. The drone of the plane's engine was quickly audible. But it was a moment longer before its form was spotted. When it finally was seen, gunners immediately reacted by swinging their guns to point to its location, targeting the craft by the blue flame exhaust it emitted. But the guns, themselves, remained mute.

Despite the distance between the ship and plane quickly decreasing, Captain Bland doggedly continued his refusal to fire upon the craft. His gunners continued their tracking, but all remained silent. The plane, itself, continued its steady flight till finally it was directly above the destroyer's deck. Still, nothing happened. Low and black, the sinister silhouette flew on without the slightest hint of aggressiveness. Obviously, Bland had done well in evaluating the situation and in meeting its challenge. Whether the plane had been a kamikaze no longer mattered. What did matter was that the ship and crew had successfully evaded the threat. And some enemy pilot was never the wiser.

Lang was destined to remain on patrol outside Lingayen Gulf through to 27 January. For the most part, this duty passed by rather quietly. And so at this date her duty at Lingayen was officially ended and the fighter-director crew, Ensign DeHart and Lieutenant Segal, were transferred to the destroyer *Dashiell* (DD-659) before *Lang* departed for her next duty.

On Luzon the fighting continued. American forces were quickly approaching the capital city of Manila, where would be fought the bloodiest urban warfare of the Pacific war. General Yamashita had ordered the city vacated by his troops but a separate 16,000 man Naval attachment under the command of Rear Admiral Sanji Iwabachi ignored the order, pledging to defend the city to their death. The battle was to last right at a month, during which the Japanese murdered thousands of innocent civilians. American casualties became staggering. And MacArthur, who had pledged never to bomb the city, finally relented to a massive artillery barrage to speed the fighting to an end. As promised, nearly every Japanese defender gave his life, and the once beautiful city was left in ruins. Elsewhere, the fighting continued, with Luzon not declared secure till 30 June, and even then many Japanese defenders remained. (Yamashita and a 50,000+ man force would dormantly hole up in the mountains till war's end, finally surrendering on 15 August).

Lang sailed for Leyte, where she safely arrived on the night of the 30th. Leyte was much quieter now. It didn't even seem like the same place. In fact, the three day layover even allowed *Lang*'s war weary crew some valuable rest, though it was far short enough. It also allowed for a welcomed improvement in the ship's chow situation. For the past month nearly all meals had been reduced to dehydrated food as nearly all the fresh provisions had been used up. During this short stay at Leyte, however, Lieutenant Kenneth Law, *Lang*'s paymaster, successfully "bummed" a good supply of fresh beef from some nearby transports. And immediately afterward the ship's cooks gained new respect from among the crew.

Another treasure waiting for the crew at Leyte was mail. Hoping many long overdue bundles were ashore in wait of the ship's arrival, Captain Bland sent a 20 man working party to Tacloban to search it out. There, to their awe, the men found about an acre of mail stacked as high as 20 to 40 feet. Finding anything destined for *Lang* looked hopeless, but they began to search through the mess anyway. And, as luck would have it, they somehow successfully gathered up 15 to 20 bags of *Lang*'s mail to be hauled back to the rest of the destroyer's crew, receiving a hero's welcome for their effort.

This stay ended on 2 February. Before departing, however, the crew did receive one more opportunity to trade with the natives. It was during this bartering session that a couple of *Lang*'s sailors were able to trade for some fighting roosters. Obviously, this acquisition was to bring some most interesting moments aboard. Soon bets were being made and the fights were begun. Cheers were soon echoing across the ship, and for a moment thoughts of the war were overshadowed by fun and games. But it was not to last, as the new sport quickly wore old, and the crew decided a much better use could be given their birds — pan fried seemed most popular.

That afternoon *Lang* was back out to sea. Setting a course eastward, she was again screening a group of transports, this time destined to return to the Solomon Islands.

The news of their destination was certain to rekindle old stories of *Lang*'s many experiences about the Solomon's chain. Younger sailors were to listen intently as the old timers again recounted their tales of Guadalcanal, New Georgia, and Vella Gulf. Most were true, but always there were some embellishments added. It almost seemed unbelievable, all their ship had survived. And now fate was to return them not only to the place where *Lang* initiated her Pacific wartime career, but also to her old base of operations, Tulagi, and reunite them once again with her old division, destroyers *Sterett*, *Stack*, and *Wilson*. Certainly the crew was hoping this gathering was to serve only as a moment of appreciation for all they and their sister ships had accomplished before given their ticket to return home. Instead, it would be registered as just one more short pause before heading back into the heat of battle and to a war that refused to end.

Chapter 13

Okinawa: Part 1

Though the war still raged in both Europe and Asia, by the month of February its finale was close to conclusion. The German's desperate December attempt at breaking the Allied offensive line in Belgium had failed, and their battered remnants were now in a hasty retreat for safety, allowing the Allied armies steady progress to the edge of the Rhine. On the Eastern Front, the Russians had at one point of their advance reached to within 33 miles of Berlin before being halted; whereby future progress was assured. Only in Italy were the Germans consistent at holding off the Allied offensive effort. In China, Allied forces had successfully reopened the Burma Road. While in the Philippines MacArthur's troops were steadily retaking Luzon back from the Japanese, in the process liberating Manila and some 5,000 American and Filipino prisoners. On the 16th, Marc Mitscher's Task Force 58 was to successfully make their first carrier borne airstrike against Tokyo, sending 1,200 planes in a full-scale offensive that would destroy shipping, factories and a large number of Japanese aircraft. And just three days later American forces under Vice Admiral Richmond "Kelly" Turner were to begin their bloody assault against the Japanese island fortress of Iwo Jima, breaking the last line of perimeter defense between themselves and the Imperial homeland.

For *Lang*, however, February was to be a rather quiet month, bringing about a most welcomed break in the action. Following a peaceful transit from Leyte, she was safely returned to the Solomons, arriving on the 11th, and anchored at Purvis Bay, Tulagi. And for the first time in long while the destroyer and crew were allowed some valuable rest.

Purvis had changed very little over the past year and a half, provoking many thoughts on *Lang*'s special ties to this important Solomons anchorage. It was here the destroyer had solidly established her name in the pages of history. Truly, much had happened since those days. The war had given cause for thousands of additional miles to be recorded in the ship's log. Many more engagements were found listed in her action reports. And turnovers in the ship's company had seen many men and many leaders come and go from her roster. But there remained enough of the old timers aboard to ensure that every member of *Lang*'s crew knew well of her exploits in the campaign to win these islands. For those veterans of that campaign the story was an endless epic of pride which they never tired of repeating.

Adding even further to the crew's renewed interest in the past fought Solomons campaign, was the fact that *Lang* was again reunited with all three destroyers that had made up the rest of Simpson's old division, now reincarnated into Destroyer Division 4, under the command of Commander W. T. McGarry. Surely this reunion could only be indicative of a good omen for the future — or so the crew thought.

Lang, *Stack*, *Sterett*, and *Wilson* had indeed all been very fortunate, they had so far survived the viciousness of the Pacific campaign (*Stack* had had a near fatal collision with the carrier *Wasp* prior to entering the Pacific war, putting her out of action for nearly two months, and *Sterett* had taken a terrible pounding during the 13 February 1942 battle at Guadalcanal, taking her out of action for over two months. *Lang* and *Wilson* had, however, so far survived without major damage). They had all fought well, having often done duty together, and always having exemplified their class in their wartime efforts. They were a proven team. But this was the first time since the Marianas campaign that all four ships would again serve together as a complete division. Thus it appeared obvious that, despite the many newer and bigger destroyers now in service, these four were destined to remain in the forefront of the action. Very soon they would indeed again face the enemy's challenge, and it was to prove a most fearful event, even to the likes of these four tough veterans.

Momentarily, while in need of some minor repairs, *Lang*'s first order of business at Purvis was a rendezvous with the repair ship *Vulcan* (AR-5). The work proved rather routine, but it did allow another opportunity for Lieutenant Law to work his procurement magic. He soon had "bummed" from the repair ship's stores a supply of fresh eggs for the service of *Lang*'s cooks, who in turn provided a fine early morning breakfast for the destroyer's officers and crew.

Later that day Law also made his way over to a New Zealand reefer ship, where he was able to acquisition some mutton. In acquiring this mutton, however, he also had to agree to take a supply of cabbage. No problem, he merely had the mutton stored in *Lang*'s meat locker, while the cabbage, which caused diarrhea, he had passed from one side of the ship to the other and dumped overboard.

Thereafter, *Lang* remained in port eight days, providing a nice period of rest for her crew. But on the 19th, Captain Bland was again directing his command back to sea, where they were to participate in a planned series of battle exercises. The next two days of gunnery and torpedo practice were to be another strong indicator to the crew that a return to the States was not likely to be a part of their ship's immediate future.

To further substantiate their expectations, once returned to Purvis the crew was quickly put to work repainting the ship. Whereas, the destroyer was soon taking on a whole new appearance. For instead of her most recent camouflage colors, her hull below the sheer was painted navy blue, everything vertical above the sheer was painted haze grey, and all decks were painted deck blue. That another major campaign was in the works seemed most obvious at this point.

By the 25th, *Lang* was indeed headed for a new mission, though it was far from a major campaign. Orders had been received directing her to search for a suspected midget submarine reported to have been seen lurking just off Guadalcanal. For the next two days the destroyer patrolled the area in search of the miniature menace, but no contacts were made and she returned to Purvis without incident.

The following morning *Lang* again hoisted her anchor and departed the confines of Purvis, this time taking the van of Destroyer Division 4 while en route to the Russell Islands. The journey was like stepping back in time; reminiscent of those days back in August 1943, when *Lang*, *Stack*, *Sterett*, and *Wilson* had served their nation so well in these very same waters. And they sailed just as proudly now as then.

That night the four destroyers arrived at their intended destination. They anchored and remained till morning, when they then departed as screen for a group of transports headed back to Guadalcanal. There they were to participate in exercises with Marines in preparation for the next campaign.

At Guadalcanal several days were utilized in the practice of landing exercises on the island's sandy beaches. Thousands of Marines participated in the exercises, riding the waves to shore aboard a variety of landing craft to then disembark upon the quiet island's edge. Meanwhile, *Lang* and the other destroyers took up positions close to shore just as they would in a real invasion, allowing many sailors the ideal position for observation of the Marines in action. But at this already conquered island there were no enemy soldiers ashore to challenge their advance. This, the crew knew, was certain to change in the very near future.

As these days of practice continued, the scuttlebutt increased. Everyone was anxious to learn just where they were headed. No doubt they would be moving even closer to Japan. With the battle for Iwo Jima winding to a close, the list of possible objectives narrowed considerably. But Formosa had been mentioned, so too had the Ryukyus, and also the Japanese homeland of Kyushu. Yet, despite their guessing, official news remained scarce. Still, everyone knew, wherever their destination, it would likely be no picnic.

By 6 March the landing rehearsals were ended and the ships returned to the Russells. There they were to remain for the next nine days in wait of their next move. Meanwhile, the crews continued to speculate about their destination.

This pause lasted till the 15th, then the fleet of ships again headed out into the open sea. *Lang* departed as a part of the screen for about 24 transports en route to Ulithi, in the Western Caroline Islands, where 6 days later they safely anchored.

Ulithi Atoll had been occupied without opposition back in September 1944. Yet, as a base, it was very unimpressive. The coral ring produced only a handful of islands, these sheltering a huge lagoon. This anchorage, however, while being along the invasion fleet's route and capable of handling the fleet's large number of ships, made it ideal for a midway layover.

At Ulithi, *Lang*'s crew was allowed a few more days of rest before their next move. Most of the crew were to spend some time ashore on the small sandy island of Mogmog; a little island set aside as a recreation area, though — other than offering a beach for swimming and an area for a beer party — its facilities lacked considerably.

Meanwhile, preparations for the next move continued, and more ships arrived to fill the anchorage. When a British Carrier Task Force arrived on the scene, several of *Lang*'s older hands were immediately reminded of their earlier experiences with their British counterparts.

Throughout the stay the whole area continued to teem with activity. The many ships were busily being refueled and reprovisioned, while numerous small boats skirted from one area to the next transferring passengers, supplies and precious mail. And the pace of this activity was to continue steadily throughout the stay.

During this time *Lang*, too, had her fuel tanks topped off and fresh provisions brought aboard. To the crew's delight, a fresh supply of beef and pork were brought aboard to be stored in the ship's meat lockers, while the previously stored mutton got tossed.

These preparations were finally complete on 27 March, and the ships departed the shelter of Ulithi for the open sea. *Lang* took her place among the screen of the Third Amphibious Force, which consisted of some thirty transports supporting two Marine divisions. And they sailed on for what was to be the next big fight of the Pacific campaign — The official word had finally been given; they were headed for Okinawa.

The island of Okinawa was only some 340 miles south of the Japanese mainland. There a strong Japanese army occupied its landscape with considerable fortification, and was fully prepared to die in its defense. The battle would be bloody and long, but it would soon be learned that the Navy was to bear the brunt of this campaign.

As the journey continued, *Lang*'s crew soon noticed a change in the weather; the previous warm climate began to turn cool while the previous calm water began to turn rough. By the 28th winds had picked up their pace considerably, and soon warnings of an approaching storm were given. In response, sailors began the process of preparing the ship for the fierce weather, securing all loose gear and heaving spare gear overboard, even as strong sprays of saltwater blasted across the decks. Some of the crew took great pleasure in the effort, allowed the opportunity to toss several cases of dehydrated food over the side; they had had enough of that stuff during the last campaign.

For the next two days the destroyer fought her way across the angry sea. Waves crashed over her bow and swept across her open decks, making ventures out upon these areas far too perilous. Therefore, the crew had little choice but to wait out the storm's fury somewhere within their ship's confines. To pass the time, stories were told and cup after cup of coffee was given attempt at consumption. Some sailors even kept record of the degrees of each roll of the ship as it tossed from side to side, while others held their breath in wait for the ship to right itself. But, as in the past, *Lang* did not fail those who depended upon her and made it through this storm — only to sail into another even more violent.

By midnight of 31 March–1 April the fleet had finally arrived off the western approach of Okinawa. It was April Fool's Day, Easter Sunday morning, and "LOVE" Day (invasion day Okinawa) all wrapped into one.

Lang began the day poised at an anti-submarine screen near a group of transports awaiting the invasion to commence. From about midnight on constant reports were received of unidentified aircraft being in the area. At 1:07 A.M. *Lang*'s radar picked up one of the unidentified planes approaching from a distance of five miles. General quarters sounded, a warning was given the other ships, and the screen immediately formed for anti-aircraft defense. But this plane never directly threatened *Lang*.

For the next few minutes things remained relatively quiet. Then, at 1:40 A.M., a second plane was picked up closing from a distance of only four and a half miles. Within a minute this plane was within 2,000 yards and racing toward the destroyer at top speed through the night's inky darkness.

Unable to get a visual, *Lang*'s radar directed the five-inch gunfire, sending high-explosive projectiles screaming toward the unseen target. The batteries pounded steadily, but to no affect. With a terrifying roar, and with only one of the ship's 20-millimeter guns able to squeeze off a short burst, the plane rushed overhead to release its deadly cargo.

Two bombs dropped from the night sky, straddling the ship lengthwise; one striking the water just some 20 feet astern, while the other struck just ahead of the bow. The ship jarred, shaking heavily all its inhabitants. Captain Bland immediately called for a damage report. Almost simultaneously, the task force commander, who thought for certain that *Lang* had been hit, was radioing to question the seriousness of the damage and requesting a casualty count. Fortunately, Bland was able to report that both bombs were misses; no damage or casualties had been received. One of the crew was even able to reflect a little humor on the ordeal by stating that "the Easter Bunny had just dropped two eggs."

Afterwards, at 3:20 A.M., the OTC ordered the screening destroyers to detach and proceed on a course to sweep ahead of the transports. Since the attack on *Lang*, all ships had remained at general quarters. But the area remained quiet, and at 3:36 it appeared that general quarters could be safely secured. Then, just 17 minutes later, another unidentified plane was once again picked up on radar, and full alert was again established. This plane, however, turned away before placing any of the ships at risk.

General quarters remained in effect at 4:19 A.M., when anti-aircraft fire suddenly erupted just ahead of *Lang*. *Wilson* was throwing up a horrendous fusillade of fire toward a rapidly approaching enemy bomber. Despite this effort, the plane's initial approach was uninterrupted by the blistering gunfire. *Wilson*'s gunners did not back down, however, and finally a determined round found its mark, exploding the plane in flames to crash just 1,500 yards off the destroyer's starboard beam.

A few hours later, at 8:00 A.M., *Lang* began a patrol near the approaches to the landing beaches. Thirty minutes into this patrol and the invasion of Okinawa began. The land battle for this island was now engaged. And, despite enemy planes continuing to threaten the area, for *Lang* the worst of this first day was past.

For the rest of this day and the next *Lang* led a screen of destroyers and destroyer-escorts in escorting transports from the ocean approaches to the invasion beaches, without incident. On the afternoon of the third day, following completing a fueling operation in the northern transport area, Bland's destroyer independently escorted the oiler *Neshanic* (AO-71) on to Kerama Retto — a small group of islands 15 miles west of southern Okinawa which provided a secure roadstead for large numbers of otherwise highly vulnerable shipping — again without incident. And that same evening, she proceeded some 13 miles south of Okinawa to rendezvous with the suicide damaged escort carrier *Wake Island* (CVE-65), also escorting this ship back to Kerama, where they safely arrived at 6:18 A.M. on the 4th.

That night *Lang* proceeded about eight miles due north of Kerama Retto to commence her first radar picket at RP#11. There were sixteen of these picket areas strategically posted around Okinawa, each usually patrolled by two destroyers, whereby early warning of either pending surface or air attack could be advanced to those areas most closely threatened. In overall command of these pickets was Captain Frederick Moosbrugger, the very same daring leader who had been responsible for the Vella Gulf operations. This night, however, there were to be no battles for *Lang*; there was a heavy overcast, allowing the destroyer an extremely quiet patrol. Yet these pickets, and especially those north of Okinawa and closest to Japan, were rarely to be such peaceful assignments, as *Lang* and crew were soon to learn.

Though *Lang* would indeed give much more service to the pickets, this first duty was to be quite a short experience. That very next morning Bland was ordering his ship to return to a patrol station near the transport area, where the destroyer was to remain throughout the rest of the day.

By evening, *Lang* had been joined in her patrolling efforts by the destroyer-minesweepeer *Rodman* (DMS-21). Again the night passed by peacefully. And by morning Bland was again directing his ship to a new assignment, departing *Rodman* to take the lead station of the screen for a group of transports headed for Saipan; whereby at 9:00 A.M. *Lang* had taken up her new duty and was sailing eastward.

Initially, this voyage was to hold much promise. Indeed, this was the orders the crew had been hoping and praying for such a long time. And the word spread throughout the ship quickly.... It was official, they were going home. From Saipan they were to proceed to Hawaii, and from there on to the States, where *Lang* was to receive a scheduled overhaul. It had certainly been a long time coming, but finally it appeared it was really going to happen. Then the promise faded, and so too did the crew's elation.

During the Philippine action the Japanese had been unable to gain definitive information on the true effectiveness of Onishi's Kamikaze Corp, somewhat limiting their understanding of its success. Fleet carriers, battleships, cruisers, and transports had been their primary targets, to which they had erroneously claimed several sunk or heavily damaged. Certainly the heavily armored capital ships had found the kamikazes to be very menacing, though rarely was their inflicted structural damage beyond superficial. Obviously, the transports were extremely vulnerable, but few had actually taken serious hits. Instead, it was the smaller, lighter vessels of the fleet that had found the suicide attacks the most devastating; whereas, successful strikes had often caused much death and destruction. Of these vessels, hardest hit were the escort carriers (2 sunk, 13 damaged) and destroyers/destroyer-escorts (3 sunk, 28 damaged). Just as critical, the crews of these smaller vessel types were quickly being demoralized by the increasing successes that the kamikazes were achieving. Yet these tallies — inaccurate or accurate — had little bearing on the Japanese command's decision to continue the controversial effort. Truth was, the kamikaze was nearly the only weapon left to their disposal with any serious punch, and they were desperately determined to use it. In fact, Admiral Soemu Toyoda, Commander in Chief of Imperial Japanese Air Forces, had early on devised a plan for defending Okinawa by use of ten massive air raids, each utilizing conventional bombers in unison with the kamikazes, this time devoting less attention to the capital ships and more to the transports and their smaller escorts. This operation was code-named Ten-Go, with each of the ten attacks designated "Kikusui." Kikusui #1 was scheduled for 6 April, numbering 366 planes, and was to prove devastatingly effective.

On 6 April, *Lang*'s transport group first received the air raid alert at 11:23 A.M., and Bland quickly established general quarters. Back at Okinawa the large force of kamikazes had struck a furious blow. Four ships were sunk, including two destroyers and a destroyer minesweeper. In addition, another twenty ships were damaged, including ten destroyers, two destroyer-escorts, and the destroyer minesweeper *Rodman*. It had been only five and a half hours earlier that this same destroyer minesweeper had been sailing within 1,000 yards of *Lang*'s stern. Truly, it appeared that luck had again delivered the destroyer from the edge of destruction.

This attack had, however, done stunning damage to the Navy. The remaining fleet suddenly found itself far short the available destroyers and destroyer-escorts needed for the proper support of all its outlying pickets and patrols around Okinawa. The results were inevitable, and sure enough, at 7:00 P.M., the destroyer *Bennion* (DD-662) was the first of the transport screen to be ordered to return. There was little doubt that *Lang*, too, would soon be beckoned back.

On the following morning, at 12:30 A.M., the crew's fear was realized; *Lang*'s trip home was canceled. She was ordered to turn around, and in company of the destroyer *Pringle* headed back for the Okinawan waters (*Pringle*, like *Lang*, had been headed back for the States for overhaul).

Back at Okinawa the air action continued, and fearfully so. *Lang* and *Pringle* returned as ordered and were quickly sent to a position four miles north of Kampa Misaki, where they were to establish a patrol. They had barely settled into this new assignment when, at 8:55 A.M., *Lang*'s observers spotted anti-aircraft fire at a distance of ten miles straight ahead. In response, Captain Bland immediately sounded general quarters. But only two enemy planes were observed, with these both diving on another destroyer at some distance away, and with both crashing harmlessly into the sea. Still, the moments proved quite nerve-wracking to the crew.

Within moments, several more attacks were reported from various areas around Okinawa. Most of these were of no affect, but the destroyer-escort *Wesson* (DE-189) was one of the unfortunate exceptions. While screening a couple LCIs in an area just north of Ie Shima, she had at 9:17 A.M. come under attack by three enemy planes, which her gunners took under fire as they crossed her bow. In the meantime, a fourth enemy plane suddenly appeared in a steep dive for the ship's starboard side and, though gunfire was diverted its way, crashed it amidship for a crippling blow.

At 9:36 A.M., Captain Bland was receiving orders to go to the assistance of the suicide damaged DE as quickly as possible. Though *Lang*'s engines were worn and tired, they yet managed to churn out 30 knots in the effort to reach *Wesson*'s position. And by 10:12 A.M. *Lang*'s lookouts had the crippled vessel in sight.

Wesson was in a bad way but far from given up. A fire that had broken out on the boat deck her crew had quickly controlled and extinguished. However, her propulsion on the port side was completely gone, and her steering was inoperable. Power in the ship's after sections kept going out. And there was considerable flooding in the engineering spaces.

The DE's crew worked feverishly at saving their ship, but they too had taken a heavy toll. Five men had been killed instantly from the hit, and two others were to die later. One man was missing. And 25 others had received varying degrees of wounds.

Upon reaching *Wesson*, *Lang*'s crew immediately set out to aid the stricken ship in any way possible. To give medical assistance, *Lang*'s doctor, Lieutenant A. J. Bernard, quickly made his way over to the wounded. In addition, a submersible pump was transferred to aid in the control of the flooding. And then a tow line was attached, whereby *Lang* slowly began pulling *Wesson* back to Kerama, where she could receive emergency repairs.

Before reaching Kerama, however, *Wesson*'s crew had successfully regained steering and partial power. And by 11:33 A.M. the tow line had been detached, and the crippled DE was able to complete the journey on her own, with *Lang* serving as screen.

Meanwhile, the remnants of the Imperial Japanese Navy had tried one more desperate attempt at striking a blow for the honor of its leaders. The fleet, consisting of the super battleship *Yamato*, light cruiser *Yahagi*, and eight destroyers, had begun their journey on the previous day, sailing from their anchorage at Tokuyama. Their mission was one of desperation, primarily a one way effort to decoy American planes away from Okinawa in order to give a wave of kamikazes easier access to the American shipping. Though some 250 American planes did fly to meet them, their mission was a dismal failure, as the kamikazes still met powerful resistance, to which no American ship was sunk and all but four of the Japanese vessels went to the ocean's bottom. As a result, the Japanese had sacrificed six more ships, including their most powerful ship left afloat, and 3,665 sailors for nothing.

That evening *Lang* proceeded back to the northern transport area, where she remained till the following afternoon. Then, at 2:45 P.M., she was directed to proceed to radar picket station #1, on the northern side of Okinawa. There she was to assist the destroyer *Cassin Young* (DD-793) in manning the picket overnight. This departure, however, was delayed a bit, as Captain Bland wanted to be certain to retrieve Lieutenant Bernard, who had remained aboard *Wesson* while continuing to treat her wounded. This done, the destroyer headed north, arriving at the picket station an hour later.

As *Lang* took her position 1,000 yards astern *Cassin Young*, her crew struggled with their emotions. It seemed their good fortune had just fizzled, and their countenance reflected their disappointment, anger and fear. From the promise of heading home, to the call to return to Okinawa, and now to the deadly northern pickets, fate had directed them to the worst possible position. Kikusui #1 had already claimed two destroyers, *Bush* (DD-529) and *Colhoun* (DD-801), at this very picket station. Certainly *Lang*'s crew did not want to be next.

This night proved peaceful, however. And on the following morning, at 6:29 A.M., orders were received for *Lang* to proceed on to RP#2, where she safely arrived on station at 7:38 A.M.

At RP#2 *Lang* relieved *Sterett*, which was to take a new assignment at RP#4. This done, both ships began their new patrols, and throughout the morning hours both stations remained quite.

It was just shortly before noon that *Lang* had her first bit of excitement, picking up a sonar contact just a short distance from her picket patrol. Having moved to the area to investigate, it was soon determined the contact to be false, and the destroyer turned about to return to her picket. But, at 12:16 P.M., a lookout suddenly sighted a body floating just some 500 yards off the ship's starboard beam. Captain Bland maneuvered the destroyer closer, and the body — identified as that of a dead Japanese pilot — was grappled by its open chute and hauled aboard.

For most of *Lang*'s crew this was the first opportunity they had had to view one of the enemy so closely. Though his face was somewhat bloated, one could easily see he was very young — 17 or 18. At six foot, he was also much taller than many of the crew expected of the Japanese. Yet his youth and stature were of little real concern to the crew. He was the enemy. More than that, he was an enemy pilot. For months, even years, they had built up a bitterness and hatred for everything he represented. Other than being a source for souvenirs, they had little use for him. His humanity did not exist. When he had been in his plane, he was merely a machine of war that had to be stopped. When he fell from the sky, no one heard his last words, saw his final expression of anguish and fear, or witnessed his final breath of life. That he probably had a family that loved him was at this point meaningless. Now, with his young, lifeless body wrapped in canvas and weighted with five-inch projectiles in the readiness to cast him to the deep, there was no one to shed a tear. Instead, when the moment came and his lifeless mass splashed below the ocean's surface, many cheered his end. But then, that is war.

With the Japanese pilot's burial at sea completed, things quickly returned to normal aboard the ship. Thoughts passed from the dead pilot to those that were still living, presenting themselves an ever present danger to the lives of every sailor who sailed the water around Okinawa. And there was a common knowledge among the crew that whatever came from Japan to strike at Okinawa, it would most likely first pass by one of the four northern pickets which they now sailed.

The crew's expectations were soon proven true. That evening, at 6:45 P.M., general quarters was sounded for sunset alert. Ten minutes later *Sterett* was reporting being under attack by six Vals.

At RP#4 *Sterett* was having an awful battle. The first attacker was driven away and the second was shot down, but *Sterett*'s gunners could not stop a third. The plane crashed into the destroyer's starboard side at the waterline. Instantly, the ship was dead in the water, without power, without steering, and without communications.

Captain Bland immediately ordered *Lang* to depart her patrol and proceed to give assistance to the *Sterett*. But after moving only a short distance, word was received that the destroyer minesweeper *Jeffers* (DMS-27), which had been on patrol at RP#3, had already arrived on the scene and was giving aid to the crippled destroyer. With no need to proceed further, *Lang* was returned to her patrol of RP#2.

For the next day and a half the sky remained eerily quiet. Not a single blip was picked up on radar, nor were any reports of contacts received from any of the other ships in the area. Such peacefulness should have helped the crew relax but it did not. They expected — and correctly so — this only a lull before the storm.

Indeed, the Japanese were busily preparing for their next major air attack. Kikusui #2, which was scheduled for 12 April, was to have a total of 380 planes amassed for the effort. Additionally, the Japanese had prepared a surprise, a new weapon that they hoped would help turn the tide — it would not.

By the afternoon of the 11th *Lang*'s radar had once again become active. Off and on throughout the rest of the afternoon unidentified planes were picked up probing at various distances. None of these planes came close enough to present a serious threat to the destroyer, still their presence allowed her crew few opportunities away from their general quarters stations.

Darkness saw the situation change very little. Throughout the night *Lang*'s crew continued to remain mostly at general quarters. Just after midnight, numerous aircraft were reported within a 100 mile radius, bearing northeast to northwest. At various times planes were picked up closing in on the destroyer, but none came closer than eight miles.

At one point heavy anti-aircraft fire was seen to erupt off in the distance, very near the location of the transport area. The flash of gunfire and the streaks of tracers penetrated deeply into the intense darkness. Shortly after, an enemy plane was seen to plummet from the sky, its flaming form arching down to a silent demise. And then the fight abruptly ended.

That next morning dawn opened quietly, and for the next several hours there was again a lull in enemy activity. *Lang* and the destroyer *Stanly* (DD-478), which had joined *Lang* on patrol at around dusk of the previous night, continued their watch on RP#2. General quarters had been secured, but the crews did not relax. Tension was high, and morale was low. Despite the previous night's inaction, the weary crews knew the enemy was up to something. And they could not help but be fearful.

Noontime continued to remain quiet but, as expected, it was not to last. At 1:17 P.M., an unidentified plane was reported at a distance of 16 miles and closing. General quarters immediately sounded and again the men rushed back to their stations. For the next several minutes they searched the sky, hoping to spot the plane early. But the intruder did not appear.

Then, at 1:47 P.M., *Cassin Young*, which was still patrolling RP#1, reported she was under heavy air attack. Assisted by the destroyer *Purdy* (DD-734) and a CAP of carrier fighters, *Cassin Young* was engaged in a fight with 30 enemy planes. The Navy fighters had kept most of the enemy well away from the destroyers, but three managed to break through to dive in on *Cassin Young*. Of these, the first two were successfully shot down, but the third made it through the ship's defenses to crash her at her port yardarm, exploding with considerable force.

Meanwhile, Commander McGarry, who still remained aboard *Lang*, immediately directed *Stanly* to proceed to the assistance of *Cassin Young*. But *Stanly* was barely able to get underway when at 2:00 P.M. she too was engaged in a fight with an enemy plane.

One minute later lookouts aboard *Lang* spotted six to seven enemy planes flying at high altitude directly above. *Lang*'s five-inch batteries quickly began a concentrated fire. Black puffs could be seen to mingle within and without the enemy formation, though apparently without initial effect. Then, just as they were escaping the gunners' range, one of the planes was seen to trail smoke.

In the meantime, the CAP had joined *Stanly* in her fight, splashing the lone attacker before it reached the ship. But this battle was far from over.

With *Lang*'s position beginning to look threatened, Commander McGarry rescinded his previous order to *Stanly* and ordered her return. As she was complying, at 2:31 P.M., a Japanese Val suddenly burst out of the sky, screaming headlong on the attack. *Stanly*'s guns began to pound desperately, and threw up such a tremendous fusillade that the plane suddenly veered away. The frustrated pilot then decided to try his luck with the smaller *Lang*, and again he charged forward on the attack.

With a determined roar, the low flying dive-bomber came speeding toward *Lang*'s port quarter. In response, the destroyer's gunners reacted quickly. They threw up everything available. Every gun hammered and pounded as the ship shuddered from their collective and continuous recoils, but the plane continued its course. Closer and closer it raced, penetrating the maze of steel thrown out by the ship's gunners with comparative ease. And, again, *Lang*'s survival was placed in serious peril.

Finally, just as the bomber had reached within a few hundred yards of the destroyer, a couple hits were observed to stagger the craft, damaging its control and causing its pilot to release his bomb just a fraction of a second too late. The bomb then skimmed over the ship, just barely above the two 40-millimeter gun mounts, to harmlessly hit the water a short distance off the starboard quarter.

In the meantime, the damaged plane had also passed low over the ship, and its pilot, evidently contemplating a suicide attack, had pulled the craft up in a sharp climb. As he did so, he exposed the full form of his plane to the ship's gunners. Such a target could not be missed, and gunfire again ripped into the plane. It did not immediately go down, however; with black smoke trailing the doomed craft, its pilot was able to nurse it out to about 12,000 yards before it finally exploded and crashed into the sea.

At the peak of this attack, those men working below decks had been warned to expect a hit. Yet being unable to see what was transpiring on the outside, they could do little but wait. For them each second that had ticked by seemed an eternity. They had stood frozen with fear and anxiety, staring helplessly at the ship's metal skin while hoping and praying for the best. Second Class Machinist's Mate Vernon Stark would later write in his diary: "I felt us get hit about ten times before he finally passed over, dropped a bomb, but missed." Fortunately, *Lang*'s luck had not ended just yet.

With this first Val downed, at 2:38 P.M. the gunners began firing on a second. As this gunfire opened, an unusual craft was observed to flop from the sky and to crash into the sea just a short distance off the port beam. Shortly after, the second Val turned away. But then a stream of smoke was noticed off the starboard beam; some new type of rocket-propelled plane was streaking straight toward *Stanly*. A few of *Lang*'s gunners were able to divert some of their fire, but the craft was too fast to set their aim. And, unabated, it slammed into *Stanly*'s starboard bow.

A violent eruption immediately engulfed *Stanly* in a huge cloud of smoke. From *Lang*'s bridge the stricken destroyer became totally hidden from view, and appearing as if she may have met her final fate. Gazing helplessly toward the stricken vessel, Captain Bland sadly thought of his good friend Lieutenant Commander R. S. "Yutch" Harlan, captain of *Stanly*. But just as he thought the worst, the stricken destroyer reappeared, sailing out from behind the screen of smoke and steam.

Encouraged, to say the least, Captain Bland immediately radioed *Stanly* to ask her condition and need for assistance. In return, the radio cracked with a familiar voice; with his usual calm tone Captain Harlan began to detail his ship's situation.

The rocket bomb had entered through *Stanly*'s starboard bow, passed through the chiefs' quarters, and on through the port side, with the warhead exploding outside the ship. Fragments of the craft, including the mangled body of its pilot, were found throughout these areas. The impact had knocked guns #1 and #2 out of action, and two men had jumped overboard, but otherwise there were no casualties.

This new and unfamiliar manned weapon was the Yokosuka MXY7 Navy Suicide Attacker (Allied code-named Baka). As *Lang*'s crew had learned, the Baka's size (right at 20 feet in length and near 17 feet in wing span) and speed (403 mph) was to make these craft very difficult for gunners to stop. And their powerful 2,646 pound warhead made them a potentially lethal foe. Yet, due to great losses of their mother craft (a specially modified *Betty* attack bomber), pilot inexperience, and malfunctions (the first craft to be seen by *Lang*'s crew to flop from the sky was later reported as a rocket that had failed to ignite) few Bakas were to have success. 12 April was to prove an exception, however, with successful strikes against both *Stanly* and the destroyer *Mannert L. Abele* (DD-733), which had been on duty at RP#14 and was to be the only ship sunk by a Baka at Okinawa.

Within minutes of this hit on *Stanly*, *Lang*'s gunners were again firing on another Val. During this effort another of the unusual rocket bombs was seen to flop from the sky and to splash into the sea some distance off the port beam. Just as suddenly, another stream of smoke was noticed on *Lang*'s starboard side, and again a rocket bomb went streaking across the destroyer's bow.

As before, *Lang*'s gunners quickly began to concentrate their fire on the demented suicider. But again the craft's speed and momentum carried it through the wall of steel. This time, however, a probable hit caused it to begin to wobble and veer slightly off course. It then proceeded past *Stanly*, just clipping the jackstaff behind stack #2, veered a sharp right, struck the water, sheared its wings, bounced back up, and plunged into the sea to explode.

In the meantime, the Val which had earlier occupied a good portion of *Lang*'s gunnery had also met its end. While making its initial approach under fire from the ship, the enemy plane had suddenly came afoul an even sharper foe; a Marine Corsair fighter had dropped from the sky to shoot the enemy plane into the sea upon its first pass.

Afterward, there was a short lull. During this time, at 3:30 P.M., Captain Harlan proceeded to take *Stanly* back to the transport area for emergency repairs. Meanwhile, Captain Bland continued to direct *Lang* about the deadly picket.

Not all was over for *Stanly*, however, and shortly after her departure another enemy plane swept upon her, missing with a bomb but turning to successfully crash close aboard. This action caused some additional damage to the ship and created some casualties, yet *Stanly* was able to continue on without assistance.

Back at RP#2 the dangers remained high, and nerves were at their extreme edge aboard *Lang*. Therefore, when at 4:15 P.M. a division of Corsairs arrived in the area, Captain Bland was all too happy to assume control of this CAP. Indeed, this friendly air cover was quite a relief to the destroyer's crew, and even more so when in the next seven minutes the flying leathernecks successfully and systematically splashed an additional three Vals.

Finally, the worst of 12 April was over. Though several additional unidentified planes were reported up till dusk, *Lang*'s batteries remained rested. Her day had certainly been quite remarkable, however. The destroyer's crew had successfully fought off continuous air attacks for almost a full hour and a half. Her guns had expanded 417 rounds of 40-millimeter, 741 rounds of 20-millimeter, and 221 rounds of 5-inch ammunition. And throughout it all, their destroyer had survived untouched.

Sadly, the same could not be said for several others. One destroyer (*Mannert L. Abele*) had been sunk, while another 13 ships had been damaged. Of those damaged, five were destroyers (including *Stanly*, *Cassin Young*, and *Purdy*), four were destroyer-escorts, and one was the destroyer minesweeper *Jeffers*. *Lang* was the only destroyer serving the northern pickets not to be hit.

As for *Lang* and her crew, their survival did not mean a break from duty; they were destined to remain on station at RP#2 a while longer. They were alone, tired, and very scared. But they had already proven their grit against the deadly kamikazes, whereby Commander McGarry best summed up their performance: "Your performance of duty has been outstanding while working with me in an isolated and hazardous radar picket station for the period 8 thru 12 April. Well done."

Chapter 14

Okinawa: Part 2

Friday the 13th of April, it appeared to *Lang*'s crew, could not have come at a worse time. Their destroyer's luck had been stretched to its very limit during the previous day's fight, and they were fearful that on this traditional day of bad luck her ability, should the need arrive, to mete out any additional good fortune just might falter. Certainly they were to pray, as never before, for this day to pass by quickly and without consequence.

At least they were no longer alone. Just a few minutes prior to midnight *Lang* had been joined by the destroyer *Bryant* (DD-665). And this was of some reassurance; for if they were to remain on the patrol at RP#2, they would now have some help.

Bryant, a brand new Fletcher Class destroyer, had just arrived in the Okinawa area, being sent directly to the deadly radar pickets for her first duty. Her captain, Commander G. C. Seay, was senior to Commander McGarry and therefore was obliged to assume tactical command of the picket patrol. He did not do so, however, without first seeking some wise counsel from *Lang*'s veteran senior officers. The previous day's attack had given him good reason to be concerned, especially cautioned by the introduction of the new rocket powered "Baka" bombs. For this reason he posed several related questions to McGarry and Bland: "Was approach of Buzz bombs from low or high altitude and did they use jinking ('jinking' refers to the maneuvering made by aircraft to avoid gunfire)? Did control of Buzz bombs appear good?" To these McGarry replied: "Approach was from medium altitude, dive starting at about 15 degrees and flattened to about 5 degrees. No jinking observed. Control was not too good; one hit and one very close on *Stanly* and two misses out of four observed."

This information seemed to satisfy the new commander. His confidence level did not appear to dissipate in the face of this new situation. Yet he had not truly experienced what the others on the pickets had already. If so, possibly his confidence would not have been so rock solid.

Aboard *Lang* it was obvious that confidence in survivability was slipping very rapidly. Her crew's nerves were shot, and their physical prowess neared the point of exhaustion. For the past 48 hours they had spent most of their time at general quarters, and their weary eyes reflected their uncertainty. For they had had little opportunity for any valuable rest, with only short, usually interrupted, naps squeezed in between alerts. And they could expect little relief in the days to come.

Nourishment had also become of serious concern. Time to enjoy a good hot meal had been completely out of the question. As a substitute, irregular meals consisting of soup (with its compliment of rice to hide reported sightings of worms) and G. Q. biscuits (with their compliment of raisins to hide reported sightings of roaches) along with hot cups of black coffee were served the men while they manned their battle stations. Such was far from a desired menu, but it remained better than nothing — though some surely would have disagreed.

Truly, to this point morale appeared beyond repair. There was simply very little left to offer the dispirited crew in the way of encouragement. There was no real opportunity for rest, no fresh food, no mail, and no guarantees of security. Then, as if to shatter what little morale that remained, that afternoon came the stunning report that the nation's president, Franklin D. Roosevelt, had died. Immediately, the destroyer became a sullen shell, her sailors thrown to silence by the shock of the devastating loss.

The fact that Roosevelt's health had been failing was of no secret. His affliction with polio and the stress of his office had taken heavy toll of him. But it was of no less shock when on 12 April a cerebral hemorrhage stole away his life.

Roosevelt had been more than a president, he had been a national symbol of one's ability to overcome the odds. The only man to serve his office four consecutive terms, he had brought his nation through some of its most desperate moments and successfully led it to a new era of power and influence. Though circumstance had set his presidency apart from others, his ability to face problems head on and his superior leadership talents made him a man for his time. Now that he was gone, a grieving nation questioned how to proceed. Fortunately, Roosevelt's successor, Harry S. Truman, would prove to be a man for his time as well.

Lang's past close association with Roosevelt made his loss of even greater impact to those aboard, especially for those few "old hands" who remembered his visits to the ship and the cruises they had shared. Those days were long past, but far from forgotten.

Few ships had been so honored. So in silence they remembered their fallen Commander in Chief.

The rest of the day passed by very slowly, the crew spending most of their time at general quarters just as they had expected. Throughout this time enemy planes were continually reported about the area, but none ever directly threatened *Lang*. And the routine patrol continued quietly, interrupted only when the ship stopped to recover what was to be identified as a Baka bomb's plywood fuel container.

Though a definite tenseness remained, the following day also proceeded quietly. Enemy planes continued to menace several areas around Okinawa, but again none were to threaten *Lang*'s position. Only the wild passing of word that "Germany had surrendered" and "Russia had declared war on Japan" gave break to the tense monotony, momentarily giving rise to the crew's spirit. But this was soon proven someone's successful attempt at spreading false rumors, quickly putting a damper on the crew's new hopes.

By this time, however, *Lang*'s continuous patrols had run her fuel supply very low, as the 12 April ordeal had also depleted much of her ammunition supply. So, at 8:00 A.M. on 15 April, Bland's destroyer temporarily parted company with *Bryant* and headed back for the transport area for replenishment of much needed fuel and supplies.

Three hours later *Lang* was once again off the southwestern approach to Okinawa. There she made an initial stop next to the amphibious force flagship *Eldorado* (ACG-11) to drop off some intelligence information on the Bakas, whereafter she proceeded on to the oiler *Taluga* (AO-62) to take on fuel. After that, having by then received 2,629 barrels of fuel oil, she proceeded to escort *Taluga* in transit to Kerama Retto.

Lang entered Kerama Retto at 6:00 P.M. After nearly an hour wait, she finally moored next to an LST in berth K-2 in preparation to receive a stock of smokeless powder. But hardly had the mooring lines been secured when general quarters alarms erupted, again sending sailors in a rush to their battle stations.

Enemy planes were reported on the approach, and throughout the harbor ships and crews braced themselves for the attack. Smoke boats hurriedly created their chemically induced clouds to aid in cloaking the many vulnerable ships gathered about. In the meantime, radarmen diligently watched their screens, prepared to relay any detection of the enemy, while gunners anxiously poised themselves in readiness for their own defense. And, if all these failed, repair parties and medical personnel prepared for the worst. Yet — three hours later — the alert ended without incident, and the anchorage returned to the business at hand.

Lang was to remain in Kerama Retto for the rest of the night, moving about only in the effort to acquire her needed stocks of ammunition. Throughout this time reports of enemy planes continued, and the destroyer's crew continued to spend most of their time at general quarters. But when daybreak appeared, *Lang* yet remained intact, having no intruder to approach her position by any closer than six miles.

Despite *Lang*'s nighttime ease, daylight was to allow no relaxation in the frequency of alerts and precautions. The enemy absolutely offered the sailors off Okinawa no breaks, his planes performing nearly round the clock sorties to strike at the American ships. Still, *Lang* continued to avoid the kamikaze's deadly sting. And at 11:15 A.M. she departed Kerama intact for a new patrol at station B-28, where she arrived 35 minutes later.

Sadly, many other ships had not been near so fortunate. This morning's attack (Kikusui #3) had again taken a heavy toll of the smaller ships. *Lang*'s old division mate, *Wilson*, had been hit. *Pringle*, the destroyer that on 7 April *Lang* had initially turned back with, had been sunk. *Bryant*, the destroyer that *Lang* had parted company just 28 hours before, had also been hit. And so too had *Taluga*, the very oiler from which *Lang* had earlier fueled from and then escorted to Kerama.

Of all the ships to take hits, however, it was *Laffey* (DD-724) which had seemed to draw the greatest of enemy attention. Serving on RP#1, she came under 22 individual attacks in a period of only 80 minutes. During this time she was hit by six kamikazes and four bombs and near missed by another bomb and another kamikaze. And somehow she had survived.

Being one of the few destroyers momentarily without obligation, it was *Lang* that was to respond to *Laffey*'s urgent call for assistance. Within minutes *Lang*'s weary engines were surging with power, shuddering heavily as they pushed the destroyer at 33 knots across the sea. Along the way she met *Bryant*, crippled but limping back to port under her own power. And again the crew pondered their own good fortune.

A short time later, at 1:36 P.M., *Laffey* was finally spotted. At a distance of ten miles, she was seen sitting dead in the water and being assisted by a sub chaser and two fleet ocean tugs which were already on the scene. As *Lang* moved closer, the severity of *Laffey*'s damage became apparent. The after section of the ship had been thoroughly scorched by fire. The after deckhouse had been wrecked by a direct kamikaze hit. The aftermost twin 5-inch gun mount had also taken a direct hit, showing a large gaping hole on its starboard side, with one gun barrel pointing upward at about 60 degrees, while the other was leveled aft. The starboard mid-20-millimeter gun tub was heavily scorched and twisted from a direct bomb hit. And these were only the most visible damages.

Of even greater consequence were the many litters of wounded which lay upon the crippled destroyer's decks in wait for transfer to the sub chaser. And then there were the dead, the covered bodies of her crew lying in wait of burial at sea.

Just how the destroyer had survived such grueling punishment was beyond the comprehension of *Lang*'s veteran sailors. Her continued existence seemed nothing short a miracle. Yet it was obvious that her crew had fought hard to save her, their fortitude of the very finest example, and they had succeeded.

Following the transfer of *Laffey*'s wounded, one of the fleet tugs took the disabled destroyer in tow. In the meantime, *Lang* began a circular patrol around the two ships, providing as much protection as possible for their slow efforts to move back to safety. Then, when a group of four Marine Corsairs arrived on the scene, *Lang* switched to a normal escort position and took fighter control of the CAP.

By 5:00 P.M., after nearly three hours of painstakingly slow progress, the group still continued on the move; they yet remained a considerable distance from the transport area. It was at this time, however, that *Lang* was ordered to temporarily depart her escort of *Laffey* for a rendezvous with the destroyer *Preston* (DD-795), from which she was to bring aboard some seriously wounded casualties for transfer back to the transport area. And, with little delay, Captain Bland was directing his ship back toward RP#1.

Thirty-five minutes later *Lang* had successfully retraced the path that had so far taken *Laffey* and her towing tug three hours to cover, and was moored portside of the *Preston*. The casualties to be transferred consisted of seven men from the support landing craft LCS 116 and four men from the *Bryant*. Several were burn cases, while all suffered from severe wounds of one type or another.

Several men from each destroyer took part in helping with the transfer, but it was the husky frame of Mitchell Sang, now a boatswain's mate, that occupied the most prominent position. With one foot upon the deck of *Lang* and the other upon the deck of *Preston*, he used his strength to ensure stability to each litter as each was systematically passed from one destroyer to the other. Perhaps his careful attention had more to do with association than duty, for he remembered far too well his own scars of battle, as Vella Gulf had forever etched into his clearly disfigured hand.

Carefully, each wounded man was successfully brought aboard. With the arrival of each one, Doctor Bernard set out to quickly examine each one to determine who was most desperate his attention. Most all the patients, it was soon learned, were in serious need of urgent medical aid, but one man quickly became the doctor's priority.

All who saw this man, an officer from off of *Bryant*, could easily see he was just barely hanging on to life. His ghostly white flesh made evident the excessive loss of blood. Quickly, Doctor Bernard called for any of *Lang*'s crew with a matching blood type, and immediately began transfusions of the life giving flow into the officer's veins. Desperately, he worked to sustain the man's life, but despite all he tried his efforts fell short; the man's life faded beyond the doctor's grasp. And on that evening Lieutenant (jg) Thomas N. Bridge died of his injuries, another victim of the deadly kamikazes at Okinawa.

In the meantime, Doctor Bernard scurried about to aid the other casualties the best he could in accordance with their injuries. By 7:15 P.M. *Lang* had caught back up to *Laffey* and her tow, slowing in order to recommence screening duties for the crippled destroyer as previously ordered. But the wounded aboard *Lang* were in need of much more medical aid than possible with Doctor Bernard's limited resources, and Captain Bland requested permission to depart the screen, so to proceed on to the transport area where the wounded could receive better care. Thirty minutes later permission was granted, and *Lang* began her run to the anchorage.

About an hour later *Lang* arrived back at the transport area. But the situation was not good. Enemy planes were being reported in the area, and the anchorage was covered with the chemically induced clouds of the smoke boats. This alert lasted yet another 20 minutes. Afterwards, *Lang* had to wait a few additional minutes to regain visibility before she could close the attack transport *Crescent City* (AP-40), whose own medical staff were awaiting Doctor Bernard's wounded patients. Finally, at 10:45 P.M., the transfer began.

Doctor Bernard continued to work with the patients, even into the LCVP which was their transport to *Crescent City*. He had already lost another man, First Class Seaman B. Riser from off LCS 116, just shortly after arriving back in the transport area. Even as he desperately worked, another man, First Class Seaman S. Ellis from also off LCS 116, died of his injuries while being placed in the LCVP. Certainly these losses frustrated the doctor greatly. Had he the facilities and had not there been so many delays, possibly all the men could have been saved. Unfortunately, war rarely provides ideal situations. He knew that under the circumstances he had done the best possible, and at the very least he had given those who remained a fighting chance at survival.

Following this transfer of wounded, *Lang* was destined to remain around the transport area. Throughout the next day and night she patrolled various stations as reports of enemy planes continued to keep the crew mostly at general quarters. But the threats remained distant to *Lang*, and in taking advantage of these quieter moments Captain Bland was able to bring aboard fresh provisions and some long awaited mail. And for the first time in a long while the crew had something with which to perk up their sagging spirits.

This break, however, was obviously not to last long. By early morning of the 18th *Lang* was once again on the move, departing the transport area as escort for LSM 234. Her orders were to provide protection for the LSM till she had successfully completed the landing of a radar team on the beach at Hedo Saki, on the northern tip of Okinawa.

During this morning's transit the two vessels passed within two miles of the tiny isle of Ie Shima. This small mass of land appeared serene. In fact, the island had been initially reported free of enemy. But nearly 3,000 Japanese troops had been in wait, and were now giving Marine invaders a real battle ashore. Most unfortunate was that during the height of this action one of America's most beloved personalities was to be lost. In the rage of the fighting, and only a few hours after *Lang*'s passing, an enemy machine gunner's bullet was to end the life of Hoosier born war-correspondent Ernie Pyle. Pyle, who had survived his many travels with the troops in Europe, had just recently arrived in the Pacific to cover a portion of this war for his faithful readers back home. He would not leave. His backlogged column would continue in print for another ten days, but his pen would no longer record his vivid stories of the ordinary soldier's and sailor's war.

By 10:45 A.M. *Lang* had arrived off Hedo Saki, and the LSM had begun its independent journey to shore to land the radar team it carried. Once the team was on the beach, and while their equipment was being unloaded, *Lang* kept a patrol some 3,000 yards off shore for cover. During this time a couple enemy planes were reported at various distances, but the operation never came under any direct threat.

The actual unloading of the LSM took a little over five hours to complete. In the meantime, however, the tide went out, leaving the landing ship stranded till high tide. So *Lang* remained till the LSM was free, finally departing the area a few minutes past midnight.

Once having returned to the transport area, *Lang* went alongside the oiler *Nantahala* (AO-60) to refuel. Afterward, she then proceeded to take station of one of the area patrols. But with the weather being cold and rainy, enemy air traffic for this day was nearly non-existent. And, therefore, the crew enjoyed several refreshingly quiet hours.

The following day, 20 April, remained cold, but the weather cleared enough to once again allow the enemy access to the sky. Just as daylight began to fade, enemy planes again appeared in the darkening air space above and about Okinawa. From sunset, when two *Betty* bombers passed by, till on past midnight, *Lang*'s main batteries were kept busy blazing away at the intruders. Anti-aircraft fire from other ships also pronounced their presence by their own thunderous shattering of the night. And enemy planes added to the nighttime color by the dropping of flares, their own effort at aiding in the location of targets on the ocean's darkened surface.

With the arrival of daylight the nighttime frenzy finally came to an abrupt end. The early morning sky was clear but the enemy did not reappear. And this unexpected but much welcomed break in the action allowed *Lang*'s weary crew a few additional moments of valuable rest.

That night, however, the enemy was again on the prowl. This time though the threat came not from above but from below. At 8:17 P.M. *Lang* made a definite submarine contact by sonar. Quickly, Captain Bland swung his command into action. Within minutes, a pattern of nine depth-charges were splashing beneath the ocean's surface in response to the enemy contact. And soon the familiar dull, jarring thuds of the detonating canisters were being followed by their gushing sprays of water.

Once the sea settled, *Lang*'s soundman listened to regain a contact with the enemy below. For the next hour and forty-five minutes a game of cat and mouse persisted between the two opposing vessels. The destroyer patiently searched the area, giving every effort at forcing the evasive enemy into making a move. But the sub remained quiet, refusing to give up its hidden position. And finally the search ended.

The morning of the 22nd passed by quietly, but that afternoon the sky again became full of the suicidal enemy. Once again deadly kamikazes fell from the sky to wreak havoc among the shipping around Okinawa. And it was not long till *Lang* was again being called to give assistance to some of the battered ships.

First, at 6:07 P.M., *Lang* was directed to proceed to give assistance to the suicide damaged destroyer *Isherwood* (DD-520). A kamikaze had crashed into the destroyer's #3 five-inch gun mount, starting several fires, one of which caused the explosion of a depth-charge on the ship's aft rack. As a result, her after engine room was heavily damaged and there were heavy casualties. But as *Lang* made her way to *Isherwood*'s position on station B-9, word was received that the damaged destroyer was proceeding to Kerama Retto under her own power, and in need of no assistance.

Lang, however, continued on to station B-9, where she was to remain until relieved. But at 8:05 P.M. she was once again on the move. This time she was to supervise in the rescue of survivors of the sunken minesweeper *Swallow* (AM-65). Just an hour earlier the sweeper had been crashed by a kamikaze, the damage incurred allowing her crew only six minutes to escape the doomed vessel. *Lang* arrived on the scene soon after the call, and spent the next two hours patrolling the area while the survivors were being picked out of the water by some smaller craft.

The next day *Lang* returned to the southern transport area. There she spent the day while her crew gathered spare parts and obtained gasoline and fresh water. For some time the crew had been forced to ration fresh water and, with the ship's reservoir now refilled, this was the first time in two weeks they were able to enjoy a refreshing shower.

Lang was to remain in the transport area for the next three days. Though during this time there were a few alerts, the sky remained unusually quiet. There was a nervous expectation that the enemy was again up to something. And, indeed, on the evening of the 27th (the eve of Kikusui #4) things again heated up for the *Lang* and her crew.

In accordance with the orders she had previously received, *Lang* had just reported back to the transport area. It was a brightly moonlit night and, due to several earlier alerts, the entire area had been covered by the chemically induced clouds of the smoke boats. In maneuvering through this blinding cover, Captain Bland had brought the destroyer in on radar and soundings and had anchored in an area near a group of transports. Shortly after, the smoke boat in front of *Lang* broke down, and a strong easterly wind had soon cleared a path through the smoke which revealed *Lang* along with a few other ships. And, in seizing this grand opportunity, a demented suicider suddenly appeared on the attack.

Lang immediately picked up the enemy plane on both its search and gunfire radars. From the information initially gathered on the plane's bearing and movement it quickly became apparent that this fast approaching enemy was heading straight for the destroyer. And, with the crew already at general quarters, the ship prepared for combat.

Unfortunately, due to several ships having been previously damaged by random firing, the anchorage was under a "no fire" order. But these orders aside, when the enemy plane reached two miles distance Lieutenant Conaway's main batteries gave no hesitation at defending the destroyer. And for a few seconds his five-inch guns hammered desperately at the yet unseen adversary.

Conaway's initial gunfire had been intense, but at a thousand yards out the radar contact was lost. The firing abruptly ended, and everyone ducked for cover. What followed was a long moment of terrifying silence, as everyone anticipated the hit. Then came the sudden roar of the plane's engine, present just a fraction of a second before the deafening blast left only ringing in the ears of the sailors.

The target had taken a solid hit. Fortunately, that target was not *Lang*. A large cargo ship a hundred yards forward and just off the destroyer's starboard bow was the one to receive the wrath of this "Divine Wind."

After being struck solidly on the fantail, the bright moonlight revealed the big ship to be rapidly settling into the depths of the sea. In response, Captain Bland quickly notified the transport commander and requested immediate help for the stricken vessel, while at the same time he direct *Lang*'s own gig lowered in the effort to assist with rescue of survivors.

It only took 11 minutes for the stricken ship, *Canada Victory*, to slip below the water's surface. Her survivors, meanwhile, could be seen frantically swimming the moonlit sea in search of help. One such swimmer was located and quickly hauled aboard *Lang*'s gig, soon to be returned to the safety of the destroyer. As this survivor was making his way aboard, one of the observing crew jokingly yelled from the forecastle, "Hey man, how come you were swimming so fast away from that ship?" The survivor then paused, yelling back his most serious reply, "If you were sitting on ten thousand tons of ammunition, you'd swim away in a hurry too!" Only then did *Lang*'s crew realize just how fortunate they really were. As it turned out, *Canada Victory* had not sank from the damage inflicted by the plane, but had been intentionally scuttled by her own crew. Had they not done so — or had the plane struck just 50 to 75 feet further forward — she probably would have exploded, as had *Mount Hood*, to take several other ships with her, including *Lang*.

A short time later the guest from *Canada Victory* was transported to the nearby beach, and *Lang* was then maneuvered out of the confines of the transport area to take up a new patrol some five miles to the west, which was to last the duration of the night. By morning, however, Captain Bland had his command back in Kerama Retto, there to refuel and replenish his stock of depth-charges. And again *Lang* got caught in a duel with a suicider.

Throughout this day *Lang*'s crew spent a considerable amount of their time at general quarter, as enemy planes continued to make their usual repeat appearances. But it was not till near dusk that the threats turned serious for the destroyer.

Initially, the first sign of major trouble came at 7:30 P.M., when a suicider slipped in undetected to slam into the unexpectant hospital evacuation ship *Pickney* (APH-2). Anchored only a short distance from *Lang*, the ship erupted into a flaming mass, sending a billowing cloud of black smoke high into the air. Those men topside of *Lang* witnessed several of the stricken ship's crew, many with their clothes aflame, jumping into the sea to escape the floating inferno. The sight was horrendous, but further attention became interrupted when a second suicider became the priority of their focus.

Just 15 minutes after the first plane's crash into *Pickney*, a second was suddenly detected by radar, already at 2 miles and quickly closing. *Lang*'s 40-millimeter guns immediately engaged the target, desperately pounding their staccato rhythm. Other nearby ships also joined the fray, adding their firepower in the effort to stop the intruder. Tracers arched through the darkening sky and black puffs of flak bursts chased the enemy's trail. Still the plane continued to race closer and closer. But the gunfire remained steady and finally a round found its mark. The plane lost control and dropped to the sea, crashing only a short distance astern of *Lang*. Yet, though measurably missed, *Lang* was not totally spared; the concussion of the plane's exploding impact was of enough force to still give the ship a good jarring.

Somehow *Lang*'s luck had held, but there was an obvious amount of uncertainty among the crew to its continuation. The rest of the night in Kerama, however, passed by peacefully, somewhat easing the crew's fear. They were even able to catch a bit of rest in the process. But at daybreak of the following morning, 29 April, their peace was again shattered.

The entire ship suddenly shuddered with an unexpected violent jar. Men who awoke to the quaking immediately jumped to their feet to rush and stumble topside.

Nearing a state of panic, their first thought had been that the ship had been hit by a suicide plane. Once reaching the outer decks, however, they soon learned the truth. Up forward to the ship's bow, the bull nose could be seen to be buckled to port. Clearly, no enemy plane had caused such damaged; they had been rammed by another ship.

That morning, at 6:40 A.M., the fleet oiler *Brazos* (AO-4) had attempted to cross *Lang*'s bow from starboard to port. In the process her captain had failed to allow enough room for clearing the destroyer's anchored bow, catching the bull nose and playing havoc with crew's nerves. Obviously, though the damage was relatively minor and did little to impede any of the destroyer's abilities, Captain Bland was furious. With over five years of service and three years of nearly uninterrupted war duty, *Lang* had received her first "bloody nose" from a friendly ship. Certainly it was a frustrating moment, but it was far from a disaster.

Temporary repairs were quickly made to the ship, and by late afternoon *Lang* was again on the move, departing Kerama as a part of the screen for the escort carrier *Makin Island* (CVE-93). Later that evening *Makin Island* joined up with an additional six escort carriers to form Task Unit 52.1.1. And for the next 41 days *Lang* was to remain with this group, performing anti-submarine duties while the carriers themselves sent their planes to attack outlying enemy held islands.

It was during this time that *Lang* received the confirmed report of Germany's unconditional surrender. Finally, there was reason to cheer. The war in Europe was ended, and this victory meant that all of America's might could now be focused upon defeating the Japanese. And this renewed the hope that this war in the Pacific, too, would soon come to an end.

Indeed, the five and a half years of Hitler's war had come to its bloody conclusion. Millions of lives had been consumed, and hundreds of cities lay ruined. Hitler had ordered the destruction of all that was left in Germany, intending to leave nothing to its conquerors, but his order was mostly ignored; those who were to carry out these orders realized such destruction would have meant only greater despair for Germany's defeated populous. Later, on 1 May, Hitler committed suicide, cheating the world of the justice it so desired, and leaving the Reich in the hands of Grand Admiral Karl Doenitz, Germany's infamous U-boat strategist. The new Fuehrer continued the war for another week, but on 7 May it was to officially come to an end, and Allied celebrations over this long sought victory began in earnest.

In the Pacific, however, the war was still raging; men, women, and children were still dying; and terrible destruction yet continued. On Luzon, in the Philippines, the enemy fought on, as they also did on Okinawa. The Japanese in Burma had been defeated but in China they stubbornly continued their resistance. To the Japanese, despite the reality of their assured defeat, surrender remained the unthinkable. On the home islands the Japanese people prepared for the inevitable Allied invasion, willing to die for their nation's defense. Indeed, as the war had so far proven, as with the suicidal civilians of Saipan and kamikazes of Okinawa, total defeat of the Japanese would require their near total annihilation as well as near complete destruction of Japan proper — not to mention the lives of tens of thousands of additional Allied soldiers and sailors. Truly, it was a cost neither side wanted to pay, but that both were determined to risk. And so this bloody war in the Pacific appeared destined to continue for at least another year.

Lang's crew understood the reality; the news from Europe was good but would not see them safely home. Their fight continued, and their survival would be greatly determined by their own performance — combined with *Lang*'s continued good fortune — and the performance of a great many other sailors and airmen. Certainly there were no guarantees. But at least now there was some light at the end of the tunnel.

By 10 June the destroyer's duty with the carriers had ended, and she was making her slow return to the transport area at Okinawa. This trip had begun unremarkably, but as they neared the anchorage a small boat was spotted floating just a short distance off the destroyer's path. Nothing or no one appeared to be occupying the vessel, so in accordance with procedure the crew prepared to sink the obstacle. Yet, while awaiting the order to commence fire, machine gunners suddenly spotted a man standing in the boat. Within the next second three more men also stood to present themselves to the ship. At first it was thought that all of these men were Japanese, but it was later to be determined that, with one possible exception, they were all Okinawan laborers.

These four men were then motioned to move their craft up next to the ship and prepare to board. As the boat approached, two sailors manned the destroyer's railing with sub-machine guns in hand, keeping the men in their sights at all times. There had been many instances throughout the war, and especially at Okinawa, of surrendering enemy carrying explosives, hoping to kill as many Americans as possible in their individual suicide mission. Therefore, one false move out of these suspected enemy and the result would have been their immediate annihilation.

After coming alongside, a line was tossed from the ship to the four men, and they began their climb to the deck. There they were immediately stripped of all their clothing, given some navy dungarees as replacements, and then made to remain in a squatting position under the watchful eyes of their armed guards.

None of the men could speak English, and there was no one aboard *Lang* who could speak Japanese. There was an attempt at interrogation, but with little success. The best that could be determined was that the four were all Okinawan civilians and that they were attempting to escape the fighting on shore. Still, no chances were

212

taken, and the four were forced to remain on the outer deck, a cold breeze whipping their half naked bodies, while under continuous armed guard.

A short time later some of the crew brought out a bucket of water and four trays of hot cakes and hash. Curiously, the four guests, evidently misunderstanding its intent, took the water, which had been intended for them to drink, and began to bathe themselves. And, as a further curiosity, the hot cakes were quickly devoured but the hash, for some unexplained reason, was left untouched — even *Lang*'s crew had had their own doubts about that stuff.

Otherwise, the trip back to Okinawa was uneventful. Once back at the transport area, the four prisoners were transferred over to the port authorities, where they would be more thoroughly interrogated. Afterward, *Lang* refueled and again headed out to the open sea, this time departing as part of the screen for a group of transports bound for Ulithi.

Finally, it appeared that *Lang*'s crew were to get a real break in the action, maybe even receive that long awaited trip back to the States. Yet, however it turned out, it was good to be exiting this deadly campaign. It had been long and hard fought, but somehow they had made it through the rough moments and escaped the horrendous possibilities of destruction. Many had not been nearly so fortunate. Since the initial invasion of Okinawa proper, 11 ships had been sunk, of which 8 were destroyers. In addition, another 157 ships had been damaged, of which 57 were destroyers. But, with the exception of her crushed bull nose, *Lang* had passed the test unscathed — not only the Okinawa test but also the Pacific war test. Indeed, though yet very much unknown to *Lang*'s loyal crew, the ship would never again fire her guns at a hostile enemy. They were going home!

Chapter 15

Final Voyage

By June of 1945 there was little doubt that the war in the Pacific was quickly drawing to its conclusion. It had been a long, bitter struggle, fought in some of the world's most inhospitable regions. The nations of Australia, New Zealand, England, Canada, China, and a score of others lesser in size, all of whom having shared in the sacrifice, remained in the fight and were to continue with the effort. Yet it had been and continued to be American forces bearing the brunt of the burden. And certainly in the intensity of these closing moments this was not likely to change.

What had changed, however, was the overall character of the remaining warfare. Now that the European war was ended, the earlier American hardships of having to deal with inadequate supplies, inferior equipment and shortages in manpower no longer existed. All of America's might could and would now be focused against Japan. For this reason alone, the Japanese were assured total defeat. It appeared that their only recourse was surrender. Instead the Imperial leadership offered only "honorable" annihilation for their people — and death to all enemies. In effect, it was to be Saipan on a much larger scale.

Indeed, Japan's ability at defense was growing weaker by the moment. Her once powerful army was now only a small fraction of the force it once was, being exhausted and without proper equipment and supplies. Despite this, it remained a force loyal to its leadership, quite determined to continue the fight, and especially brutal to those who were to stand in its opposition. As for the Imperial Navy, including its merchant counterpart, it had but a few ships remaining, leaving the home islands nearly cut off from the rest of the world. Therefore, access to needed raw materials was ended, and war production slowed to a near standstill as industries starved. What remained of the Japanese air arm, now emaciated and antiquated, was mostly in reserve for a last ditch offensive, which would be a continuance of the kamikaze effort so successfully used against American shipping off Leyte and Okinawa. And, outside this, all that remained was an army of civilians; men, women, and children trained to fight with grenades, explosives, and even bamboo spears to their own deaths.

In this respect, now that the thousands of miles of hopping from one island to the next had culminated to the point of invading Japan proper, it was of little wonder the amount of anxiety that existed among the American leadership. That the Japanese must be totally defeated was without question, but the price to be paid for such victory would no doubt be staggering — to both sides. Yet such cost seemed inevitable. Therefore, they could only hope and pray that it be done quickly and with as little pain as possible.

There remained other complications, however. All the recent changes in world leadership affected a new worldwide instability, creating many uncertainties for the war's conclusion and aftermath.

Hitler was dead, as was Mussolini (shot by Italian partisans on 28 April), and Doenitz was now in prison, leaving Japan isolated and without any allied support.

Japan's notorious Premier, Tojo Hideki (due to the military's many failures), had lost face and had been forced out of power in July of 1944. Yet, despite assured defeat, his successors proved themselves equally without merit and seemed just as determined at driving their nation to even further ruin. Only the godlike Emperor Hirohito, had the power to overrule the powerful civilian and military leadership, though he had so far been hesitant to interfere.

Stalin, remaining in power in Russia, being both an ally to the U.S. and at treaty with Japan, could not be trusted by either side, as his regime was in many ways just as evil as the one in Germany he had helped to destroy. Certainly a Russian war declaration against Japan could hasten the war's end, but with it would come their assured inclusion in the aftermath's settlements, which the U.S. would just as soon avoid.

In England, Churchill's party had lost its majority and he, the man almost solely responsible for holding his nation together during its darkest hour, had been replaced as Prime Minister by Labor Leader Clement Atlee. Still, it appeared at this point that England would stay in the fight to the end.

And in the United States, Roosevelt's death had left the reigns of authority in the hands of Truman, a man previously in obscurity but now suddenly placed amidst one of the most difficult moments of decision making in modern times.

Obviously, despite their severity, such political uncertainties were of little concern to the common soldier and sailor. While the world's politicians jockeyed for positions back home, it remained the serviceman's blood being spilled on the battlefields. They were the ones shouldering the load which truly depended the victory. And though the war may indeed have been approaching its conclusion, it was no less intense to those who fought on the front lines, and no less deadly.

Lang's crew understood far too well the reality of the front line Pacific conflict. To be there was to face down death, defy it as long as possible, and then pray for an escape. Many aboard had been a part of this reality as far back as Guadalcanal. For this reason, they were everyone eager to depart its insecurity for safer ground. And so, there was little wonder that the farther from the turbulence they sailed the broader their smiles became.

But they had sailed this way before, and had seen their expectations dashed. This the crew remembered all too well. Therefore, they purposely cautioned themselves at allowing their hopes to rise too high too fast. Even so, with the gain of each additional mile, the crew's confidence levels could not help but steadily increase. And, as the reality of a voyage back home became more and more a certainty, morale was seen to take flight and soar to new heights.

Helping to add to the crew's promise was *Lang* herself. Like her war weary crew, she too was in desperate need of a long leave from the front line actions. Besides the repairs required to fix her bent bull nose, the destroyer had other important needs: her engines were tired and in desperate need of a long overdue overhaul; her screws were pitted and chipped, causing the ship terrible vibrations at high speed; the gears and bearings of her main batteries were worn, causing the guns to oscillate and jerk while being trained; and much of her electronic equipment was in need of replacement with newer and more up-to-date versions. Indeed, if *Lang* was to continue to the next level of the Pacific war, these needs required immediate attention, and were certain to guarantee her return to the States.

As hoped, the easterly course continued, as did the promise of a return to the West Coast. More and more the war faded from the crew's thoughts, replaced by visions of civilization, home, and family. Still, many doubts about the future remained. Despite Germany's defeat and the assurance that all of America's and England's military and industrial strengths would now be focused against Japan, the Pacific war's conclusion continued to be a fearful proposition. And any separation from its deadly violence was certain to be temporary and short.

Indeed, the heritage of the Japanese people, a people never before defeated in war, would not likely allow a quick surrender. Japan's leaders had vowed to fight to the bitter end, with millions of civilians promised to engage in the defense to their own deaths. In addition, thousands of planes were said to be reserved for use as kamikazes, pledging an additional rain of terror and death upon any invading fleet. Certainly no less could be expected of a people so devoted to the ritual of death. And such seemed to assure that each acre of Japanese real estate would exact a high price in human blood.

Momentarily, though, all that mattered to *Lang*'s crew was the trip back home. Obviously, they remained somewhat cautious. But, despite their distrust, the first leg of the journey passed by nearly uninterrupted (detoured only once, this to investigate and attack a sonar target, which again produced no indications of a kill), whereby the destroyer arrived safely at Ulithi on 17 June. And there, for the first time in 82 straight days of operation, *Lang*'s tired old engines were finally secured.

At Ulithi, the crew was also to enjoy a rare evening of rest, as many, having just been entertained by a movie on the destroyer's outer deck, elected to remain outside to sleep beneath the tranquility of a beautiful starlit sky. By the following morning, however, Captain Bland had again directed his ship and crew back out to sea. Still, the destroyer's bow pointed eastward. And three days later, following a near constant 20-knot pace, she safely arrived at her next destination, Eniwetok.

At Eniwetok, *Lang* spent her first morning next to an oiler for refueling. Such an operation should have been routine. But not this time. Just a short time into the procedure, a sharp eyed *Lang* sailor, while surveying the area around the ship, suddenly spotted a lone Army nurse standing on the deck of a nearby transport. Within seconds the news of his sighting had spread throughout the ship, and in immediate response it seemed every man aboard had found his way to the ship's railing. It was a wonder the sudden shift in weight did not capsize the destroyer; no doubt she was given a heavy list.

Obviously, the crew had not seen a female "in ages," and, like the deprived men they were, each one struggled desperately for a good vantage point from which to view the rare sight. Hundreds of arms waved violently and half as many voices cheered in the effort to gain her attention. Surely she must have been flattered. If not, certainly she had good reason to be thankful for the blue moat that separated her from the crazed group of destroyermen.

That afternoon, with her fuel tanks finally filled and her crew reluctantly back at their posts, *Lang* returned to sea. Happily, however, she did not deviate from her promised course, and the journey back home continued, next stop Hawaii.

This next leg of the voyage also passed by peacefully and without interruption, and by 10:00 A.M. on the 26th *Lang* had again returned to Pearl Harbor. It had been over a year since the ship's last visit here, and the base had changed some, but there still remained a few reminders of the "infamous" attack of three and a half years earlier. Of these, most notably was the sunken remains of the battleship *Arizona*, her flag still flying defiantly and a good portion of her crew eternally manning her interior. It was a sad sight, but as *Lang* passed nearby, her crew stood proud, knowing they had played a valiant part at seeing that justice was being served to those guilty of the crime.

Soon after, *Lang* was at anchor, and almost immediately a boat came alongside loaded with nearly a hundred bags of long overdue mail and packages destined for the ship's crew. It was a wonderful surprise! But it was only the beginning. No sooner did this boat leave when another came alongside stocked full of milk, ice cream, and fresh pies. Then there appeared a base recreation officer, making his way aboard to explain to the officers and crew of a special welcome arranged in their honor; that afternoon half the crew would go ashore to a beer party, having all the beer and sandwiches they wanted, while that evening the other half would go to a chicken dinner and dance at a millionaire's mansion. If this were not enough, after the officer's departure, there yet appeared another boat, this a small stores barge bringing new clothes to replace the hopelessly worn and stained wardrobe that the past year of non-stop campaigning had left the crew. Obviously, the men were overwhelmed. They had never before experience such a wonderful welcome. And still more remained.

The following day *Lang* received an even greater honor, as her rich history was used in helping to promote a war bond drive. Over the radio airwaves were sent accolades of her wartime achievements, reminding all who listened, including *Lang*'s crew, that though the end was near the war was not yet over. Victories of the past, such as *Lang* had shared, had been made possible by the strong financial support of those back home. And, even if the war could be ended quickly, paying the price for the victory would remain a struggle for some time to come.

Indeed, this visit to Pearl had been unlike any *Lang*'s officers and crew had before experienced. Still, when on the evening of 27 June the destroyer's anchor was drawn and she headed back to open sea, no one felt disappointment at the departure. Instead, every man went about his duties with gleaming countenance. They knew their next stop would be "the good old U.S.A., happy day." In essence, this was the last leg of a journey that had taken them over a year to complete, that of a hard fought round trip directly through death's domain. And it was finally coming to a long awaited end.

Howbeit, this journey home was to prove neither quick nor easy. Despite everyone's impatience, Captain Bland determined that in order to conserve fuel the ship should not exceed 16 knots. And in slowing the progress even further, the weather quickly deteriorated, causing each nautical mile to be gained only by the extra efforts of both ship and crew.

By 2 July the sea's swells had increased so that huge rollers were regularly sending tons of water crashing across the destroyer's outer decks. Visibility also decreased, as heavy fog encompassed the ship. *Lang*'s progress slowed further. But no less determined, the ship's officers and crew continued to encourage her along.

At this point they were less than 24 hours away from their destination — and very impatient. Lookouts desperately searched forward, hoping the fog would lift so their view would increase and display before them the wonderful land they so sought. But it did not happen quite so quickly. Finally, on the following morning, radar picked up a huge mass stretching before the ship. Then, through a break in the fog, it was seen. Land! And the crew gave out a joyous cheer.

A short time later *Lang* was met by a harbor craft, and a harbor pilot was soon aboard to aid in the entry to San Francisco Bay. The pilot was hardly needed, however, as Captain Bland, displaying some of his own impatience, exhibited the destroyer's ability to navigate the fog covered channel from one buoy to the next by use of its radar. Minutes later he had the ship passing beneath the totally fog consumed Golden Gate Bridge, and safely entered into the bay. Truly, this was a very "happy day."

Afterwards, the ship stopped long enough to unload its stock of ammunition. Then it proceeded on to Mare Island. And there it met yet another grand reception.

From the Mare Island docks came the sound of festive music. Awaiting the ship's arrival was a Navy band and a large gathering of friends, relatives and wives. In the forefront of this group stood Lieutenant (jg) K. C. Gummerson, *Lang*'s Engineering Officer, who had departed Pearl in advance of the ship to deliver its work orders to the shipyard. And it was he who was largely responsible for the dock-side gathering, especially for the wives, whom he had made sure were present.

As *Lang* continued to move closer, the music grew more spirited, and the cheers and congratulations became increasingly louder. Wives, with their eyes shedding forth tears of joy, intently waved their arms in anxious anticipation of once again placing them around the man in each of their lives. In return, various ones of *Lang*'s proud crew searched the shore for that special someone. Even *Lang* added her own grateful response to the heart touching reception, giving forth a mighty blast of her whistle. For, indeed, they had made it. They were finally home — really home. And now it was time for them to enjoy their long awaited reward.

Lang was soon secured to the dock, and those men with leave began their departures down the gangway to make their happy reunions. The smiles that followed were broad, the tears were many, and the hugs were long and full of emotion. Even those men who were to remain on duty aboard ship could not help but feel good about the moment.

Truly this welcome home was very special. So much so, in fact, that with all the excitement few of the crew, if any, had given much notice to the vessel next door. Certainly they had seen this vessel many times in the past, and there appeared no reason for their attention to be drawn her way. Despite the fact that repair activity to the ship was unusually heavy, no one seemed to give her a second look. Obviously, *Lang*'s crew, as even her own for that matter, could not have known the key role this ship was about to play toward the war's end — or the sad fate awaiting her. Therefore, her presence and the activity around her did not at all seem out of place.

A cruiser of the Portland Class, *Indianapolis* was commissioned into the U.S. Navy on 15 November 1932, and had been in the thick of the Pacific fight from the outset. Stationed at Pearl Harbor at the time of the Japanese attack, she had fortunately been out of port that Sunday morning, engaged in a simulated bombardment exercise just off Johnston Island. With the declaration of war that followed, she immediately engaged in the earliest efforts to strike back at the Japanese, screening the carriers *Lexington* and *Yorktown* during the March strikes against the enemy ports of Lae and Salamaua, in Huon Gulf, New Guinea. Afterwards, she moved to the North Pacific region, playing an important role in the battles for the Aleutians, moved back to the South Pacific for the Gilberts campaign, then on to the Central Pacific to be involved in the Marshalls, Marianas, and Palau operations. After a brief return to the States for an overhaul, she quickly returned to the western Pacific regions to take part in both the battles for Iwo Jima and Okinawa. It was at Okinawa, however, that a Japanese plane slipped in on the ship, noticed too late by her crew, and successfully dropped a bomb on the after deck before itself crashing the ship's port side. The plane did little damage, but the bomb, which passed through every level of the cruiser to exit out its bottom, exploded directly underneath, blasting two good sized holes in her hull. Yet, though hurt, she was not finished. With emergency repairs stabilizing her wounded structure, she departed for a stateside drydock, successfully making the long trip back to Mare Island under her own power.

As a result, *Indianapolis* arrived at Mare Island ahead of *Lang* by just a few days. This arrival, as it turned out, was timely, as new developments would soon require her service for a top secret, high priority mission. And yard workers worked around the clock at getting the cruiser ready, unknowingly helping to set into motion the events that were destined to bring the war to an early end.

For some time the United States had been secretly working to develop a new, powerful bomb, a super-weapon far beyond anything the world had so far seen. This effort, under the name of the "Manhattan Project," resulted in the manufacture of three atomic bombs (one to be used for testing purposes), each capable of a blast equal to that of 20,000 tons of TNT. The procurement of this new power suddenly placed the United States in a unique though uncertain position. As it was, no one, not even the scientists who were its creators, was certain of just what effect this new, deadly weapon of mass destruction was to actually have. Its effect on the Earth's atmosphere, the true force of its power, and its long-term radioactive repercussions were unknowns. Still, the weapon's potential at bringing the war to an abrupt halt was too enticing of an option to be overlooked.

President Truman, his cabinet somewhat split on the issue, studied this new option carefully, weighing the pros and cons of its use, as pressure mounted on him to make a decision one way or the other. Certainly he hoped the Japanese would wake up to their untenable position and make his decision unnecessary. But the Imperial leadership — despite a sincere search for an "honorable" way out — rejected the "unconditional surrender" demanded by the United States. There were suggestions that assurances be made to the Japanese that the Emperor would retain his throne, and Truman did consider making such assurance in the effort to allow some room for a positive response; but bad timing and public opinion — as such a move this late in the game would give an appearance of weakness, not only to the Japanese leadership and American public but also to the Russians — deterred the possibility. At this point compromise by either side was out of the question. Truman knew that use of the bomb, though it brought Japan to the treaty table, would be controversial. Yet his only other option, it appeared, was to make a costly, all out invasion of Japan proper. With this in mind, despite the assured controversy, Truman made his decision, risking many uncertainties to bring the war to a quicker conclusion, and ordered the bomb to be deployed.

In the meantime, far from the decision makers in Washington but unknowingly sitting next to an extension of their newest policy, *Lang* had begun her badly needed overhaul. It had been 21 months since the Mare Island yard workers had last done such work on her, and since that time she had steamed over 150,000 miles in the struggle to push the Japanese back across the Pacific. Certainly these yard workers, by their own efforts, were just as proud of this destroyer's accomplishments as were her own officers and crew. For, indeed, they had had a hand in her many successes. And for this reason they were very much determined to see this second job was of no less quality.

During this time about half of *Lang*'s crew received 20 days of glorious leave. Those who remained behind enjoyed easy duty and many good liberties. Of these liberties, though, most were to be spent "on the town," oftentimes at bars and clubs in notoriously rough areas. And it was during one such visit that the life of one of the ship's crew befell a tragic end.

Second Class Torpedoman William S. Bates, a Virginian, had become a part of *Lang*'s crew back on 21 December 1941. He had served the destroyer honorably throughout all her many perils in the Pacific. And he had earned a special respect and friendship from among all who had sailed with him.

Most noted of Bates was his well developed skills at boxing. This, and the fact that he was a toughened veteran, made him pretty fearless when given challenge. Like many of his *Lang* comrades, he rarely turned away from a good scrap. But the guardian angel who had seen him through all his past adventures in the Pacific failed him at home. For on 14 July, while visiting a bar in a rough section of Vellejo, he was stabbed and left to die in a pool of his own blood. After all he had been through in the Pacific, Bates' untimely death came just one month shy of victory.

Just two days later *Indianapolis*, fully repaired but untested, hurriedly made her important departure from Mare Island for her special rendezvous with fate. Upon her deck was the important cargo entrusted to her care, a canister, eighteen inches in diameter and two feet high, which was the top secret uranium core for the atom bomb Truman had so recently ordered deployed, target Hiroshima.

On 19 July, while *Indianapolis* was yet seven days away from delivery of her cargo, *Lang*'s officers and crew were gathering for a dinner and dance at the VFW Hall in Emeryville. The occasion was intended to be a lively and joyous celebration of their safe return home. But in at least two ways it was marked by considerable sadness. First, there was the moment set aside to pay homage to Torpedoman Bates. Captain Bland stated of their lost shipmate these solemn words: "His passing has caused to each of us a deep sense of personal loss, as his popularity and comradeship provided an inspiration to his shipmates during their many periods of trial. His name will long be remembered for those qualities of a bluejacket he so displayed within the highest tradition of the Navy." At that point celebration seemed rather out of place. The death of this friend, a man who had met the challenge of war only to have his life stolen by one of his own kinsmen, seemed so brutally unfair. Especially when it appeared that the war was so close to its end. Which reminded all, in a second moment of sadness, that life remained fragile. Even in the security of home there could be no guarantees. Such made their past survival in the war torn Pacific seem that much more phenomenal — and the suspected return for its finale that much more fearsome.

Indeed, for the most part, *Lang*'s officers and crew expected their stay in the States to be only as long as it took for the work on the destroyer to be completed. After which they felt assured of their return to sea in preparation for the long talked about invasion of Japan. Certainly such was a fearful thought, as each veteran of the Pacific campaign could well imagine the cost in the attempt.

Truly, for the most part, it appeared there was little hope of an early end to the war with Japan; but on 6 August the lone bomber "Enola Gay" with a single mission suddenly and drastically gave such prospects new promise. The news of the atomic bomb and its devastating blow on Hiroshima was as shocking to all Americans as it was to the rest of the world. And its powerful introduction immediately changed the character of the Pacific war — not to mention the character of all future wars.

This new development did not immediately end the hostilities, however; not till a second bomb was dropped on Nagasaki, on 9 August, did Japanese leaders finally determine any further continuation of the war as futility. Even then, not all of Japan's warlords were ready to quit. But Emperor Hirohito, facing possible assassination, determined to intervene, saying enough was enough. After which, the world's brutally long war suddenly ended. And on the evening of 14 August President Truman officially announced Japan's decision to surrender, pronouncing a two day holiday in celebration.

Tragically, the vessel so key to having successfully delivered the bomb's most important element, would not be a part of the celebrations. She was no longer around to enjoy the victory. At near midnight of 29 July the cruiser *Indianapolis* had been struck by three torpedoes fired from the Japanese fleet submarine I-58, and within the 12 minutes that followed she was gone. Of her complement of 1,119 officers and crew, some 800 survived the initial sinking. But, due to a series of mishandled information, her loss or overdue status was not immediately recognized by fleet command. As a result, *Indianapolis*'s survivors struggled in the elements for nearly four days before finally being rescued. In the end, only 316 men were to survive, making this late war disaster one of the worst and most embarrassing in the history of the U.S. Navy.

Lang's crew also found their participation in the victory celebrations interrupted, though for much different reasons. Inspection for the day had not passed Captain Bland's high standard, and as a result he had the crew restricted to ship. He would later admit his regret in the decision, noting that he remained somewhat reluctant to allow his crew ashore due to the recent loss of Bates. At any rate, he did not waver in his decision, and the crew could only celebrate among themselves, all the while whistles, bells and sirens sounded and while thousands of people rejoiced in the streets of town.

On the following morning Captain Bland relaxed the restriction, but it came too late. So much of a mess had been made in the Frisco area the previous day and night that all military personnel were now restricted to base. To say the least, there were few happy sailors aboard *Lang*. But, for most aboard, the reality that they were home to stay soon overcame any petty anger.

Ten days following the war's end, *Lang* finally reappeared to stand out of San Francisco Bay, a completely rejuvenated destroyer. The yard workers had done their jobs well. Looking impressively like a new ship once again, the mid-day's sunlight gleaming brightly against her freshly painted hull, *Lang* made her way toward a new destination, San Diego.

With her recent overhaul *Lang* had received many new modifications: New FC radar had been installed, additional twin 40-millimeter guns mounts had replaced the old midship twenties, and new batteries of twin twenties now replaced the old forward single barrel twenties and the torpedo mounts on the main deck. Even new faces appeared aboard her decks, as several of her veteran crew had now been discharged. Yet, despite all these new modifications and changes, and though only a little over six years old, the war had brought forth so many newer classes of destroyers that she was now obsolete. Her service was quickly coming to an end — though not just yet.

It was on the following morning, and while still steaming just short the ship's destination, that a lookout spotted a raft floating some distance ahead. As the ship maneuvered closer to the fragile craft, two men could be seen protruding from its confines. Both could be seen to be in a bad way, but with the careful aid of a truly experienced crew the two men, civilian survivors of a small plane that had crashed, were soon safely aboard the destroyer and receiving medical aid.

The pilot was found to be badly injured and both men were suffering from severe exposure to the elements, but were quickly stabilized at the capable hands of *Lang*'s new medical officer, Lieutenant (jg) W. A. Hinrichs. A short time later, at San Diego, the two grateful passengers were transferred by ambulance to medical facilities ashore. And this would prove to be the last of many successful rescues for the destroyer.

For the next several days the crew was kept busy making test and training runs with their newly overhauled ship. This duty was easy and several liberties were made during this time, many of the sailors spending their free time "south of the border." There, bull fights and bars were popular places to visit — while jail was a popular place to avoid.

Then, on 13 September, *Lang* was once again sailing the open sea. Her orders had come, and she was to proceed to New York, via the Panama Canal. This was to be her final voyage, the trip to her decommissioning.

Proceeding south and east, for the first time in many years *Lang* traveled the night without darkening ship. For the many veterans who still served upon her decks this was truly a strange experience. Throughout the war such an act was unthought of and would have been considered an act of suicide in the face of so many enemy threats. Despite the fact that the war was now over, the fears that had been etched upon the minds of these sailors during that turbulent time were not easily erased.

Continuing her voyage, it was about the third day out of San Diego that *Lang* rendezvoused with another ship, SS *Thomas Pickney*, and took aboard a sick second mate. Once getting the sailor situated in the sickbay, the destroyer then proceeded on to her destination of the Panama Canal, where later the sick passenger would be transferred ashore. This opportunity provided for the destroyer's a final act of servitude at sea.

Arriving at Balboa on the morning of 21 September, *Lang* proceeded to make her way through the canal. After taking a little over ten hours to accomplish this lock to lock transit, the ship finally arrived at Coco Solo Naval Base, Colon. There the ship managed one more occasion of good fortune.

While that evening *Lang* remained in port, Quartermaster Eldon Coward found in checking the ship's portfolio of charts that there were no east coast navigation charts.

An absolute necessity in order for the ship to proceed, he immediately rushed to the Coast and Geodetic Survey Office to acquire the needed material. But upon his arrival and to his dismay, he found that the office was also without such charts. So many ships were making the transit from west to east that all available charts had been quickly snatched up, with additional ones not expected for several more days.

Not knowing exactly how best to handle the situation, the quartermaster headed back for the ship. As on the way he contemplated the problem, he came upon a docked submarine chaser and noticed a lonely looking sailor standing upon its deck. After speaking a greeting, he found the other sailor was also a quartermaster and immediately struck a conversation. To the amazement of Coward, he also found the other sailor to have the same problem as he, only his ship was headed west. So being, in what could only be described as an act of fate, each had the charts that the other needed, already corrected and ready for use. A swap was soon arranged and quickly accomplished. And afterwards, each man parted his way to happily return to his respective ship, both still caught up in the wonderment of their day's lucky break.

The following morning *Lang* was fueled and provisioned. A short time later she then departed Colon on the last leg of her journey to New York. As the destroyer proceeded north through rain and rough seas, a handful of old timers recalled the last time they had sailed these waters; the journey they had taken a little over three years earlier while heading the opposite direction in preparation for the invasion of Guadalcanal. It now seemed a lifetime had passed since that fearful occasion; the moment the destroyer carried her crew into the vast unknowns of a cruel Pacific war. She now returned as a victor over the vanquished and a proud warrior whose talents were no longer needed. The end of her admirable career was quickly drawing to its close.

After another four days of calm sailing, *Lang* and crew finally made their arrival at Brooklyn, New York, tying up at the 35th Street Pier. She was to sail no more, as there the ship would remain for the decommissioning process, as all her various equipment were to be inventoried, tagged, and removed for storage.

Then, on the morning of 16 October 1945, with the last group of enlisted men and all but three of her officers preparing for their departures, and in accordance with orders of the Commandant of the New York Navy Yard, the USS *Lang* (DD-399) was formally decommissioned. The time was 10:30 A.M., and the moment was solemn as the "colors and commission pennant were struck."

Three officers, Lieutenants (jg) Lyle Beattie and James Clark and a young Ensign named P. C. Ewing, were destined to remain aboard the destroyer as armed guards till early November. Then on 6 November, with *Lang* having been struck from the Navy list on 1 November, these three men departed her decks for the final time. In so doing, Lieutenant Beattie became the last of her crew to depart the now vacated vessel and to walk down the gangway. As he did, he paused momentarily to take one last look at the ship that had been his home for the past year and a half, and then turned and solemnly continued on his way.

Left behind, *Lang* remained proud in stature, enduring and endearing to those many men who had served upon her decks. Her stripped hulk was destined to be sold for scrapping on 20 December 1946 to George H. Nutman, Inc., 153 Pierrepont St., Brooklyn, New York. Despite this end, her name, like others of her time, was solidly etched into history. Her spirit, which would carry on far into the old age of the hearts of those young men whom she had mothered, was destined to live many additional years. And though her former officers and crew were certain to return to their respective families and continue their lives in a multitude of capacities, she was always to remain a part of them — even if only that she had brought them safely through to be as they had become.

Truly an era had ended. The great ocean-wide contests of the scale fought during this Second World War were, by their own innovations, destined never to be repeated. Those naval campaigns were bloodily vicious, involving five world class navies. In the end, three of these navies (German, Italian, and Japanese) were to be nearly wiped out, another (England's Royal Navy) was left humbled, and the last (the U.S. Navy) became the dominant force left afloat. The American victory at sea had been absolute, and *Lang* had been a part of it from beginning to end. From neutral observer to determined defender to victorious veteran, from the Caribbean to the Atlantic to the Mediterranean to the Pacific, and from untested man-of-war to battle hardened warrior, she had done her part and much more.

Indeed, *Lang* had played a very important role in the overall Allied victory. For her Second World War service she had received 11 battle stars — few ships would earn more. Her guns had eliminated large numbers of enemy troops, destroyed numerous shore installations, sunk enemy ships, and downed several enemy planes. The Vella Gulf battle, to which she shared equally in victory, has been determined one of the most (if not the most) perfect fought naval actions in U.S. Naval history. And, for those many pilots and sailors she had grasped from the clutches of the merciless sea, she had been the angel to which their extended life was owed. Of even greater amazement, however, had been her survivability. Though heavily involved in nearly every major campaign of the Pacific war, she had survived it all with hardly a scratch. She had lost but three men (a third sailor, Seaman First Class Hugo Babka, had been killed in a bus/train accident while on leave from the ship in 1943) throughout the entirety of her wartime service, and this with a service turnover estimated at a little over 700 men. In fact, not a single member of her roster rolls received the slightest enemy inflicted wound. No other U.S. Naval warship could boast such a record over such an extended time involving an equal number of actions.

Certainly to no other event in history — or possibly in the future — has America as a nation arose to a cause with such unity; not only with vocal support, money, labor and sacrifice, but also in prayer to an Almighty God. Whether one wishes to believe that prayer has power and influences events is of one's own concern. At least for those veterans of the crew of *Lang*, however, there was — and is this day — a great awareness of the many times it had not been the support from home or their own skills which had brought them through some moment of darkness. However, it happened, either by providence, fate or luck, it is certain they had not been alone. For *Lang* had carried them to death's doorstep, and they had all survived.

Bibliography

Angelucci, Enzo, *The Rand McNally Encyclopedia of Military Aircraft 1914–1980.* New York, Military Press, 1980.

Boyd, Carl and Akihiko Yoshida. *The Japanese Submarine Force and World War II.* Annapolis, Naval Institute Press, 1995.

Dull, Paul S. *A Battle History of the Imperial Japanese Navy 1941–1945.* Annapolis, Naval Institute Press, 1978.

Francillon, René J. *Japanese Aircraft of the Pacific War.* Annapolis, Naval Institute Press, 1988.

Griffith, Samuel B., II. *The Battle for Guadalcanal.* Annapolis, The Nautical and Aviation Publishing Company of America, 1979.

Hara, Tameichi, Fred Saito, and Roger Pineau. *Japanese Destroyer Captain.* New York, Ballantine Books, 1961.

Harms, Norman E. *Hard Lessons Vol. 1: U.S. Naval Campaigns, Pacific Theater, February 1942–1943.* Fullerton, CA., Scale Specialties, 1987.

Hashimoto, Mochitsura. *Sunk: The Story of the Japanese Submarine Fleet 1941–1945.* New York, Henry Holt and Company, 1954.

Hoyt, Edwin P. *The Battle of Leyte Gulf.* New York, Playboy Press, 1979.

Ienaga, Saburo. *The Pacific War, 1931–1945: A Critical Perspective on Japan's Role in World War II.* New York, Pantheon Books, 1978.

Inoguchi, Rikihei, Tadashi Naaajima, and Roger Pineau. *The Divine Wind: Japan's Kamikaze Force in World War II.* Annapolis, Naval Institute Press, 1958.

Jensen, Oliver. *Carrier War.* New York, Simon and Schuster, 1945.

Bibliography

Leeward Publications. *Ship's Data 1, USS North Carolina (BB-55).* Annapolis, Leeward Publications, 1975.

Lott, Arnold S. *Brave Ship, Brave Men.* Indianapolis, Bobbs-Merrill Company, 1964.

Morison, Samuel Eliot. *History of United States Naval Operations in World War II, Vols. I–XV.* Boston, Atlantic, Little, Brown and Company, 1984.

—— *The Two-Ocean War: A Short History of the United States Navy in the Second World War.* Boston, Little, Brown and Company, 1963.

Nichols, David. *Ernie's War: The Best of Ernie Pyle's World War II Dispatches.* New York, Random House, 1986.

Preston, Antony. *Destroyers.* New York, Galahad Books, 1982.

Roscoe, Theodore. *United States Destroyer Operations in World War II.* Annapolis, Naval Institute Press, 1977.

Sherman, Frederick C. *Combat Command.* New York, E. P. Dutton Inc., 1950.

Stafford, Edward P. *Little Ship, Big War: The Saga of DE-343.* New York, William Morrow and Company, 1984.

Steinberg, Rafael. *Island Fighting.* Time-Life Books, 1978.

Toland, John. *The Rising Sun: The Decline and Fall of the Japanese Empire.* New York, Random House, 1971.

Tregaskis, Richard. *Guadalcanal Diary.* New York, Random House, 1943.

U.S. Army, Office of the Chief of Military History, *U.S. Army in World War II: The War in the Pacific.* Series:

—— Cannon, M. Hanlin. *Leyte: The Return to the Philippines.* Washington D.C., 1987.

—— Crowl, Philip A. and Edmund G. Love. *Seizure of the Gilberts and Marshalls.* Washington D.C., 1955.

U.S. Navy. *Dictionary of American Naval Fighting Ships, Vols. I–VIII.* Washington D.C.

U.S. Navy, Office of the Chief of Naval Operations. *History of Ships Named Lang.* Naval History Division (OP-09B9), Ship's Histories Section, Washington D.C.

U.S. Navy, The Joint Army-Navy Assessment Committee. *Japanese Naval and Merchant Shipping Losses during World War II by All Causes.* Washington D.C., 1947.

Watts, Anthony J. *Japanese Warships of World War II.* London, Ian Allan Ltd., 1966.

Unpublished Materials:

Coward, Eldon (QM 2/c USNR). *USS Lang Diary, Oct. 29, 1942–Dec 15, 1945.*

—— *A Few Sea Stories.* A collection of stories while serving on the USS *Lang* from June 1943–Oct. 1945.

Lihosit, Francis (RM 3/c). *USS Lang Diary, Aug. 26, 1944–Jan. 19, 1946.*

—— Collection of original dispatches of the USS *Lang*.

Bibliography

Mcintyre, Scott (SM 2/c). *A Biography of Routines, Actions and Events At and Subsequent to the Attack on Pearl Harbor on December 7, 1941.*

Novak, Raymond P., Alex Telfer, and Charles W. Stirrup. *USS Lang Fifth Anniversary, 1944.*

Potthoff, John (RM 2/c). *USS Lang Diary, Dec. 1940–Oct. 1942.*

Stark, Vernon (MM 2/c). *USS Lang Diary, Jan. 1, 1945–June 27, 1945.*

Walden, William (SoM 3/c). *USS Lang Diary, Oct. 31, 1943–Jan. 22, 1945.*

Archive Materials:

Task Group 31.2 Action Reports for Battle of Vella Gulf, 6–7 August 1943.

Task Group 31.2 Action Reports for Vella Gulf Encounter, 9–10 August 1943.

USS Lang Action Reports 1942–1945.

USS Lang Log Entries 1939–1945.

Index

Index

Index